ALL LIFE LONG
THE SAME QUESTIONS,
THE SAME ANSWERS

All Life Long
The Same Questions, The Same Answers

REINTERPRETING SAMUEL BECKETT

CHAMAN AHUJA

MANOHAR
1996

First published 1996 by
MANOHAR PUBLISHERS & DISTRIBUTORS LTD
2/6 Ansari Road, Daryaganj, New Delhi 110002

ISBN: 81-7304-163-6

Typeset, designed and produced by
BNV ASSOCIATES
Printed in India by
PRINT PERFECT
A 6/2 Mayapuri Industrial Area, New Delhi

Contents

Preface

Even though I cannot believe it myself, this book has been on the anvil for almost two decades—of course, with long and frequent breaks when I would get involved in other projects.

I made my acquaintance with Samuel Beckett sometime in the mid-sixties when it was fashionable in India to talk about the Theatre of the Absurd—without having seen any Absurdist play, of course. Frankly, I did not understand *Waiting for Godot* when I read it for the first time—not even with the help of whatever little criticism I could lay my hands upon. The award of the Nobel Prize to Beckett in 1969 not only increased my curiosity but also my bafflement because the spate of interpretations was too varied to reconcile. The turning point came in the early seventies when I chanced to discover a whole set of Beckett's major plays in the personal library of a friend. It took me quite a few readings to disorient my tradition-bound imagination. And, then, one fine morning I got seized by a hunch that has been my obsession these twenty years.

As this study was started soon after my doctoral programme, it had originally the format of a dissertation. During the long spell that the project remained shelved, that kind of scholarship lost its glamour for me; what is more, I have learnt the hard way the virtue of readability. Consequently, I had to take extra pains to minimize quotations and the concomitant documentation. Since the idea is not to deny credit where it is due, I wish to express my indebtedness to all critics mentioned in the 'Bibliography' for their contribution to the making of this book. In this connection, it is necessary to mention the fact that one's benefit from critics' opinions is not always direct. Invariably, these stimulate one's thinking and thus help form such arguments as are quite unrelated to the originating ideas. Such a 'creative' use of secondary sources, I believe, is more valuable than a mechanical incorporation of others' views, howsoever well-documented.

Notwithstanding all this, I should wish to offer my apologies as well as thanks for any such 'borrowings', direct or indirect, conscious or unconscious, as a traditional critic would normally document.

While acknowledging my indebtedness, I must place on record my gratitude to the Panjab University, Chandigarh, not only for the study leave that enabled me to complete this project but also for the travel-grant which facilitated my visit to Britain in the summer of 1990. In that connection, thanks are due also to the British Council for subsidizing my visit through a grant from Charles Wallace India Trust. During the visit, I tapped the resources of a number of libraries at Oxford, Cambridge and London, but I feel most obliged to the Beckett Archives at the University of Reading for the rare material that I could not have possibly consulted anywhere else. With gratitude I recall my visits to the BBC and the London University Audio-Visual Centre where I could hear or see dozens of Beckett's plays on audio and video cassettes in the exclusive sessions arranged for me. The visit to UK afforded me also the chance to discuss my approach with a number of Beckett scholars. Indeed, I shall never be able to forget the spontaneous help and advice rendered by Prof. James Knowlson, Prof. Ruby Cohn, Prof. Katherine Worth, Dr John Pilling and Mary Bryden. I was, indeed, overwhelmed when John Calder did me the honour of going through my typescript and offering his opinion. My thanks to all of them! In India, too, I had the privilege of benefiting from the resources of dozens of libraries in Delhi, Bombay, Madras, Hyderabad and Chandigarh, but I owe a special word of thanks to L S Ramaiah, Librarian, Central Institute of English and Foreign Languages, Hyderabad. Thanks to his invaluable system of updating the collections in his library, I never had any problem regarding the availability of the latest published Beckett material.

Chandigarh CHAMAN AHUJA

A Note on Abbreviations

In the parenthetical documentation within the text of this book, the following abbreviations before page numbers refer to the works and editions mentioned against them:

Dj	*Disjecta* (London: John Calder, 1983)
Eg/Endgame	*Endgame* (Faber Paperback, 1964)
WG	*Waiting for Godot* (Faber Paperback, 1965)
HD	*Happy Days* (Faber Paperback, 1966)
M	*Murphy* (London: John Calder, 1963)
MMDU	*Molloy, Malone Dies, The Unnamable* (London: John Calder, 1959)
NK	*No's Knife* (London: Calder and Boyars, 1967)
P	*Proust* (New York: Evergreen, 1931)
W	*Watt* (London: John Calder, 1963)
WH	*Worstward Ho* (London: John Calder, 1983)

Wherever page numbers unaccompanied by any abbreviation are provided, the reference is to the *Collected Shorter Plays of Samuel Beckett* (Faber, 1984).

1 Godot: A New Interpretation

Waiting for Godot has proved, like *Hamlet*, to be the Mona Lisa of literature. For Ihab Hassan, it is an enigma that a sphinx might dream.[1] Even while thrilling its spectators, it has baffled most readers and proved the despair of critics. Early critical reactions to the play are epitomized in John Fletcher's remark, 'I did not understand it, but it made an impact.'[2] Bert Lehr, who played Estragon in the New York production, when asked what the play was about, answered cryptically, 'I have no idea.'[3] The directors too by no means claimed any better understanding, so much so that the famous Peter Hall, who directed the first London production in 1955, made no secret of his utter bewilderment: 'Haven't really the foggiest idea what some of it means.'[4]

Could it be that in this play Beckett had played a hoax on the high-brow—like that notorious lecture on 'Le Concentrisme' that he had delivered in Dublin before Modern Languages Society? Anyway, there is no dearth of those who treat it as a play for play's sake and, talking about its having no definite meaning, declare it a stunt. Needless to add, equally fervent has been the defence offered by Beckett proponents like Bamber Gascoigne who argue that having no one meaning does not necessarily mean having no meaning at all.[5] Some of them go to the extent of attributing a positive virtue to this opacity. It is argued that the refusal of the play to divulge its meaning liberates it from the restriction of the playwright's outlook and thus leaves the spectator/reader free to raise the possibility of all kinds of ideas—a process that facilitates his penetrating below the surface. It is customary, therefore, to attribute to Beckett's characters the quality of 'x' in algebra: what 'x' means depends on what we want it to be. It is not surprising, therefore, that Eric Bentley could find in the play the mark of all possible attitudes—intellectual, pro-intellectual, anti-intellectual, non-intellectual, etc.[6]

The first-ever review of the play in *La Liberation* (7 Jan. 1953) by Sylvain Zegel was prophetic. Declaring that the play would be spoken of for a long time, it talked of the people's embarrassed laughter and questioned, for the first time, the identity of Godot:

> They [the audience] don't know. And in any case, this myth hasn't the same form, the same qualities for each of them. It might be happiness, eternal life, the ideal and unattainable quest of all men—which they wait for and which gives them the strength to live on.[7]

So fantastic has been the ingenuity of the critics in inventing ever-new interpretations of Godot that it is not difficult to imagine the kind of pandemonium that the play might raise if there were to be a conclave of Beckett scholars.[8] Possibly, Martin Esslin would begin by observing puckishly that Godot is Godeau, Balzac's funny cyclist in *Marcadet*. Eric Bentley might nod in assent while Josephine Jacobsen and W R Mueller stand up to point out that etymologically Godot (= Godeau) could be a synthesis of the English God and French 'eau'. However, John Fletcher insists on Godot being *Godillot*, French for boot. Yes, yes, shouts some one, it is the hob-nailed boot of the Gestapo during World War II. But, counters another voice, Godot here is awaited expectantly, not fearfully; if anything, it should be De Gaulle. Cut it, snarls Jean-Jacques Mayoux from a corner; Godot is just the way the Irish pronounce God—nothing more, nothing less. However, for Father Nathan Scott, Godot implies the absence of Godot and not his presence. The suffixing of 'ot', he argues, signifies negation. At this, Edith Kern is seen jumping in her seat to point out that 'ot' signifies diminution (as in Charlot), not necessarily negation. Even as the speakers start disputing whether Godot is white-bearded Jehovah-Daddy, an anthropomorphic image of God, or a cynical saviour (need of God spat-on), Robert S Cohen tries to relate the play to Simon Weil's *Waiting for God* as its literary source. That provokes Melvin Friedman to assert that that credit should go to Tom Kromer's *Waiting for Nothing*, Nothing being interpreted as Non-being, i.e. Death. Yes, here too is waiting for death, as in *Endgame*, it is pleaded. Meanwhile a suggestion has emerged that, in Ruma, God means a 'Year'; so Godot is possibly not so much a spiritual signpost as a temporal symbol—Father Time or Time Future. G S Fraser, once again raking up the question of literary source, points to Clifford Odets's *Waiting for Lefty*.

When some one points out that Godot is the name of a Paris street for call girls, the colloquium turns into catechism. Isn't God-er a slang for erection? And Godillier one for fornication? And why can't it be 'God-dam', the French slang for a drunken Englishman in a brothel? Exasperated by this 'slanging' match, Alan Schneider pointedly turns for a definite explanation to a man sitting smilingly in a corner. It is Beckett himself who answers with a shrug, 'If I knew, I would have said so in the play.'[9] When pressed further by Colin Duckworth, Beckett asserts that the misunderstanding is born of the critics' own obsessive tendency to impose an allegorical or symbolic explanation on a play which is striving all the time to avoid definition.[10]

The way Beckett tries to steer clear of the controversy reminds one not only of what he said elsewhere—'Art, an arrangement of the inexplicable, never explains'—but also of what he said about Joyce: 'He is not writing about something, it is that something itself' (*Dj*, 27). Perhaps one could take the last remark literally and say that Beckett's concern in the play is not with waiting for Godot but with just waiting. After all, one may argue, the original French title was ***En attendant*** without any mention of Godot in it. Even the present French title, *En attendant Godot* means 'while waiting for Godot'. Once it is conceded that 'while waiting' is more important than the identity of Godot, the question about Godot's coming or not ceases to be important and the central issue becomes whether or not to wait. But, then, what does this waiting itself imply? Is it Miltonic waiting ('They also serve who stand and wait') or Micawberian waiting for something to 'turn up'? For Nathan Scott, waiting implies absence, and therefore the play epitomizes a typically twentieth century experience—the banality of a world deserted by God.[11] Since faith in Him had lent meaning to the human adventure, His absence has brought back the original sense of the absurd. Be that as it may, when the play was performed at San Quentin, the prisoners there had felt as if the play depicted their own fate—a Sisyphus-like suffering without end.[12] Indeed, waiting for one thing or another is so common that nearly all of us have been in the situation of Vladimir and Estragon, even if the situation is totally mundane—for example (as Alec Reid has pointed out) while waiting for an aeroplane, for the last bus, for a letter, or even for the opening of a bar.[13] Anne C Murch and Linda Ben-Zvi have recorded how the adaptations of the play in Australia and Israel were geared to certain specific situations peculiar to the local life there and left a profound impact.[14] The audience had no problem in understanding the play because it was all part of their daily experience.

The approach to the characters of the play has been equally varied as a look at the Dec. 1966 number of ***Modern Drama*** and Friedman's article 'Crritic' in it shows. Not too inclined to accept the characters as individuals on a realistic level or even as assumed names of historical figures, critics have generally tended to regard them as symbolic or allegorical beings. Going by their names, they have often been seen as representatives of various nationalities—a French Estragon, a Russian Vladimir, an Italian Pozzo and an English Lucky. From this, the popular conclusion is that together they represent European man or even Everyman—a picture of humanity fiddling its way through life. For Ihab Hassan, the four persons are, in a sense, the same person as well as all of mankind because the play lends itself easily to social, political, theological and psychological interpretations of the human situation.[15] G C Barnard, on the other hand, believes that they correspond to the four Zoas of Blake—Imagination, Reason, Passion and Sensation.[16] Some critics prefer to go by pairs thus clubbing Vladimir with Estragon and Pozzo with Lucky to suggest that the twin couples represent existential human polarities—eternal and temporal, tragic and comic, subjective and objective, static and dynamic, contemplative and practical, and so on. Yet another approach is to regard them as two separate couples that are not necessarily related to each other. Thus Didi and Gogo are supposed to represent id-id and ego-ego, respectively, in the relations of man and woman locked in matrimony. For Norman Mailer, on the other hand, they are homosexuals.[17] G C Barnard sees in them the twin selves of a schizophrenic personality—the alienated inner self and the pseudo self.[18] As regards Pozzo and Lucky, they have been shown to represent master and slave, capital and labour, wealth and art, politics and intellectualism, even Joyce and Beckett. Even when they have been taken separately, they are treated not as individuals but as symbols. For example, Pozzo has been regarded as a Nietzschean overman, a tyrannical Jehovah, a crucified god, a swaggering soldier, a dreaded Gestapo, while Lucky is supposed to be an articulate editor/professor, a Christ-figure, even a degenerate intellectual. The most interesting thing, however, is that Beckett would not accept any of these interpretations. Rather, he is on record as having warned against the hunt for symbols 'where none intended'. To Alan Schneider he once wrote:

If people want to have headaches among the overtones, let them. And provide their own aspirin. Hamm as stated, and Clov as stated, ne tecum nec sine te, in such a place, and in such a world, that's all I can manage, more than I could. (*Dj*, 109)

Despite Beckett's unequivocal declaration, critics by no means have ceased their search for new interpretations. If anything, the quest has gained in intensity. Without claiming to offer the last word, the present writer offers an entirely fresh approach; what is more, it affords a consistent interpretation not only of this play but also of the entire work of Beckett. Of course, it leans heavily on symbolic and allegorical interpretation of the characters—something that Beckett would never have approved of; but, in the arts, the artist's intention is only half of the creative business, the other half being what is actually received. Surely, it is safer to trust the tale than the teller.

The interpretation being offered in this study is based on either textual facts or such suggestions as have come to enjoy near-consensus. In brief, the basic assumptions are:

(a) that Godot is not exactly God or god but a diminutive version—less than god but more than man;
(b) that since Vladimir claims that 'all mankind is us' and Pozzo, responding to both Cain and Abel, is declared to be 'all humanity', the characters are more than individuals;
(c) that the names of characters justify an onomastic-cum-symbolic approach;
(d) that the play depicts mankind as waiting for a superhuman being whose exact identity is not known;
(e) that the process of waiting has already taken so long that mankind is fed up and is tempted to give up;
(f) that while waiting, mankind is merely biding its time and doing absolutely nothing;
(g) that even as the messianic hope is perpetually deferred, things are going from bad to worse and mankind finds itself wasting and pining;
(h) that since the seed of the play was Luke's account of the crucifixion of Christ and St Augustine's perfectly shaped paradox—'Do not despair: one of the thieves was saved. Do not presume: one of the thieves was damned'—the vision of

the play is related to that fearful symmetry;

(i) that Pozzo's obsession with time is thematically a pivotal rather than peripheral concern;

(j) that Time here runs on two scales, eternal and historical, and that it is at once creative and destructive;

(k) that the fate of mankind projected here is at once tragic and comic;

(l) that any interpretation of the play must get related to and/or explain (i) significance of road and tree, (ii) characters' clowning, tramphood and journeying, (iii) hat and boot business, (iv) verbal games, (v) repetition of 'Nothing to be done' and 'Let's go' (*They don't move*), (vi) Lucky's speech, (vii) dog-in-the-kitchen song, (viii) changes in Pozzo and Lucky, (ix) the boy's visits, and (x) the duplication of action in Act II.

The awaited one being Godot and not God, the two must not be treated as identical; at best, Godot can claim a kinship—something akin to God, i.e. God-like. Such a one, I believe, is the much-awaited Superman of the vitalists. As the myth goes, since the very creation of the world, guilty of the Original Sin, man has been suffering incessantly in the hope of eventual salvation which would spell escape from damnation. In the modern, secular terminology of the Darwinians, salvation and damnation mean survival and extinction, respectively. Thus may one interpret soul as an urge of the Life Force which aims at the creation of a better species until man becomes perfect, i.e. god-like or Godot. When that stage is reached—that is to say, when Superman (= Godot) arrives—it would hopefully imply cessation of all human misery. Until that time, man must suffer and wait patiently. If he gives up too soon, it shall spell his damnation, i.e. extinction as a species. Wait he must even though he has not the slightest idea of what exactly that Godot-superman would be like, or when (if at all) he would arrive. The play, I suggest, dramatizes this waiting.

Now, man's evolution has been marked by ups and downs, and many a time has he escaped extinction by the skin of his teeth. Witness, the rise and fall of the Aryan, Egyptian, Greek and Roman civilizations. Created as a freak in nature, man as a species faced imminent physical extinction but he has been trying to evade that fate through strategies of survival devised by his superior (albeit by no means perfect) mind. In practical terms it has meant experimenting with nature, religion, philosophy, art, science, etc., as the bases of different civilizations, but in each case maxima has been followed by minima. No wonder, even today, in the much-bruited age of high technology, perfection is not within sight. At the zenith of each civilization, man has always felt as if the long-awaited superman were round the corner; but each time the hope has proved illusive and man has found himself at the starting point once again. Thanks to his evolution-cum-atrophy, man's progress along the road of evolution has been not linear but curved, almost circular—like the coil of a spring. For want of a better word, one could describe such tenor of evolution as anthropocycloid. Already man has been on this road for millions of years without making much progress. Perhaps he will take, as G B Shaw had envisioned in his *Back to Methuselah*, millions of years more before he becomes Superman—that is, before Godot arrives. Or possibly the task is eternally endless and would be completed only at the end of time—like the infinitesimal division of Zeno's millet grain. Thus seen, Godot becomes the digit at the end of a recurring decimal which will be reached only when time itself stops. An individual man—or, for that matter, any particular age—placed in the context of that eternity, cannot but feel frustrated with the futility of the immense labour and might even think of giving up in despair. But then comes the consideration that no one man or age has any right to undo the efforts of so many millenia. In short, even though man is not sure of survival, i.e. Godot's arrival, yet he must keep waiting. Of course, such endless waiting for one whom you don't even know appears almost absurd; but, then, the only other alternative being suicide, i.e. certain extinction, man has to persist. In this impasse, the chances of his ultimate survival (i.e. the arrival of Godot) are delicately balanced. Like the two thieves in the gospel, man too has even chances of survival and extinction. He must not despair too much for, after all, one of the thieves was saved; but he dare not presume too much either because the other thief did suffer damnation.

If *Waiting for Godot* is the dramatization of the story of evolution, in which Godot is the never-arriving Superman, who are Vladimir, Estragon, Pozzo and Lucky? They are what Erich Auerbach calls 'figuras'. Together they comprise composite Everyman. To my way of thinking, Vladimir and Estragon represent the timeless existence of Man, the time-bound historical aspect being represented by Pozzo and Lucky. Born without the means that could protect him against the wildness of nature, man was doomed to extinction, but he has managed to survive because of his mind. Though relatively superior, the mind of man is imperfect; what is more, it is imperfectible. Realizing only too well his comparative mental strength and physical vulnerability, man has been busy creating, in the big macrocosmic universe of God's making, a smaller microcosmic world of his own—a world governed not by the inexorable laws of Nature but those devised by his own imperfect mind. However, man cannot simply dispense with the natural self and has therefore continued to be handicapped by physical disabilities. This living at once on the rational and the physical planes has resulted in a dichotomous schism. Thus seen, Vladimir and Estragon represent, respectively, the mental and the physical aspects of human personality, in uncomfortable interdependence on each other. The physical self would rather be free of the mental self because the moral laws of the mind's devising are unnatural; but as that freedom would spell his own extinction, the physical aspect has to barter away his freedom for protection. The trouble is that since the human mind is not perfectly rational, it keeps changing its laws. That inevitably necessitates continuous effort at readjustment. The mental self, of course, aims at modification, but betterment on the mental level does not necessarily imply a corresponding betterment on the physical level. On the contrary, more often that not, it leads to physical deterioration. This is ironic because, if allowed full scope, the growing process of physical deterioration would also lead to extinction from which the mental self has been trying to save the physical self. This dialectical relationship between the physical and mental aspects of human personality explains not only the rise and fall of civilizations but also the fact that, even after millions of years, man remains where he was. Indeed, with progress always countered by regression, the net result is bound to be zero. In other words, howsoever frequently man may change the strategies of survival and transvaluate his values, the sum total would always be the same. It is like filling of water tank that has an exit-pipe as wide as the tap itself, or like carrying of a number of milk-cans from one end of a platform to the other, and back. Perhaps, this absurd story of man's paradoxical evolution-cum-degeneration would continue ad-infinitum, like the story of the dog-in-the-kitchen sung by Vladimir in the beginning of Act II.

Since man rules the world because of his intellect, the mental aspect has been named Vladimir which literally means the ruler of the world. No wonder, too, his preoccupations are related to hat and to his stinking breath (= words). Estragon, on the other hand, recalls the name of a French herb, Terragon, which means earth-bound. Indeed, he is earthy, of the earth. His troubles being sensory, they are related to boots (= feet) and he cannot think of anything beyond problems related to physical appetites—for example, the choice between carrots and radishes. Since the only gain resulting from their coexistence has been mere survival without any perceptible progress, Vladimir and Estragon remain at the end of the play where they were in the beginning. The business of man's waiting for Godot-stage being endless, what we have in the play is, so to say, a finite moment in the progress of eternity. It is like one digit in an infinitely long series of recurring decimals. Although presenting only a moment in the context of eternity, yet in temporal terms the business of the two acts covers two stages of an epoch—the rise and fall of a civilization. As Man waits to become Superman, civilizations come and go. In each social system, the wielder of power prolongs his tyranny by exploiting the intellectual and cultural heroes, but absolute power makes him blind even as the mainsprings of culture go dry. That is precisely what happens to Pozzo and Lucky who stand for civilization and culture, respectively. Civilization and culture always go together, tied to each other, as it were; when civilization declines, culture follows suit. In short, taken collectively, Pozzo and Lucky stand for the ethos of an historical age; taken individually, they are two complementary forces which determine the shape of life within that society.

For a set, we have a near-empty stage. That is as it should be because the stage is a metaphor for existence. Just as man is trying to fill the existential vacuum through unending but inconsequential activity, Vladimir and Estragon, representing that man, fill this stage with their incessant movements. Their activities never assume the proportions of momentous, dramatic action because that would be contrary to the quintessential tenor of human existence. As they wait, they invent one pastime after another—a symbolic representation of the innumerable strategies of survival devised by man. One of the pastimes with these tramps is talking—speaking when they have nothing to say. They talk for the sake of talking, so to say. This corresponds to Man's obsessive preoccupation with 'word'. So, indeed, they go on and on—the actors on the stage, like Man in the universe.

In the traditional epics, the hero's progress is depicted through a journey which symbolizes, as it were, obstacles to be overcome to reach a goal. Consequently, road has come to be treated as an emblem of progress and arrival. Very aptly, therefore, we have a road in the play to prepare us for the heroic adventures of mankind. But, then, it is a road that does not lead anywhere. It is not used to reach a desired goal, nor is there any indication regarding the whence and whither. That is as good as saying that in the tiresome journey of evolution, man has neither reached anywhere nor is there any certainty about his direction. In any case, this is not a highway but just a country road—a line where the realms of civilization and nature intersect. In the set, there is also the tree which is bare in Act I but covered with a few leaves in Act II—a change suggesting rebirth, a development which would ordinarily appear incongruous because Act II depicts degeneration and not regeneration; but if we remember that it is a willow tree, we realize that the absence of leaves signifies hope, and their presence, grief and despair.

Although the time of action in each Act is evening, it does not symbolize the same thing in both the cases. Evening is the time when day matures, its being followed by night corresponds to the ripeness of a fruit which gets rotten thereafter. Such indeed is the zenith of the Pozzo-civilization in Act I. Evening is also the time when the sunlight of reality yields place to the moonlight of illusions; thus at the end of Act II, as the sun of the Pozzo-civilization sets, the talk of 'tomorrow' embodies the illusion of hope. Of course, 'todays' and 'tomorrows' are to be interpreted metaphorically, not literally. Act I is not separated from Act II by a single revolution of the sun; rather, as I have been maintaining, these represent distinct stages of a long aeon—the peak of a civilization and its decline. In the ordinary concept of time, these stages might be separated by decades or even centuries, but in the framework of eternity, a year would be no more than a fraction of a second. Such time gaps can, therefore, be referred to as yesterdays, todays and tomorrows—at least by the near-eternal Man represented by Vladimir and Estragon. That they are timeless and not bound to the narrow confines of a time which is measured by clocks is underlined by the fact that Pozzo alone is watch-conscious in Act I. Pozzo's watch may have some role within the limited context of a civilization, but it cannot measure the evolution of man which covers an endless series of civilizations. In that eternal framework, the temporal bounds of any particular civilization lose all significance.

Thus the play acquires a universal dimension and what is presented in Acts I and II could be treated as happening in any civilization, anywhere. Or, to borrow Beckett's own manner of putting things, the scene is nowhere and the time is nowhen.

As the curtain goes up, Estragon is seen on a low mound. Low, indeed, because the action does not represent any high moment in the evolution of man. Although there is nothing in the stage directions to indicate his looks and age, or Vladimir's either, the two are invariably presented as old tramps. Old, indeed, because man as a species has inhabited the universe for such a long time. And since man does not seem to be particularly at home on planet earth, he is a kind of a tramp, too. Also, since from the opening moments, we have a lot of clowning from Vladimir and Estragon, it is customary to attribute a touch of the circus harlequin, music-hall cross talk, etc., to them. This is as good as saying that man is a veritable clown of the universe. With only episodic bits rather than the central part assigned to him, a clown tries to assume significance and project himself as the protagonist; precisely in the same way, man too has been trying to give the impression that he is the most important performer in the drama of existence. In other words, the world is a great circus in which human activity is amusing but without any intrinsic significance. When Aesop wanted to show the animal in man, he inverted the position and showed animals behaving like men. Likewise, the clown's representing humanity here implies mankind being clownish.

Like a typical circus clown, Estragon is seen trying to take off his boot, the foot-gear; Vladimir's clowning later would be related to head-gear, i.e. hat. These are significant hints to suggest that they represent the physical and mental aspects, respectively. I have already referred to the fact that Estragon stinks from his feet while Vladimir stinks from his breath which is the chariot of words and thought. This is confirmed by their pet-names, too. Gogo suggests going, i.e. footwork, while Didi suggests talking to those who are aware that the French word 'dire' means 'to tell'. Anyway, what does Estragon's trouble with the boot signify? The function of boot being protection against the wildness of nature, it could be a symbol of any such institution as man has invented to protect himself from the thorny laws of nature. That is to say, the boot here could be a sort of value-system which gets outdated and out-of-shape with the passage of time.

Man would like to get rid of it but cannot.

Before the very first speech is uttered, Estragon pulls at his boots until, exhausted, he gives up saying, 'Nothing to be done' (*Godot*, 9). Indeed, man's struggle for survival has been going on and on for such a long time and his efforts have proved so futile that man has reached the end-of-the-tether situation. If he has continued so far it is primarily because of the mental self who would resist quitting in despair. However, now even he is getting desperate: 'I'm beginning to come round to that opinion' (*Godot*, 9). Earlier, all his life, Vladimir (the mental aspect) explains, he had been putting it off him by arguing to himself that he hadn't yet tried everything. This reference to 'haven't yet tried everything' (*Godot*, 9) is important in the context of man's never-ending urge to invent ever-new social modes, ethical mores and cultural values as strategies of survival.

From the conversation that follows it appears that Estragon and Vladimir are meeting again after having separated last night which the former spent in a ditch where he was beaten up, 'as usual'. All that it means is that, in the evolution of man, there are moments when body and mind get fed up with each other's company and tend to separate. However, since that implies return to primitivism (ditch-stage) and being beaten by the physically stronger species, the physical self is compelled to return to the mental self. Mind is, of course, only too happy at this reunion. But, frightened by the prospects of yet another spell of existentialist torture, the physical self, in a mood of despair, cannot muster a matching enthusiasm. Mental self resents this coldness and reminds the physical self that, but for the protection of mind, man should have been an extinct creature, or a fossil, by now:

VLADIMIR: 'When I think of it...all these years...but for me...where would you be...? (*Decisively*) You'd be nothing more than a little heap of bones at the present moment, no doubt about it.' (*Godot*, 9)

When Estragon rejoins with 'And what of it?', he seems to underline the fact that not much has come anyway out of their prolonged coexistence—a reminder that makes Vladimir gloomy. Nevertheless, he seeks to console himself by saying:

'...What's the good of losing heart now, that's what I say. We should have thought of it a million years ago, in the nineties.' (*Godot*, 10)

'Million years ago' is not merely an idle mannerism of speech.

Beckett had in mind the stage when, millions of years ago, Man, just created, was in a precarious condition. At that stage, leading a less perverse and more natural existence, he was at least less grotesque and more presentable. Now it is too late. That 'a million years ago' is followed immediately by 'in the nineties' is a characteristic trick of Beckett who is trying to present man on the two scales of time—chronological and eternal. That the progress of man involves both physical and mental suffering is underscored in their repeating the same sentence: 'Hurts! He wants to know if it hurts!' (*Godot*, 10). They are referring, of course, to their respective troubles—Estragon's trouble with the boot (adjustment with man-made values) and Vladimir's with pissing (imperfect intellection).[19]

Soon, Vladimir is assailed by a new doubt: of the four evangelists, only one speaks of a thief being saved. Could one be justified in basing hopeful calculations on just this 50 per cent chance and that too from only one of the four evangelists? Why believe Luke rather than the other three who have recorded, instead, the death of both the thieves? Ditto for the secular evangelist, Darwin. To bring home this Darwinian link, Beckett makes Estragon reply, 'People are bloody ignorant apes' (*Godot*, 13). To prevent the audience from thinking only of the Biblical evangelists, Beckett mixes the roles of the saviours—Christ who would save from Hell (*Godot*, 12), i.e. damnation, and Godot who would save from death (*Godot*, 13), i.e. extinction. In this connection, it would not be out of place to surmise that Beckett possibly imagined that the two tramps standing before the audience were to look like two thieves. Thus, in a sense, the question could appear: which of these twin aspects of human personality stood any chance of survival—the mental self or the physical self?

The conversation that follows Vladimir's first announcement that they are waiting for Godot appears pointless but not when one keeps in mind the suggestion that Godot stands for Superman. Surely, there being no certainty of time and place regarding man's growing into Superman, he has to keep waiting until that actually happens, i.e. until Godot arrives. As the locale of the story of human evolution has been changing from civilization to civilization, the actual place of the tryst with Godot is inevitably uncertain, the only thing certain being the presence of a tree—the symbol of anima mundi. Intriguingly enough, this tree appears at once a shrub, a bush and a willow, but in fact it implies an interesting deduction. As these descriptions bring to mind their traditional associations with life-giving greenery, sex, and death, respectively, one immediately perceives the close proximity between life and death (via sex) in the functioning of Life Force. Likewise, about the time of Godot's arrival, the only thing known is that the day of the tryst is Saturday—Sabbath day, after a full week of labour. In terms of evolution that would mean after the tedious waiting of millions of years. Vladimir looks wildly about himself, as though the date were inscribed on the landscape itself (*Godot*, 15). That is an apt reaction because the time of evolution is to be measured in terms of geological rather than chronological clock.

On that eternal scale, a whole age separates 'yesterday' from 'today'. At the even-time of every civilization, there is an illusion that Godot-stage has been reached. But instead comes night followed by the dawn of another 'day'—a new civilization which gradually matures into another 'evening' when the illusion is revived once again. This is repeated civilization after civilization, i.e. 'day' after 'day'. In this context, it is understandable why Estragon cannot recall what had happened 'yesterday', and why every messenger boy disclaims having visited earlier. At the time of these 'evenings', the physical self, feeling exhausted, falls asleep even before the night-fall and sees nightmares of impending collapse—something that the mental self is not even prepared to hear about.

But, then, if they cannot share their secret dreams, shouldn't they better part company? (*Godot*, 16) Even if they do, Estragon, the physical self, cannot go far. The only other alternative is suicide (*Godot*, 17), but Vladimir, the mental self, would not have that. He would rather prefer to wait until Godot told them how they stood. That is to say, until they knew if, even as Superman, man would have any more meaningful life. What a pity that man has taken upon himself this ordeal of endless waiting without any commitment on the part of Godot! The promise was not only tentative but also conditional: he was to 'see' after consulting his family, friends, agents, correspondents, books, and accounts (*Godot*, 18). This, one feels, is a way of saying that man's survival is subject to his own track-record and reputation as a species. The reference to man's being tied to Godot (*Godot*, 19) implies man's living not in the present but for some future hope. This hopeless hope is like the proverbial carrot—ever-dangling but never realized. Hence, Estragon's preference for carrots. Anyway, while physical self is still bound to natural laws of surfeit—'the more you eat the worse it gets' (*Godot*, 21)—the mental self claims to get used to the muck as he goes along. That is to say, the essentials do not change; only one learns to live with things. Indeed, there is nothing that man could ever do. Repetition of 'Nothing to be done' (*Godot*, 21) at this stage not only swings the play back to the starting point but also underlines the quintessence of the problem—man's progress being just an interplay of creation and decreation to maintain the zero-situation.

This process of creation and decreation is illustrated by showing how a civilization rises, falls and vanishes, leaving things as they were. That is the dramatic function of the two visits of Pozzo and Lucky in Acts I and II. Now each civilization has a peculiarity of its own and its hero is one who embodies the spirit of the time. Since the values that serve as the basis of a civilization are exploited by its hero, the culture of an age is a kind of slave without which a civilization cannot survive. In other words, each culture is tied to its civilization, but it is a tie that represents symbiosis as well as submission. Such is the position of Pozzo and Lucky who represent respectively, as suggested earlier, the civilization and culture of an age.

Of course, the fate of Pozzo and Lucky resembles that of all civilizations and cultures; but, just as Vladimir and Estragon together stand for Man in both individual and collective sense, the Pozzo-civilization could be treated as both specific and archetypal. In any case, writing the play in the late forties, Beckett could not help projecting in the play the attributes of mid-century Europe which was then witnessing the collapse of the civilization identified with Italian Fascism and German Nazism.[20] A hero may not be a superman but to lesser mortals he appears to be a demi-god. That is why, for a moment, Vladimir and Estragon mistake Pozzo for their much-awaited saviour. But that illusion is short-lived. Heroes are, after all, men; Superman, on the other hand, would be more than a man—a category apart.

Against the overbearing Pozzo, Lucky is an effeminate 'half-wit'. That Lucky is to have only the bones while Pozzo is to have the wine-and-chicken is an ironic comment on the fate of cultural heroes in the service of political bosses. It is possible to see in the dinner-parade the rigorous regimentation in the Fascist, Nazi and Soviet camps. An echo of British imperialism is heard in Pozzo's complaints of Lucky's tyrannizing over him through over-usefulness—a near-satirical variation of the notorious 'white man's burden'. Obviously, Pozzo represents a kind of civilization which should suit man physically rather than mentally. That is why Estragon is keen to stay on but Vladimir feels ill at ease. If Pozzo's kind of civilization and mental self cannot adjust, nor can its culture and the physical self. That is why Lucky gives Estragon a powerful kick and receives back a spiteful spit—a veritable way of saying that culture spurns senses and senses spit on culture.

Apropos of that lyrical recitation about the setting sun, its manner and contents correspond to each other. Towards the close, inspiration vanishes and what appeared to come like a bang ends up in a whimper. 'That is how it is on this bitch of an earth', adds Pozzo (*Godot*, 38). That, indeed, is the way the civilizations rise and fall. A similar impregnation of meaning in the style may be seen in the tenor of the dialogues. Questions are raised but not answered. These are picked up again and yet again, even when rendered redundant; sentences are begun but not completed. There is incessant repetition but the entire chatter is inconsequential. That is precisely the tenor of human life, too—marked by inconsequentiality, redundancy, incompleteness, repetition, incessant verbosity, constant questioning. As for the progress of civilizations, it is essentially a matter of eating, drinking, making polite conversation, mutual exploitation, bragging—all epitomized in what Pozzo does and says. Nothing significant is done and said by any of the characters because these no-role-to-play actors are supposed to represent a species that has no role to play in Life. In the same way, Pozzo keeps losing things one by one—pipe, vaporizer, watch, and sight (in Act II)—to underline the fact that the process of civilization implies not only addition but also discarding of such things as have been cherished possessions once. And that, in a way, reinforces the fundamental theme of the play regarding creation going hand in hand with decreation.

In fact, Beckett loses no opportunity of reiterating this theme whenever he gets an opportunity—of course, with varying metaphors in different situations. For example, when he brings the thermodynamics of emotions: 'The tears of the world are a constant quantity. For each one who begins to weep, somewhere else another stops. The same is true of the laugh' (*Godot*, 33). Since in the syndrome called life, as one symptom is eased, another is made worse, the progress of evolution amounts to naught. Thus, for all practical purposes, any given generation is as good as the preceding or the succeeding one—perhaps better in one way but worse in another. That is what Pozzo implies when he adds, 'Let us not then speak ill of our generation. It is not any unhappier than its predecessors. (*Pause*). Let us not speak well of it either. (*Pause*). Let us not speak of it at all' (*Godot*, 33). Indeed, human effort at evolution is fated to remain barren because the soil is so unproductive.

The absolute inability of man to grow is precisely what Lucky declares in his 'speech' (*Godot*, 42-5)—in his own round-about manner, of course. But before 'thinking' comes his dance. Lucky's dance has been described by the other three characters as 'The Scapegoat's Agony', 'The Hard Stool', and 'The Net' (*Godot*, 40).[21] Taken together, the labels imply that, entangled in the net of fate, man may wriggle in agony right and left, up and down, like the mythical scapegoat, but for those viewing things dispassionately the whole exercise is as comic as the passing of a hard stool. This dance for the amusement of the characters tends to be entertainment-within-entertainment—like play-within-play. For the audience, however, it is a kind of dumbshow before the play proper, encapsulating semiotically what is to follow verbally in Lucky's speech—the self-entanglement of man within the circumstances and mutually cancelling strategies of survival.

Lucky's 'thinking' is a great piece of writing. More than the words, it is the form which conveys the theme. The speech is not logical like a philosopher's well-knit argument; it is, instead, a network of uncertainties through 'desperate retchings' from the pell-mell of thought, torrents of broken sentences, imprecise expressions, repetition of phrases, etc. All this corresponds to the tenor of human evolution. Instead of a logical and integral development, what characterizes the story of man are irrational starts, inexplicable interruptions or terminations, sudden resumptions, repetitive efforts, etc.—a chaotic mess, indeed. If man's evolutionary stream is suggested in the flow of rhetoric, his turning from nature to religion, to philosophy, to art, to science, to technology, etc., without trying any one of them to the logical end, is conveyed through the threading-cum-jettisoning of one argument after another. The irrational pomposity of man's claim is brought home effectively by parodying the typically philosophical style in such a manner that arguments invariably lead to contradictory deductions, and even abortive speculations are ejaculated with the vigour of exclamations. Repetition of phrases, as in a broken gramophone record, suggests lucidity being transformed, through centuries of subservience, into mindless parroting. This is to hammer home the fact that on the level of evolution also, man has been behaving as if he were stuck in some groove, for he has been repeating the same pattern of existence for thousands of years without making any fundamental progress. The entire speech is so structured that, even as it goes on and on, it exudes decadence and decomposition. That is precisely the theme of the speech, too: as man goes on and on with his evolutionary strategies, he has been only wasting and shrinking.

As Anselm Atkins points out, structurally the speech has three parts.[22] The first part, which ends with the phrase 'better than nothing' (*Godot*, 43), presents theological and philosophical arguments in the rational, geometrical mode of Descartes and Spinoza: 'Given the existence of God, *then*...' The next part is an incomplete fragment of a rational argument—like the last half of an objection. This part is a self-repeating verbal trap created by the interweaving of the cycles of time (autumn, summer, winter, etc.) and varying spaces (like Feckham, Peckham, Fulham, Clapham, etc.), with a collage of contradictions and malapropisms. The last part begins as a second objection but, later, discarding all syntax, lapses into complete aphasia. The phrases in this part are either repetitions of the previous parts or poetic words introduced for the first time.

Is Lucky's speech meant, as Lawrence E Harvey believes, to deflate the intellectuals, to satirize the specialized professional and vocational categories, and to highlight the fact that despite vitamins, sanitation and physical education, man is shrinking?[23] Or following Norman Mailer, may one see in the speech 'intuitive lunges into the nature of man, sex, God and time?[24] Or is G S Fraser nearer the truth when he surmises that the speech seeks to dismiss Liberalism, Progress, Popular Education and what Peacock used to call the March of Mind?[25] Frederick Hoffman asserts, instead, that the speech deflates biblical literature[26]—a hunch echoed by Edith Kern who regards it as a mock-serious satire of the Corpus Christie cycles.[27] Linda Ben-Zvi, on the other hand, sees in the speech three themes—the indifference of heaven, the dwindling of man, and the earth as an abode of stones.[28] All these are useful insights and any satisfactory summary of the speech must reckon with all of them. Here is, indeed, the summary offered by G C Barnard:

> Given the existence of a personal God with white beard who loves us so dearly (with some exceptions) and suffers with those whom (for reasons unknown but time will tell) he has damned and plunged into hell; yet it is certain that man, both potential and actual, wastes and pines; in spite of all science and medicine, sports and physical culture, man shrinks and dwindles.

In short, humanity suffers and we know not why.[29]

While Ruby Cohn[30] and Jerold J Savory[31] paraphrase the speech in their own abbreviated versions, they also highlight these points with only this difference that the former lays additional stress on 'skull fading fading' and the latter on 'abandoned unfinished'.

In short, despite want of critical unanimity, critics agree that Lucky's speech laments the ironic outcome of God's love—man's shrinking as a result of his incessant efforts at growing. It would not, therefore, be unfair to suggest that the speech sums up what we have been projecting as the very theme of the play—that, despite the labour of thousands of years, involving artists, philosophers, professors of divinity, scientists, and physical culturists, man has not evolved much; instead, if anything, he is dwindling. This fate has inevitably resulted in his ever remaining 'unfinished, unfinishing, unfinishable'. Perhaps that explains why the speech ends with such words as 'abandoned', 'skull', 'stones', etc. Indeed, abandoned by God, subjected to mortality, and fated to live on barren rocks, man cannot but find his labours always unfinished. Since in a situation like this, he cannot reach the stage of Superman, he must of necessity keep waiting for Godot.

The senselessness of Lucky's speech suggests that life is meaningless like the speech but, before that view is absorbed as total truth, the vague feeling of a latent sense at a deeper level is felt. Consequently, what comes home is a conviction that behind the absurd in life there is some divine purpose. The message seems to be that 'anthropopopometry' (*Godot*, 43)—i.e. measuring the growth of man—is a riddle because alimentation and defecation run concurrently, simultaneously in such a manner that it is difficult to tell for certain whether man is progressing at all. This mystery has confounded all kinds of thinkers who yet continue with their never-ending 'quoi, quoi, quoi' in the hope that some day 'Time will tell'. Man's mind is too imperfect to realize this paradox of human growth and yet mankind has placed all its hopes of survival on such a flawed mind.

Why do Vladimir, Estragon and Pozzo react to Lucky's 'speech' the way they do? Pozzo is disgusted right from the start because it is an outright condemnation of human civilization. It is equally painful for Vladimir and Estragon but they alternate their protests with attentiveness. They are impressed by big words but grow violent when evolution is condemned in plainer phrases. At last, Lucky is dispossessed of his hat and silenced—a process that is completed off the stage. In Act II, Lucky is dumb and Pozzo blind. Lucky's fate signifies the gradual loss of cultural values parallel to the decline of a civilization. This is, in a way, a telling comment on the dialectical relationship of interdependence and antagonism between culture and civilization. Culture tries to adjust to the changes in a civilization as if it were a slave but, at the same time, artists are the ones who point out the weaknesses of a civilization, for which they may be silenced, but then that proves the end of the civilization, too.

Corresponding to the loss of Lucky's hat is the loss of Pozzo's watch, signifying the loss of time-sense. Thus the departure of Pozzo and Lucky denotes not just the departure of two individuals, or of a specific age, but of every one of the innumerable civilizations. The departure in Act I is much more prolonged than it would be in Act II because a civilization at its peak lingers on while a declining one merely collapses. The passing of one epoch, or of a few generations, does not mean the end of life or of human existence; in fact, the waiting for Godot continues eternally, age after age, generation after generation. That is the precise point made when Pozzo leaves shouting, 'On! On!' (*Godot*, 47) and both Estragon and Vladimir echo him.

Lest the passing of a civilization induce depression in man awaiting Godot, an element of hope is injected through the message from Godot reviving the promise of a visit. That the messenger is a 'boy' is not without significance. Being a link in man's continuity in the chain of evolution, every child is, as it were, a harbinger of the hope that man may yet become a Superman, if he persists. Vladimir thinks that the boy is the same as had brought a similar message the previous day, but the boy assures him that he has come for the first time. That is as it should be. After all, the boy stands for future age and the 'future' in each age is always different, even though to Man as a species it would naturally appear to be the same. This boy minds the goats and is liked by Godot while his brother who minds the sheep is often beaten by their master. This is obviously an ironic reversal of what we have in the Bible, for it was Abel who tended sheep, goats being under the charge of Cain. Possibly here is a Nietzschean reversal: Godot-superman patronizes not the sheepish creatures lauded by meek Christianity but those who can whore like goats.

As the boy leaves, night falls and the moon rises. After all, even a dark age is not without illusions and the fate of man is not very different from that of the moon. Both are pale for weariness in their efforts to climb to heaven—man's heaven being the Godot-stage. That makes Adam's suffering even more excruciating than crucifixion because, unlike Christ who died quick, man languishes bit by bit. But, maybe, tomorrow will be better (*Godot*, 52), as the message brought by the boy implies. But, strangely enough, it suggests the thought of suicide to the tramps. They agree, however, that it isn't worthwhile *now*. They also agree to go, but do not move. This is significant because, in this situation of hopeless hope, 'going' for Man may mean either going ahead or going away from the road of evolution; neither being possible, they remain where they are. Mankind is still where it was, despite all the fuss between body and mind, despite all the glory of civilization and the labour of culture.

That things remain unchanged is reiterated by repeating the opening situation of Act I in Act II. In fact, it is customary to sum up the action of the play as 'Nothing happens, twice'. Of course, it is not exactly the same situation; after all, between the two Acts, time has passed and what was ripe then has become rotten now. The irreversible line of descent on the one hand and no-change-in-essentials on the other may appear contradictory but not when one relates the two to the chronological and eternal scales of time, respectively. The line of descent in a century or two would be a mere dot on the graph of eternity; and since in the meanwhile there might be an upsurge of another civilization, the next upward dot would give the impression of there having been no change whatsoever.

As the curtain goes up, three things catch one's eye: Estragon's boots, Lucky's hat, and four or five leaves on the tree. As suggested earlier, they stand, respectively, for social mores, the intellectual component of culture, and the instinct for procreation. The implication of the setting, therefore, is that, (a) although discarded, the old moral values persist; (b) intellectually also there is no displacing or progress; and (c) only anima mundi being active, the population has increased. While the appearance of the leaves, symbolizing renewal of life, makes Vladimir feel fervishly excited, he is disgusted at the putrefying boots that represent outdated morality. The hat is ignored possibly because it symbolizes the unpleasant reality embedded in Lucky's speech. As the leaves on the tree bring into Vladimir's mind the thought of recurrence, infinite continuity, and the analogical deduction that the repetitive process of evolution also implies eternal recurrence, he starts singing the song, 'A dog came in the kitchen'. The tenor of the story of the song corresponds to the progression of man's evolution—story-within-story-within-story-within-story...ad infinitum, although it is the same story all along. It is like the unending line of images created by placing two mirrors parallel to each other. The linear progress of the story is effected through repetitive circularity—like horizontally placed coil of a spring. Here is an ironic comment on man's fate in which linear progress is made contingent on the Viconian cycles.

When Estragon comes in, he behaves peevishly, because he has been beaten once again during another night spent in a ditch. Characteristically, he would not be touched, questioned or even spoken to, but he wants Vladimir to stay with him. All this reiterates the dependence of the fragile senses of man on the relative strength of his mind. But so great is their mutual incompatibility that the senses resent the company of mind. Mind, too, feels better when left to itself—for it can piss (i.e. think) without trouble—but self-centredness breeds melancholy, too. Estragon reports that he has been beaten again although he was not doing anything. On one level it would appear an unmerited punishment; on the other, it might underline the very crime of human existence—that is, man's ***not doing*** anything but just letting time pass. Instead of doing something positive towards his own evolution, man has been just content to wait and thus get entangled in a network of routine. No wonder there is nothing exciting about life—only unending boredom.

The conversation between Vladimir and Estragon turns sour and once again the latter suggests that it would be better if they parted. 'The best thing', he proposes, 'would be to kill me, like the other'...'like billions of others' (*Godot*, 62). These billions should mean the innumerable species that have become extinct. But since killing is out of the question, they must continue to carry their own crosses, and thus they decide to while away time through conversation. The banter that follows is about the inexhaustibility of man and the dead voices of the ages that have flown away. Surely, for Vladimir, it is not enough 'to have lived' and 'to be dead' (*Godot*, 63); therefore, he would have man think, too. Man did think once upon a time, but now, since there are only skeletons of thoughts, human life has become a sort of charnel-house (*Godot*, 64). Should man start again in another direction? Characteristically again, Estragon suggests a turn towards nature. But Vladimir retorts that they have tried that, too. Indeed, hedonism did not serve man any better than rationalism. It is possible that man could do without thinking but thinking is by no means the worst thing that he can do.

Is man better equipped today to solve the riddles of the universe? Perhaps not. He doesn't know anything—not even why he does not know. And still this congenital fool of the universe claims to be rational in evolving values—a point brought home through Estragon's boots. The pair is there but only changed in colour. What used to be black or a kind of grey is now brown and a kind of green (*Godot*, 67). Perhaps the idea is that medieval standards of morality with white and black categories, or the Renaissance standards that merged black and white into grey, are yielding place to a morality that is less vigorous (brown) but more colourful (green). The suggestion that the pair might have been left by some one else for whom these had grown tight possibly implies a reference to the ethical system of one country or age being adopted by another even after they have been rejected in the country of their origin. (Witness, for example, the current craze for orientalism in the West and for the westernization in the East.) Mysteriously enough, the pair fits Estragon; rather it is too big for him. If it is Estragon's own original pair, it could mean that what appears a morality too strict in one age might appear too liberal in the next, and vice-versa. Of course, there is also a simpler way of explaining this phenomenon on realistic level: boots are too loose now because Estragon has in the meantime shrunk, as lamented by Lucky in his speech on anthropometry.

The pair having talked themselves to exhaustion, Estragon wants to go to sleep and Vladimir sings him a lullaby: 'Bye bye bye bye...' (*Godot*, 70). No words are actually used but the tune, an echo of 'Rock-a-bye, baby', awakens in the mind of Estragon the memory of the lines of that well-known song: 'When the bough breaks, the cradle will fall/Down will come baby, cradle and all.' That, in turn, leads to the stimulation of such associations in his subconscious as precipitate an archetypal dream: 'I was falling...I was on top of a—...' (*Godot*, 70). Perhaps this is the dream dreamt in Act I, too; but, as earlier, Vladimir is not interested. It could be Adam's fall haunting Man's collective unconscious, or else a fall consequent upon the breaking of a bough of the tree of evolution. At this stage, Lucky's hat is noticed. The two tramps pass the three hats around in different combinations (*Godot*, 71-2)—a typically Beckettian trick to suggest the variety of permutations, effected in different ages in respect of the interlacing of sensuous, intellectual and cultural values. The whole business of culture is seen to be purely clownish when Vladimir plays Lucky and imitates his thinking and dancing. More ridicule follows when they affect the polite behaviour of 'after you' only to find themselves shouting at each other. Significantly, these are all verbal games. This is as good as saying that man is seeking to establish his significance not through action but through words. Starting playfully but getting serious through involvement, these games mirror the human situation in which men and women do seriously what is intrinsically as absurd as these games. Equally absurd is the game of evolution involving such symbolic exercises as 'movements', 'elevations', 'relaxations' and 'elongations' for they produce contradictory and self-cancelling results—'to warm us up' and 'to calm us down' (*Godot*, 76). To bring home this point visually, they 'do' the tree and stagger. The implication of this staggering vis-a-vis the tree of evolution annoys Estragon so much that he brandishes his fists and orders God to have pity on him (*Godot*, 77).

As if in answer to this angry prayer, Pozzo and Lucky arrive on the stage. But now Pozzo is no longer the tyrant he was in Act I; instead, he is blind and led by a dumb Lucky. Thus, against the zenith of civilization in Act I, Act II represents its nadir. In the interim, Vladimir and Estragon, of course, have not undergone a comparable decay because together they stand for the essence of mankind and, according to Beckett, essentials do not change. The mental and physical selves continue to struggle, to adjust; only civilization and culture rise and fall.

A declining civilization needs help from individuals in both physical and mental aspects. But characteristically enough, the physical self, Estragon, will help only if Pozzo ensures his sustenance (bones) or pays a price for the help rendered. The more altruistic mental self looks upon the situation as an opportunity to prove that he belongs to a worthy species. However, even as Pozzo lies crying for help, Vladimir starts soliloquizing, like Hamlet, on what distinguishes man from animals. Very like Hamlet, Vladimir tells himself to act but does not. Indeed, in every age, man has a chance to help the process of evolution; but he does not contribute much because thinking prevents action. Interestingly, Vladimir prologues his 'soliloquy' with 'Let us not waste our time in idle discourse' (*Godot*, 79). In this he is like Polonius who begins by declaring brevity to be the soul of wit and yet goes on to inflict a long and overflourished harangue. Like the Prince of Denmark, this ruler of the world (as the name Vladimir literally means) also takes to self-accusing comparisons with a tiger bounding to the help of his cogeners without the least reflection. There is a direct echo of Hamlet's most famous soliloquy when, weighing the pros and cons with folded arms, Vladimir incorporates in his utterance the most emphatic clause of that celebrated soliloquy, '*that* is the question' (*Godot*, 80). Then he himself answers with Miltonic consolation—'they also serve who stand and wait'. Of course, he puts it differently, 'We have kept our appointment, and that's an end to that. We are not saints, but we have kept our appointment' (*Godot*, 80).

Obviously, Beckett is indicting rather than endorsing these Shakespearean and Miltonic stances. Are we really serving the interest of evolution, Beckett seems to ask, if we, like Hamlet, brood without acting and flatter ourselves with the delusive idea that we have done our duty in waiting? That such puerile waiting, without the accompaniment of action, won't suffice is underlined immediately: to Vladimir's question as to how many people could boast of having kept the appointment, Estragon replies, 'Billions!' (*Godot*, 80). What is more, he highlights the quality of man's imperfect reasoning when he adds aphoristically, 'We are born mad. Some remain so' (*Godot*, 80).

Even when Vladimir and Estragon turn to Pozzo to help him, it is more by way of diversion from boredom than out of any compassion. Can a fallen civilization be rescued in such a half-hearted manner? More likely than not, it can mean setback to man on both physical and mental levels. That is why Vladimir and Estragon are soon seen among the entangled beings. Since this makes Pozzo at once the agent and victim of the fall, he responds to both Cain and Abel. In this connection, taking a cue from Frederick Busi, who suggests that Pozzo literally means, 'I can, I am able',[32] I suggest that we may read Cain as 'Can't' and Abel as 'Able'. Thus seen, Pozzo becomes the image of both the impotence and the potential of man. To put it differently, every civilization has in itself the seeds of both the survival and extinction of mankind. When Estragon and Vladimir decide to get up, they do—a simple question of will power. What it implies is that human will alone is the guarantee of evolutionary progress.

Does this 'rising' signify the continuation of the Pozzo-civilization or the advent of some other? Beckett does not commit himself. After all, the evening of one civilization may or may not usher the dawn of another. That is why Estragon and Vladimir start disputing whether the twilight pertains to sunset or sunrise. Anyway, evening being evening, night must come. As one cannot measure time at night by looking at the sky, the notion of time is rather bewildering. So much so that reference to time is a torment to Pozzo. Hence his outburst. After all, what difference does it make when a thing happened or would happen; the only thing important is that it did happen or shall happen *one* day, or *one* second (*Godot*, 89). The division of time into years, months, days, hours and seconds is meaningless. On the scale of eternity, the duration of an individual's sojourn on this earth is so short that one may see one's birth and death as simultaneous activities: 'They give birth astride of a grave; the light gleams an instant, then it's night once more' (*Godot*, 89). Interestingly, this comes from Pozzo who used to be so time-conscious in Act I. Once its vision is blighted, a civilization moves without any direction, as if in the void of timelessness. The only thing that it must do is to keep going as long as it can. Thus Pozzo leaves while shouting 'On!', but this time without a single goodbye. Lucky doesn't dance, think or sing because he is dumb. Indeed, when a civilization declines, all its attendant springs go dry. Of course, Lucky had a new hat this time which amounts to saying that a declining age too has its own philosophy—bleak and mindless, which is usually not articulated at all.

Pozzo's outburst leaves Vladimir wondering if time is all that meaningless: is birth really astride of a grave? Perhaps not, he argues to himself: 'We have time to grow old. The air is full of our cries' (*Godot*, 91). It is habit that deadens our sense of time. As they prepare to leave, Vladimir tells Estragon to pull on his trousers. Pants must be pulled 'on', if they cannot be taken 'off'—a Camusian alternative of resumption to suicide. In this myth of Sisyphus, the real point is not the intensity of unending torture but the hero's courage to restart, to go on. Likewise, Vladimir and Estragon's decision to continue waiting is an act of Sisyphean heroism.

Thus shall Estragon and Vladimir go on till eternity. If instead of two, the play had three Acts, or even umpteen, in each case, at the close, Vladimir and Estragon would be seen together, bound in ambivalence, ever-bored, ever mutually dependent, ever encountering civilization and culture, ever trying suicide, ever the same, and always ending up to give themselves or Godot (which is, of course, the same thing) yet another chance. In the evening of every civilization, either Vladimir or Estragon would ask, 'Well, shall we go?' and the other would reply, 'Yes, let's go', but they shall not move. Such, indeed, is human life. Man can neither go ahead nor go away. As the essentials do not change, endless waiting has become the essence of existence. Absolutely absurd is this situation of man because his absolute need to evolve is perfectly countered by his absolute inability to evolve. Man does want to change his life for the better but he has absolutely nothing to build his new existence on. His experiments with nature, religion, philosophy, art, science, etc., have yielded new patterns but by no means any real progress towards perfect existence. In fact, starting from emptiness, every step forward, even though heroic in itself, has brought him a step closer to total emptiness.

In the light of this tenor, will man ever become superman; will his waiting be rewarded with the arrival of Godot? Beckett's answer lies in that perfectly shaped sentence of St Augustine about our neither presuming too much nor despairing too much. Perhaps Godot will never come; perhaps he will but only at the end of eternity. Since infinite time cannot be measured by the infinitesimally small units of today and tomorrow, finite man cannot decide whether it would be worthwhile to wait or to give up. The irony of ironies, however, is that even if Godot does arrive in the long run, it is not certain if he would make worthwhile this eternally long ordeal. After all, Godot being infinitely away, finite man cannot visualize who or what Godot is. Perhaps Beckett meant precisely this when he told Schneider, 'If I knew, I would say so in the play.'

In short, *Waiting for Godot* dramatizes the situation of horizontal man caught in vertical time and circular evolution. In this situation, a step forward is, by definition, a step backward. It is a situation like the one in *The Lost Ones* in which the injunction is on the one hand, 'Do not come up the ladder, there is nothing at the top', and on the other, 'Do not go down the ladder, they have taken it away'. In *Murphy*, too, humanity is presented as a well with two buckets—one going down to be filled, another coming up to be emptied (M, 44).[33] Caught on the horn of this dilemma, man knows not what to do, what to expect, whether to leave or persist. Being such an angel of darkness, man is, in the words of Colin Duckworth, limited by his achievement: '...he will never reach infinity. Perhaps to within one step of infinity but never there.'[34] Thus do Yea-saying and Nay-saying coalesce into a 'perhaps' and it becomes impossible to tell whether to treat the end as a measure of triumphant courage or one of pathetic impotence to break the illusion. Indeed, finite man's attempt to attain the infinite can be seen as Greek tragedy on the one hand and as quixotic farcicality on the other.[35]

To make all this possible on the neutral ground of tragicomedy, Beckett has filled the play with mutually cancelling suggestions.[36] What might appear inadvertent contradictions are, in fact, well-planted verbal traps. The big idea is to put the audience into the mould of the tramps—foiled rationalists who find that any effort to reach a one-sided rational conclusion is inevitably aborted. The more they rationalize, the more they are left with doubts, uncertainties, irresolutions and still more questions.[37] Even at the end, the problem remains unresolved; the argument about the thieves does not end, nor does the story. This inconclusiveness is only as logical a conclusion as the end of any moment in the process of eternity. Only in such a situation a text may suggest a thousand equally plausible keys without validating any one of them completely.

Instead of precipitating catharsis or crystalizing a definite viewpoint, the play wilfully obviates any unidimensional stance. Since the interplay of incessant but mutually cancelling actions results in virtual inaction, nothing eventful happens and the overall tenor appears to be repetitive like a gramophone needle stuck in a groove. Hence, too, the eternal counterpointing of binary oppositions that tend not to negate but to balance each other—Vladimir against Estragon, Pozzo against Godot, Act II against Act I, self against 'others', discourse against meaning, cyclic against linear, hope against despair, tragic against comic. Indeed, instead of telling one story, the play tells innumerable vestigial stories. Taken together, they comprise a miniscule version of the story of mankind in its floundering evolution within the prison of time and space. Only thus can one explain why we have here heroic grandeur on the one hand and the stench of dissolution on the other. For a play like this, even tragicomedy won't be an adequate label. Instead of juxtaposing, alternating or interlacing the tragic and the comic, here everything is simultaneously and concurrently tragic and comic.

2 Prophet of the Mess

Why won't Godot come?

The answer does not lie just in *Waiting for Godot* but runs through the entire gamut of Beckett's works, taken together or individually. The question tends to touch the essential core of Beckett's view of life and, in a sense, each of his poems, novels or plays is a fragmentary expression of that vision. But, then, what exactly is that view of life? Beckett scholars have been at pains to evolve that view by seeking connections among various thinkers that are mentioned in his works or are known to have been studied by him at one stage or the other. Though by no means peculiar to Beckett scholarship, this is perhaps the most questionable tradition in literary criticism. After all, a writer's mind is not an eclectic, all-embracing computer, retaining whatever he reads and assimilating it in a most rational manner. The creative process is marked by far more complex intricacies.[1] Indeed, anything said about an impact has to be a mere conjecture. The situation becomes all the more ticklish when the writer concerned might be on record having disclaimed all such influences. Whereas critics like Edith Kern, Nathan Scott, Hugh Kenner, Ruby Cohn, John Fletcher, Richard Coe, Ihab Hassan, Cormier and Pallister, J D O'Hara, G C Barnard have referred to all kinds of philosophical, psychological and Christian undercurrents or overtones, and David H Hesla, Steven J Rosen, Lance St John Butler, etc., have come out with book-length studies on Beckett's intellectual concerns, Beckett would not admit any such connection. Once he told Gabriel d'Aubarede, 'I am not an intellectual. I am only a sensibility. I conceived of Molloy and the rest the day I became aware of my stupidity.'[2] He went to the extent of declaring, 'I never read the philosophers, I understand nothing of what they write.' Elsewhere he observed, 'When Heidegger and Sartre speak of a contrast between being and existence, they may be right, I don't know, but their language is too philosophical for me. I am not a philosopher.'[3]

Surely no body can take these statements on their face-value, for not only had Beckett studied literature and philosophy most diligently and published such learned critiques as 'Three Dialogues' and 'Dante...Bruno.Vico..Joyce', but also written a whole thesis on Proust. What is even more, all kinds of thinkers not only get mentioned, quoted, explained in his creative works but appear to have served as the fundamental source of his inspiration.[4] The fact of the matter is that Beckett did read most of the philosophers from Aristotle to Sartre. If he openly disavowed interest in philosophy, it was not because he was indulging in mock-modesty but because he found himself unable to endorse any one of them totally and consistently. Probably it is the echo of his own mind that one hears in the refrains of ***Molloy***: 'It is not certain'; 'I don't know'. After all, endorsing any one philosopher or any one school of philosophy implied accepting a straitjacket which he would not. He insisted, instead, 'I'm not interested in any system; I can't see any trace of any system anywhere.'[5] Seen closely, what these statements actually imply is not Beckett's want of knowledge or incapacity to understand but his refusal to follow the traditional mode of reducing things to theories and formulae. That tendency to evolve philosophical constructs Beckett disapproved even in criticism. That is why in 'Dante...Bruno.Vico.. Joyce', he warned against the dangers inhering neat identifications and went on to declare that literary criticism is not book-keeping! (*Dj*, 19)

A writer with such attitudes is bound to elude the grasp of traditional critics who are always on the look out for labels and pigeonholes. Not surprisingly, they have been discovering symbols where none were intended, and insisting on defining even what was meant to defy all definitions. No wonder, too, Madeleine Renaud once advised that the best way to understand Beckett is to read his works without looking for any philosophy.[6] But I think that that is an advice that must be taken with a lump of salt. Surely, one can have a view of life without being a philosopher or without studying philosophy as a discipline. In fact, Beckett's 'philosophy' is rooted in his distrust of the philosophers' presumptuous certitude. Beckett turns to philosophy not for solutions but for questions that the philosophers ask. His works raise these questions without offering answers. To quote John Pilling, 'Beckett does not dismiss the traditional roads to truth; all he rejects is the palace of wisdom at the end of the road.'[7] A man of such a genius can be profound and thought-provoking without being academic or intellectual in approach. Even otherwise, a true artist must not be a theorist. As Goethe used to advise, a writer must know all philosophy but keep it out of his art. Beckett does not exactly keep the philosophers out of his works but brings them in just to prove that they are all undependable as guides. Instead of interpreting Beckett's works as lacking in philosophy, a more realistic approach would be to regard him as an anti-academic,[8] anti-intellectual philosopher. He explored the entire gamut of philosophy to reach the stage where he could confidently deny the very possibility of knowledge, rationality and coherence.

Contrary to an academician's way of studying a thinker's ideas in depth, Beckett invariably gave them parodic twists and touched them with irreverent ridicule. Instead of building up arguments or explaining philosophical concepts, Beckett would offer counter-arguments and create dialectical paradoxes. To put it differently, he adopted philosophers' intellectual procedures only to debunk philosophy and intellection; he parodied the logical and rhetorical devices of the philosophers as well as their habit of raising questions, indulging in jargon-mongering and name-dropping, and sounding impressive even about trifles. No wonder a reader might feel all along that something profound is being said even when Beckett is actually implying the impossibility of man ever being capable of profundity. In the light of the above, perhaps the safest approach would be not to allow the philosophical citations or literary allusions to mislead us into finding connections with the writers mentioned or suggested. Beckett does not belong to any school, unless it be a school of his own—the school of anti-intellectual philosophy.[9]

Indeed, declaring Beckett as an amateur dilettante would be as wrong as to piece together all the philosophical bits with a view to synthesizing them into a world-view. Being primarily an artist rather than a philosopher, Beckett's basic interest is in life. On realizing that philosophical thoughts reduced life to abstraction and offered contradictory conclusions which made things even more confounded, he undertook to make a new, creative use of philosophy. He created layers of philosophy only to debunk philosophy so that life could be seen in its essence. He wanted to lead his readers to the realm of experience—a realm beyond ideas. Thus, in Beckett, we do have a collage of scraps of learning, tags of ideas, and a jumble of wisdom, but only to serve as foil to life. One by one, Beckett removes the fripperies of ideas and drapery of rhetoric to show human condition pared to bare bones. All this serves to bring home the realization that whatever meaning life has can be only experienced, not explained. The futility of philosophical labours is communicated through the repeated raising of the same questions concerning what, why, where and whither of life. Beckett's aim is to enable the reader to realize that, although answered differently by diverse philosophers, the age-old questions remain still unanswered and probably would remain so for all times to come. This is supposed to turn the reader from theories to facts of life. For any meaningful study of his genius also, it would be helpful to turn to life and to study his intellectual and cultural background; we must not, at the same time, forget that his mind was essentially both protean and parodic.

Born in 1906, Beckett was still a student when the Great War ushered in 'modernism' which, as Ihab Hassan puts it, brought about a 'revolution of sensibility'.[10] Brought up in the midst of an intellectual ferment, this sensitive young student of languages and literature at Trinity College, Dublin, chanced to spend two years (1928-30) at Paris in the frequent company of the literary giant of the day, James Joyce. Here he was exposed to the temper of the times—the 'modern temper', as Joseph Wood Krutch[11] calls it—which saw modern man at the zenith of civilization on the one hand and at the nadir of culture on the other. While technological advancements flattered modern man into believing that he was an omniscient god, all else pointed to his utter insignificance. Evolutionary forces predicted his onward progress while the nuclear inventions threatened him with extinction. Even as he boasted of his scientific outlook, modern psychology underlined his irrationality. Likewise, social engineering reduced him to a social unit while both capitalism and communism treated him as an economic unit. No wonder, the age came to be known for desublimation, alienation, nihilism, empiricism, other-direction, traditionlessness, agnosticism and incertitude. No wonder, too, it produced debunking naturalism, schizophrenic expressionism, faceless cubism, mechanistic futurism, neurotic surrealism, the grotesque novel and the absurd theatre.

It is reasonable to believe that the young Beckett was familiar with many of the intellectual concepts that everybody in the academic circle was talking about. For example, the theories of Darwin, Nietzsche, Marx, Pavlov, Einstein, Hegel, Herbert Spencer, J S Mill, F H Bradley, Bergson, etc. Most probably, Beckett had read the books that had enchanted the intelligentsia of that time or at least known what these books were about—for example, E H Haeckells' *Riddle of the Universe*, Bertrand Russell and A H Whitehead's *Principia*

Mathematica, Wittgenstein's *Tractus*, C K Ogden and I A Richards' *Meaning of Meaning*, Freud's *Civilization and Its Discontents*, T S Eliot's *The Waste Land*. Unable to accept any one approach at the cost of another, and being the child of an age which had repudiated the values of the Enlightenment, rejected idealism, liberalism and individualism, produced Joyce and Picasso, and projected Hitler and Mussolini as its heroes, Beckett could not but embrace anti-intellectualism and speak in paradoxes. In any case, Beckett had his stimuli coming alike from theology and biology, ethics and mathematics, physics and metaphysics, ideology and historiography. Not surprisingly, Beckett turned out to be an enigmatic jesting Pilate who would ask questions but not wait for an answer.

To get at the real meaning of Godot, let us also place this jesting Pilate in the midst of the historical events of his time: the Great War, the Depression, the rise of Hitler, World War II, the nuclear holocaust, and the Cold War—events that forced practically all the thinkers of the day to talk about the rise and fall of civilizations. The apocalyptic tenor of contemporary history raised questions about the future of man as well as of life in general. Surely it couldn't be a mere coincidence that, during this period, Vico came to enjoy popularity and, taking a cue from Oswald Spengler's *Decline of the West*, Arnold J Toynbee came out with his *Study of History* and Nicolas Berdyaev with his *Destiny of Man*. Evolution and atrophy came to occupy in the mid-century intellectual ethos the same position that salvation and damnation had in the god-oriented Medieval Age or individualism in the man-oriented Renaissance.[12] While other thinkers saw evolution on one level—genetic, geological, historical, sociocultural, or cosmic—Beckett would see all simultaneously. His habit of seeing parts individually, in relation to one another, as also in relation to the whole, left him feeling that, despite all the evolutionary flux, the net result appeared to be stasis—if not actually degeneration. He was amused to see the circularity resulting from the linear movement of history, nature and the evolutionary process in general. Here was, in short, the situation of an axle—always in motion and yet not moving at all. The more Beckett brooded over man's Being and Becoming, the more convinced he became that man was a self-destroying animal who, in his effort to evolve, was succeeding only in becoming more and more degenerate. Obviously, the Cartesian bicycle of mind and body was a most defective machine. With such perceptions, Beckett could not have possibly endorsed Descartes when he speaks of roads leading to goals or a pilot leading the ship. Instead, to Beckett, the so-called progress appeared a myth and thus the entire race seemed to move along a dead-end road.

Most probably Beckett found his views endorsed in a book that appeared in 1941: G H Estabrooks's *Man—The Mechanical Misfit.*[13] Projecting human brain—nature's unique gift to man—as a vampire, the work went on to establish that man is 'not a rational but a rationalizing animal'.[14] Estabrooks has shown that civilization being an organ-grinder, far from moving up, man is skidding down the ladder of evolution. The doctor who insists on prolonging a patient's life by circumventing nature is inviting the wrath of Nature which is interested in the survival of the fittest. Consequently, as the title of the closing chapter has it, 'the wages of biological sin is evolutionary death'. Of course, there is no known evidence that Beckett read this book, but I have a strong hunch that *Godot* was a typically Beckettian twist to an episode narrated by Estabrooks. A southern preacher often used to talk of 'the people who didn't wait'. Once when a parishioner asked him what he meant, he said, 'Well, brother, it is this way. When the Lord made men, he made them from the dust of the earth. Then he stood them up in a row and said, "You all wait here till I go get you some brain." But, brother, some of them didn't wait.'[15] Possibly while reading this, Beckett countered with a most characteristic chuckle, 'And how about those who did? They are still waiting!' Or, maybe, he had yet another chuckle when he added, 'In any case, what difference did it make in the case of those who waited? What kind of brain did God bring?' Indeed, that is the ironic core of Beckett's work: those who waited are no better than those who left. That is to say, there is little to choose between extinction and survival.

Of course, Beckett had already acquired a view of life which prompted him to react in this way—a view that marks most of his major fiction which preceded *Godot.* The underlying idea of this book is that Godot theme (as I interpret it) pervades the entire range of Beckett's work—alike in poetry, fiction and drama. If I have started with *Godot*, it is not because it was the starting point but because we have here the most comprehensive expression of that theme.

Now, as already maintained, an artist's mind is subject to numerous kinds of formative influences but, more often than not, some factors do comprise the core; everything else gets fitted around that core as it serves as the agent of action, reaction or absorption. In Beckett's case, Proustian thought was such an agent. This is not to suggest that

Beckett was consciously influenced by Proust more than by any other writer or thinker. The study of Proust in the most formative period of his life bred in him the habit of seeing man in relation to time; the next logical step was to see man in relation to space. That resulted in Beckett's seeing man, on the one hand, related to the place around, to the world at large, and to the cosmos, and, on the other, in the context of eternity, history and subjective time of involuntary memory. It is possible to say that Beckett's dissertation on Proust was a most creative piece of literary criticism in which interpreting of Proust served as an excuse for clarifying his own understanding of man. That is why most of the significant statements made in *Proust*[16] can stand on their own—independent of Proustian context; or else they serve as Beckett's credo as much as Proust's.[17] Really, it should be possible to attribute to Beckett what is, in fact, Proustian riddle: 'How am I, an atemporal being imprisoned in time and space, to escape from my imprisonment when I *know* that outside time and space lies nothing, and 'I', in the ultimate depths of my reality, am Nothing also.'[18]

As if to resolve this Proustian paradox, Beckett went beyond Proustian concept of time and made it look more than a double-headed monster—a trinity that creates, preserves and destroys. In Beckett, time is at once personal, impersonal and interpersonal; subjective, objective and eternal; cyclical, linear and static. Convinced that man consumes time and time consumes man, Beckett went on to treat Time as the protagonist of human comedy as well as the antagonist of human tragedy. With such notions, Beckett could not have been content with treating time as a mere structural element as it has been in the traditional drama; in his plays, time is subject, character and structure.

When Beckett tried to reconcile his early interests in Descartes and Proust with his growing concerns with Vico and the vitalist evolution, he was probably amused as well as amazed by the contradictory pictures on the two sides of the coin called Man. On the one hand, man appeared so heroic, claiming credit for all the progress in the world and determined to outlast eternity itself. On the other hand, he seemed a mere speck in the universe, subject to mortality, torn by innumerable ever-changing selves, lost in sheer routine, always pestered by memory, and all his activities confined to dish and pot. Encompassing self-at-zero at one end and possible absolute at the other, man looked an epitome of all kinds of dichotomies resulting from the coexistence of body and mind, being and becoming, self and the other. As was his wont, Beckett saw man in relation to the universe, to the world, to other creations, to other human beings, to the civilizations of the past, to his present and future, to his various selves as an individual. In this appalling vision, it appeared well-nigh impossible to tell whether it was a process of creation or decreation, growth or decay.

In the framework of this mystery, treating man with contempt as a tiny dot would be as foolish as his own conceited boast about his role in the evolution. In a situation like this, nothing can be more inane than raising questions about the chances of man's survival and extinction, salvation and damnation. Nothing can be more meaningless than philosophizing about the meaning of existence, nothing more absurd than talking about the absurd in life. Endowed with such a binary vision, Beckett felt that what man had achieved might not be very impressive intrinsically, but it was there. If man's goal is unattainable, so is his exhaustion. Maybe, man has been only creating and decreating values to produce self-cancelling results, but that has enabled him to evade the fate of becoming a mere fossil. What if another symptom becomes worse, at least the first one has eased! Maybe, redemption and enlightenment have proved only myths and we are left with cultural junk, but at least each civilization had had its moments of glory. The big thing is that this infinitesimally small particle on the energy wave of Life Force is determined not to give up. In short, Beckett's poetics of failure celebrates human persistence despite heavy odds. That makes man like a true artist who keeps giving his best even when he knows that his best has not been good enough. Indeed, man could say in self-defence what Beckett said about himself, 'That's all I can manage, more than I could' (*Dj*, 109).

Grasped intuitively rather than cognitively, this is nothing but the acceptance of the mess with all its chaos and contradictions. Indeed, if Beckett talked of the 'mess' quite frequently, it is because it represents the very core of his view of life. It pertains both to man's Being and Becoming—to the position of man in relation to the universe on the one hand and to the world around him on the other. Even while the macrocosm continues to baffle Man as an inexplicable irrational mess, the result of his efforts to create a more rational microcosm of his own has also proved chaotic and messy. Indeed, man's claim to be the law-giver is as much out of harmony as the Universe. In fact, the source of the mess lies in man's mind, in its imperfectibility.

Unable to perceive the pattern or the logic beneath the complexity of the universe, when Man declares the universe itself senseless and chaotic, it is only a measure of the puerility of his own mind.[19] One has to place man's quintessential being in the context of the universe as well as the eternal time to realize how little he knows, how insignificant are his achievements, and how bloated are the tall claims of this arch-egoist. It is like a mole claiming its molehill to be the only and the most magnificent residential structure ever made. How silly of a floating straw to declare that it is the sole reason for the flow of the river! Equally presumptuous would be the peevish decision of man to refuse to live a life of insignificance in this universe. After all, can a straw will itself out of a river? In short, helpless as man is either to mend or to end the situation, he has to continue in the so-called mess of the universe which is, of course, of man's own divining rather than intrinsic.

The 'mess'-business has prompted critics to regard Beckett as a grave-yard humanist whose revolt takes the form of metaphysical disgust. He strips away, it is averred, one value after another in the manner of onion-peeling until one is left with total wreckage of human institutions. In Beckett's world, it has been suggested, Keats's well-wrought urn has been replaced by empty cans. It is a world peopled by men who are always haunted by an overwhelming sense of the uselessness of body, the horror of sex, the imprecisions of words, the inaccuracy of sensory perceptions, and the indefinability of personal identity. No wonder there are critics who find Swift a great affirmist by contrast with Beckett. While Gulliver's pockets, it is argued, had watch, gold, pistol, etc., Beckett's protagonists have nothing more than pebbles, burnt matches, strings, etc. Here, happy days are associated with such superfluities as toothbrush, lipsticks, medicine bottle, little hat, music box, etc.; what is worse, even these trivial things are on their way out. This 'lessness' is supposed to signify the absence of meaning, pattern, hope, ambition or will in a dehumanized existence. Perhaps it is to express disgust with this life that Victor in *Eleutheria* lies down at the end with his back turned on humanity and Dr Andre Piouk even goes to the extent of recommending the destruction of mankind by all possible means.

But, then, there are critics who find so much positive along with the negative that they see in his nihilism an inverted reflection of his hunger for good and pure. According to them, Beckett projects nothingness of man's 'being' to highlight the richness of the realm of his 'becoming'. Thus seen, the essence of Beckett's thought seems to lie not in nihilism but in his inability to go nihilistic. To put it differently, in Beckett, stark pessimism is counterbalanced against rhapsodic vision of an exhilarating future in such a manner that the zest for life appears as strong as the longing for death. That explains why the regret for having been born is as overwhelming as the will to continue. In fact, to this Beckett traces the very mystery of life. No wonder he told Tom F Driver: 'If there were only darkness, all would be clear. It is because there is not only darkness but also light that our situation becomes inexplicable ... where we have at one and the same time darkness and light, we have also the inexplicable.'[20] This binary outlook accounts for open-ended brinkmanship in Beckett. Since uncertainty about universe, about existence, and about identity results in a kind of affirmation that verges on negation and vice-versa, Beckett's metaphysics has a touch of the dialectical paradox. Here existence and essence, past and present, freedom and determinism, tomb and womb—all tend to become identical. In such an impasse, one can neither speak nor remain silent, neither have the courage to end nor the strength to go on. Indeed, a writer imbued with such dialectical vision would neither endorse any philosophy nor reject all philosophies altogether.

Beckett's works are, in a way, a series of counter-arguments to blast philosophical assumptions regarding man's identity, progress, integrity, significance and rationality. It is as if he were saying to the entire race of philosophers beginning with Descartes, 'Did you say, Sirs, that man is a thinking animal, uniquely endowed with rationality, governed by logic, shape and orderliness, and that whatever meaning is there in this universe is of man's creating? Maybe you are right, I don't know. You say that what makes man unique is his rationality; to me it appears to be his irrationality.' Saying this, he proceeds to place microcosm in the framework of the macrocosm. That instantly highlights the isolation of man in the universe, the mechanical nature of his life, the estrangement of the individual from his self, the ever-changing flux of the self that remains undefined, the pointlessness of human existence and the consequent cyclic pattern of human history. Dealing at so many levels, Beckett gives the impression of creating life in its entirety but, in fact, it is the mess inhering human life that he underlines. The claims of such a non-knower and non-caner as man to be the repository of all the rationality of the universe and the creator of the most rational system makes him a veritable clown in the cosmic farce. No wonder, unlike the archetypal hero who proceeds on an adventurous journey, Beckett's Man is projected as a fool prancing around a spot and looking on a wrong road for a goal that does not exist.

If Beckett undermines all philosophical consolations, it is not to effect Kierkegaardian leap to faith. He cannot endorse any religion because, after all, all theology too is the creation of man's imperfect mind. Of course, Beckett's plays abound in christology, but the Biblical and Eucharistic allusions have parodic associations and ironic digs. Here Cain and Abel tend to become one, Paradise leans close to Hell, Christ emerges as a being misled, salvation turns out to be a fairy tale. God is referred to as a bastard who doesn't exist; He refuses to fulfil his promise of upholding all that fall; His creativity comes in for an unfavourable comparison even with a tailor's craft. In short, Beckett would not have theology any more than any ideology.

Refusing to follow any one system, Beckett reacted to each system differently in some peculiar way of his own. Thus, he would take the assumptions of one, the methodology of another, and the vision of yet another to echo, parody or distort each one, to reach a new conclusion, or else to establish that no conclusion is possible. For example, if he took from Bruno the idea of finiteness of material universe, Niebuhr contributed the concept of man's being at once limited and limitless. The notion of self-cancelling coexistence seems to have come from Heraclitus who believed, 'We step and we do not step into the same river; we are and we are not.' The power to effect the harmony of opposites was a natural corollary of Pythagoras's belief that mirth and grief come to the same thing in the end. And all these got accommodated in the oriental approaches that project Nothingness as an absolute value. Anyway, this synthesis is done in such a manner that the originating ideas are changed beyond recognition and any effort to follow any one line of thought lands one in a most ridiculous situation.

That is precisely what makes so difficult the task of relating Beckett's world-view to specific philosophers who did contribute individually, in tandem or collectively, directly, adaptedly or unconsciously. As maintained earlier, thanks to the complexities of the way human mind works, tracing of an influence is always problematic; it is almost impossible in the case of several inter-related influences and that, too, in the mind of one who was known for anti-intellectual approaches and for parodying philosophers. Beckett neither assimilated ideas nor rejected them; he only disjected. He had stored all kinds of views in his mind and when he visited this mental junkyard, like Hamlet in the graveyard, he would kick some items and kiss some others. In this playful mood, he would at times discover unexpected correspondences among ideas and then proceed to transmute them beyond recognition.

Can one trace the intricate contours of these transmutations? The task assumes one's sitting in Beckett's mind watching the phenomena at work—an impossible assumption, indeed. Besides, if analyzing of the process of logical and deliberate assimilation in a philosophical mind is riddled with doubts, it should be too presumptuous even to attempt such an exercise with regard to the interaction of random ideas in a mind that was basically protean, parodic and anti-intellectual. What is more, critical tradition demands that every such formulation should be not only logically deduced or induced but also suitably substantiated. But, maybe, there is something of fatal fascination in the way ideas get related in Beckett because every critic of his has talked about it. I, too, don't claim to be an exception. It is necessary to assert, however, that what I am offering are mere hunches; my only justification for this exercise lies in what I have maintained above—that all talk of intellectual tempering is always conjecture work. And like all conjectures, my hunches too transcend logic and rationality. Indeed, every statement that I am going to make in what follows is, at best, a mere possibility, an assumption—what seems or appears to me rather than anything known or ascertainable. My effort is aimed at suggesting—not proving—that in the evolution of Beckett's world-view in general and Godot-theme in particular, the diverse philosophical ideas may not have played the role of forging a rational synthesis, but their echoes can be heard nevertheless—however dim or distorted they might be. In a sense, I am playing Beckett's own game—the game of perceiving unexpected correspondences among ideas intuitively rather than analytically. In this connection, I should wish not only to anticipate the charge of reductionism but also to plead guilty.

Most characteristic of Beckett was the way he played with the Proustian concept of time as a double-headed monster to make it a complement of Cartesian philosophy. With 'hour' changed into 'whore', we have 'Whoroscope' in which Descartes is the narrator. In a way this is a phenomenon of seminal significance because, in most of Beckett's works, his concern is on the one hand with the passage of time and on the other with the Cartesian bicycle.

Divining man as an angel riding the bicycle of spirit and matter, Rene Descartes talked analogically of roads leading to goals and pilot leading a ship, etc.; for him, body and mind are spiritually related via the mediation of God. The imp in Beckett took God out and showed how that bicycle was a defective, almost non-functional, machine. For want of integral interdependence, the two pedals of this machine were seen to be involved in a non-stop motion that yields no forward movement. Thus, according to Beckett, instead of dynamic ascent, the system is resulting in a veritable stasis. The source of the trouble, Beckett believed, lies in the fact that although the physical aspect that suffers and the mental one that perceives are part of the same human personality, yet they are so radically different that each may disown the other as 'not-I'. Such coexistence of body and mind has resulted in a permanent schism which makes man a cosmic clown. When Beckett dramatized this image of man, the result was Cartesian framework but a totally non-Cartesian conclusion. Reading Cartesian axiom, 'I think, therefore I am', literally so as to mean, 'Man survives because of his mind', Beckett proceeded in *Godot* to underline the vulnerability of such a belief.

If Descartes talked of a bicycle, Giambattista Vico talked of cycles, but in the puckish imagination of Beckett, the two got related and thus he interpreted Viconian cycles in conjunction with the Cartesian machine. Vico discerned a circular process in human history. According to him, following the pattern of biological progression (birth, maturity, decay, death), the theocratic, heroic and human civilizations climax in the barbaric and thus prove the starting point of another cycle. Beckett saw such cyclic pattern in human history in which a maxima proves the starting point of a descent towards a minima. It is like the twin pedals of a bicycle, one of which goes up as the other goes down. For Beckett, what keep the wheel of history moving are the twin pedals of mind and body which alternate in their positions of maxima and minima. With man alternating thus between a thinking animal and a sensuous angel, human progress is condemned eternally to cyclical rise and fall, without any chance of a linear march forward to reach the Godot-stage.

Thus seen, Beckett's concern was not only with individuals but also with mankind as a whole; his contexts were not just generations, periods and ages but also eternity. That put him in the position of a child looking at an opened clock and feeling intrigued by the way one wheel stimulates another and thus sets in motion the network of wheels within wheels in such a manner as to move the hands of the seconds, minutes and hours simultaneously but at different rates. Beckett was also fascinated to notice the intricate patterns of evolution and atrophy inhering the progress of humanity. The uniqueness and opacity of Beckett's works lies in this insistence of his on seeing at once isolated parts, parts in relationship to one another, parts in relation to the whole, and the whole as a whole. The more minutely he observed the process, the more acute became his consciousness that the rate of evolution at the geological, the genetic, the societal and the cosmic levels is far from uniform and that there is a sort of tension, even conflict, between organic and societal evolutions. In fact, there is a dialectical interplay between evolution and atrophy in each era in general and each civilization in particular so much so that each generation is a form of degeneration. That brought Beckett close to Giardano Bruno who talked about the circularity of transmutations. According to him, the maximum of corruption being identical with the minimum of generation, corruption is, in principle, a form of generation. Here were, so to say, the laws of thermodynamics at work in the field of evolution—projecting of evolutionary energy as a constant quantity, the gain in one field being equal to the loss in the other.

This gain-loss equation may not be always perceptible because of the constant process of change in the quality of energy. When a certain kind of energy is converted, its non-availability to run the system threatens to devitalize the system itself; to save itself from a dead halt, the inner mechanism reverses the process and facilitates the reconversion of energy and return to the former state. Exactly in the same way, in the evolutionary process, growth implies automatic decline even as an inevitable rise inheres the fall. In a man's biological system also, at every stage of growth, there is a latent level of degeneration. That is to say, one starts dying the moment one is born. That is what Beckett would call being born astride of a grave. In a situation like this, always living in the shadow of death, a man can never achieve full vitality, nor possibly reach the stage of non-being. Ditto for the evolution of mankind. Man as a species will neither become extinct nor reach the stage of perfection. No wonder, representing mankind, Beckett protagonists keep repeating that they cannot go on and yet they must go on.

About this paradoxical role of civilization in overcoming death by devitalizing life, there is something Hegelian, too. According to Hegel, without such contradictions, there cannot be any life; only what is dead remains without contradictions. To live through the process of oppositions, contradictions and the resolution of contradictions, Hegel believed, is the higher privilege of living beings; what is and what remains merely affirmative is and remains without life. This led Hegel to regard history as an interplay of dialectical contradictions. Refusing to endorse the sombre implications of Hegelian dialectics, Beckett characteristically indulged in simplistic reductionism to show that positive and negative, Being and Non-Being, tended to become identical. Hegelian phenomenology thus led to typically Beckettian deduction that, despite the never-ending process of change, life never changes and remains basically the same—like water changing into steam that condenses again into water.

This does sound like a variation of the 'eternal recurrence', but the implications are not purely optimistic. Whereas Friedrich Nietzsche has used the concept to affirm life Dionysiacally and to urge 'living dangerously' so as to facilitate the emergence of Overman, Beckett uses it to underline that the evolution of a higher type is a will-o'-the-wisp. Having seen the horrid realization of Nietzschean vision in the brutality of Nazi culture, in which Hitler had projected the Germans as a super-race, Beckett seems to have turned against the concept of Superman itself. For him, the working of the 'eternal recurrence' was a tale told by an idiot, full of sound and fury signifying nothing. Nietzsche had once posed a question: if a demon were to come to propose that man live his life as it is innumerable times, without any change or novelty, experiencing all the unspeakable small and great things in the same sequence, what should man say? The answer implied in the question was a 'yea'—in the hope of Overman. Beckett being Beckett, he took up only the question and sketched picture of what that kind of life would be like. According to him, it would be Sisyphean labour without any prospect of a Superman at the end—an eternal wait for Godot who would never come.

Beckett's approach was, in a way, based on Henri Bergson's assumption that elan vital is something disorderly, ever-changing and unpredictable, but characteristically he used it to counter Bergson's theory of creative evolution. Equally characteristic are Beckett's tricks to treat literally what was meant to be metaphorical. He would do that kind of thing without any warning, analogy or reference—a ruse that helped him distort and parody the implicit deduction without saying so. Thus, when Beckett talks about a well with two buckets, one going down to be filled, the other coming up to be emptied, a lay reader might regard it as something obviously amusing; but the one who knows Heraclitus would know immediately what depth is thus sought to be plummeted. Beckett might change this into milkcans being taken from one end of the platform to the other and back, but it serves his basic purpose of making Heraclitus a party to the philosophy of eternal recurrence. Likewise, a common reader may go through Beckett's works without ever thinking of Martin Heidegger, but the great philosopher himself could not help exclaiming, 'The man [Beckett] must have read Heidegger![21] The fact is that although Heideggerian postulates are never stated, they are very much assumed. These don't come to us direct because, in his most characteristic vein, Beckett lent Cartesian dimension to the realm of Heidegger. Starting with the Heideggerian assumption that man has only history and no fixed nature, Beckett would trace in the relationship between man and his world such kind of relationship as Descartes had seen between body and mind.

The references to Heidegger, Nietzsche and Camus might suggest Beckett's being an existentialist, but I must hasten to recall what I have maintained all along—his refusal to adhere to any one school the whole hog. He was, indeed, an existentialist insofar as his concern was not with characters but with the condition of living—***how-it-is*** and not ***what-it-means***. He, too, divined man as a being condemned to be free and therefore doomed to fend for himself in this universe without any help from God. However, he would not entrust man with any role to change this situation through Sartrean commitment or Camusian revolt. In fact, finding this condition of living—being without becoming—endless, Beckett would leave where he started. Thus, what we have in his works is existentialist approach rather than existentialist philosophy. Indeed, as Richard M Goldman has put it, while existentialists dispute between the priority of essence and existence, Beckett writes about the essence of existence—life departicularized, its processes cut off, its contexts abrogated, its battles not joined by either side.

Must man, then, commit suicide? Beckett's answer was a Camusian 'No'. Like Sisyphus, man must go on. However, Beckett was content with depicting the Sisyphean labour as the very essence of human existence, without any implication of dignity, indignation or transcendence.

In short, Beckett's works are a way of reworking fundamental existential problem—'to be or not to be'. Of course, he puts it in his own peculiar way—the inability to speak and the inability to be silent, even when there is nothing to say; ever-floundering but never giving up, even when there is no predestined goal; the female will to procreate, together with the male determination to kill children, even when both are sterile; telling stories and asking questions even when there is no one to listen or answer. All this piles up to give the impression that in this inexplicable universe, mystery will never be resolved because life is as much a reality as death. However, the way life and death are seen to be interacting to yield patterns of creation and destruction at different levels of time and space, one feels an urge not to give up but to continue this non-game. In other words, Beckett's answer to the worthwhileness of life is neither a yes nor a no but perhaps.

Now, 'perhaps' signifies one's being convinced despite the promptings of rationality to the contrary. It is a kind of situation one faces in the case of irrational number: you know that it is somewhere but you cannot put it precisely—so close to rational limits and yet never final. It is generally presumed that only at the end of eternity, such an irrational number would become exact. So would Beckett expect us to accept the irrational life in the hope that it would ultimately, at the end of eternity, yield rational results. The endless labour involved in the process might appear to be Sisyphean, but this at least guarantees continuance till eternity and thus an escape from extinction—the fate of all other species. Thus is finite made infinite. Seen thus, death appears a continuum of life, the next step to eternity. Conversely, every birth signifies eternity entering finitude and thus being subjected to mortality. In other words, Beckett wanted man to accept his position as a mere particle on the energy-wave of Life Force. As for the philosophers' obsession with significance of living, Beckett finds it equally irrelevant because man has never known what it means to be alive. The only thing he does know is that he is alive; beyond that he cannot possibly know for certain.

Finding life full of inexplicable and inexpressible experiences, Beckett sought their explanation with the help of philosophy, but his readings proved rather counter-productive insofar as they added to his confusion. Confronting 'absolute absence of the Absolute,[22] and doubly disillusioned in the abortive efforts of human intellect to explain things, and finding the normal channels of communication totally inapt, Beckett turned into a 'prophet of the mess'.[23] This being his basic problem, his oft-quoted statements in this regard sound like a credo:

'I am not a philosopher. One can only speak of what is in front of him, and that now is simply the mess.'[24]

'The confusion is not my invention .... It is all around us and our only chance is to let it in. The only chance of renovation is to open our eyes and see the mess.'[25]

'... there is nothing to express, nothing with which to express, no power to express, no desire to express, together with the obligation to express.'[26]

To conclude, according to Beckett, man continues to be irrelevant to the universe, despite all his efforts and claims of achievements and significance. The root of his endless and fruitless ordeal lies in the fact that man is not properly equipped for the struggle. Being neither a pure animal nor a perfect angel, man finds that the mental equipment available to him to overcome the fundamental flaws of physical existence is basically faulty. The more he tries to seek independence of either body or mind, the more acute becomes his sense of dependence on both. The more he systematizes, the greater is the disorder created by him; the more he tries to confront reality, the greater grows his need for illusions; the more he tries to rationalize, the greater is his realization about the inadequacy of his reasoning faculty. Since man has come into existence without vital, organic roots that could ensure healthy growth, his position is like that of the little girl about whom Carl Jung had once said that the trouble with her was that 'she had never been born entirely'.[27] A creature that lives without being born personifies, as it were, the will to continue. It is this position that has made man a kind of seeker who forgets what he is seeking and yet continues to seek—seeking for the sake of seeking, even without the consciousness of being a seeker. Though futile, such a search can be endless; and full of dramatic potential, it can be pathetic as well as hilarious. Such, indeed, has been man's effort to attain godhood—his waiting for Godot.

And that, I believe, is Beckett's theme throughout. Thus, his heroes, representing mankind, live a life without any action or development, raise again and again those philosophical questions—Where now? Who now? When now? They fail to find any definite reason for living and yet they continue to live without knowing what is life, what is good or bad, what to believe, and what happens after life. Thus, without any desire for life, without much hope, with no idea of a true basis for existence, man goes on and will go on in the hope of realizing a possible absolute that has always eluded him. If that ideal is ever realized, man would become a superman, god-like. But when will that Godot-stage be reached? Who knows? Maybe, never; perhaps at the end of time. Until then, man must continue, and wait!

3 Poetics of Failure

Endowed with a dialectical outlook, Beckett found Man struggling in this world without the strength to go on or the courage to end. Creating and decreating, trying to give shape to the mess only to make more chaos, man has in hand an endless business that can never yield the desired results. It is comparable to sexual effort of the chronically impotent, philosophical undertaking of the chronically ignorant, logical construction by the chronically irrational, or faith-mongering by the chronically uncertain. Depicting of this situation implied piling together of 'less-ness', composing of decomposition, creating of degeneration, projecting of disorder as a form of new order. In such an undertaking, the position of Beckett was not much different from that of Man. For him also discovering of a shape for this mess was an almost impossible task; it required the knowledge of the unknowable, the expression of the inexpressible, and affirmation of nihilism itself. Concerned with the totality of the human situation in general and the circularity of the evolution in particular, he was expected to show moments in the context of eternity, finite man related to infinite universe, Being without time, and Becoming without end. How could he accommodate endless labour and inconsequential nightmare, the obsession to commit suicide and the will to go on? In practical terms, it called for the reconciliation of zero as well as infinity, fixity and flux, impetus and atrophy, life and void, potential and impotence, absence and presence, activity and actionlessness, time and timelessness. Obviously no traditional form of mimesis could help Beckett present such dialectics of static evolution because it meant projecting as hero an anti-heroic non-knower and non-caner in pursuit of an unattainable quest. What is more, the quest is not only utterly devoid of glory but also at once inward, outward, forward, backward, upward and downward. Surely, it needed a new poetics of failure that might erase the distinction between life and art, illusion and reality, hope and despair.

Traditional drama either evokes an emotive response or stimulates the intellect in varying degrees. Beckett wanted instead a theatre that would prompt the reader to raise questions without expecting answers. To affirm life as it is with all its mess, the reader must stop thinking about life so as to become truly alive. To evolve such a theatre, Beckett had to invent a number of strategies that subverted traditional responses. In his plays, therefore, instead of verisimilitude we have the grotesque, instead of heroics we have self-amusing antics, instead of drama or anti-drama we have the pure theatre of the circus in which words are juggled around the way a clown plays with balls. Likewise, instead of a vision, message or epiphany, Beckett presents us with pure experience. Here dialogues are no longer important; situations are freed from all elements of naturalism, social setting and external plot. In this format, metaphysics and music-hall entertainment go together and dreaming is brought to the level of doing. Here reality is reflected not in one mirror but in a hallful of self-reflecting mirrors. It does tend to become somewhat obscure but it is a calculated obscurity. The aim was to imbue 'action' on the one hand with universal significance and on the other with the power to yield newer meanings with every new reading.

Corresponding to man's incessant urge to live on, however meaningless, Beckett found within himself an irrational urge to communicate his understanding of the mess, however puerile. In presenting the process of artistic creation itself as a metaphor for living, the mess could be given a shape by removing the distinction between form and content. In practical terms it meant evolving a self-contained art in which form may not exist as a separate concept but get subsumed in the general pattern of the content. For example, instead of a story about nothing, there could be images embodying nothingness—say, an empty stage, activity without dramatic significance, performers without roles. To communicate the insignificance of existence on a stage that has always been a signifying place, the distinction between the signifiers and the signified had to be minimized. Beckett tried to do that by concentrating on the inter-relationship of the signifiers. Thus, an initial image or incident is not developed but progressively torn threadbare until it approaches chaos. Details are deleted, any system of chronology or causality destroyed, and an alternative arrangement evolved in a manner that emphasizes not logic and order but just the pattern. By not giving details, he makes all details possible and omission becomes a form of inclusion. By striking a blow to the spectators' habit of assuming that drama has one meaning and that it has nothing which does not contribute to that meaning, Beckett suggests innumerable meanings and projects meaninglessness itself as a profound meaning.

Indeed, to achieve his end, Beckett has employed a new dramaturgy which subverts the traditional responses. His drama is so designed as to obviate the expectation of sequential action and the usual correspondences between language and gesture, between recognizable emotion and physical movement. These being plays of absence rather than presence, here more important than action is what does not take place. And what does take place is as unaccountable as man's presence on the earth. To effect decantation of meaning to that effect, Beckett takes up themes of many kinds—religious, social, aesthetic, psychological, philosophical—without allowing any one of them to become the central motif. To these he adds a talk which is so anti-intellectual that it defies all intelligibility. Since Beckett's play of impasse tends to deny the dramatic in life, it could not be built on such usual tensions as result from the ambivalence of forces in life. That explains why the structures of Beckett's plays are both cyclic and contrapuntal. In fact, everything here is an echo of the pattern of life itself. Hence, deliberate incoherence, repetition, irrelevance, etc. All this is expected to intrigue the spectator and force him to evolve an attitude in which creation and destruction tend to become one. The big idea is to prompt him to refrain from the customary one-dimensional response of accepting or rejecting values; Beckett would rather have them disjected. Moving forward in life being no different from going backward, Beckett wanted his novels and plays to have a format where reading forward, backward, or at random should yield the same sense of feeling.

The most effective strategy in Beckett's play is minimalization—reducing everything to the barest minimum and impregnating it with maximum suggestiveness to lend it a universal dimension. It is a strategy that yielded the advantages of symbolism without employing symbols. For example, by reducing verbal means, depth of expression is increased because words tend to become Artaudian 'animated hieroglyphics' that have meaning beyond words. A similar advantage is gained when the language of the body is also broken down into its rudimentary elements—like walking, frozen gesture, restricted movement, immobility, disembodied voice, isolated organ, exclusive facial expression, etc. Likewise, by putting men in urns and dustbins, Beckett not only effects desublimation but also creates the entire existential situation. In the same way, repetition with Beckett is not just reiteration or multiplication; it becomes something akin to variations in a musical score which produces the desired effect slowly but surely. Thus treated, the elements in hand not only assume symbolic associations but also have the flexible power of evoking different meanings in every new situation. In this format, Beckett could project even suicide as a pastime, waiting as the quintessence of life, the repulsive comicality of old age as the fizzlesome dissolution of mankind, or a chess-board as the battle ground of man's war with the universe. Only in such a framework could Beckett indulge in his characteristic games—affirmation through denial, addition through subtraction, presence through absence, order through disorder, form through formlessness.

Beckett's minimalism signifies not only reductionism and negativism but also the condensation of the whole into a part in such a manner that form becomes content and content form. It is like letting an atom or a cell contain the essence in its entirety. As stripping the action of consequences frees it of linearity, it enables us to concentrate on the centre. Likewise, stripping a character of individuality, nature or motivation frees him to represent the tenor and hopes of all mankind. In the same way, by churning words through repetition, Beckett impregnates them with such freshness as enables him to say more by saying little. No wonder, while the play becomes shorter, the story gets refined. In such a situation, 'at this place' comes to mean the entire universe; at this moment comes to signify eternity. Indeed, this minimalism helps Beckett create comedy out of tragic material and truly vital plays about the decay of the human species.

Beckett's basic problem as an artist—to express the inexpressible—being so akin to man's urge to evolve without any means, he resorted to inverted allegory of fictionalization. As he tells the stories of story-tellers, everything becomes a fictive sign of its own self. Thus, to depict human living as an art without resources, the narratives start at a point from which there can be no continuation and yet they proceed obstinately. Thus is human evolution projected as a contrived and pedestrian labour of the imperfect mind of an artisan, without the divine inspiration of a true artist. To suggest this, Beckett's writers are incessantly busy constructing, deconstructing and reconstructing in the spirit of hit and trial. In the same way, to implant the idea that man's progress is endless and foredoomed, Beckett's writers are seen struggling to write despite their unending lament about the impossibility of writing. To represent man's art of creating himself, we have writers writing about writers writing. In each case both the creator and the creature are equally tired of the process of creation. Anyway, the quest of 'I' for the 'I' that is questing for another 'I' goes on until we arrive full circle and laugh at the absurdity of it all. Laughing with the one that he is laughing at, the artist becomes his own clown—a symbol of the cosmic clown that man is.

A clown, Beckett felt, would be the most apt metaphor for the human situation because, in his case also, success lies in failing and falling. As a clown's strength lies in his quintessential vulnerability, he cannot afford to get stuck on any stereotyped role but has always to shape new games. No wonder Beckett's dramatic work is full of Chaplinesque tramps—symbols of humanity reduced to zero but always busy trying to start afresh. Even otherwise, life being a play of assumed roles, man in the world is best represented through a performer who 'acts' in such a manner that each act of his resembles action without being one. Also, human history being an exercise in passing time, life is a play in the sense of pastime, a game—a game the rules of which are not prefixed but get evolved as it goes on. Such a game may not end in defeat or victory but continue indefinitely like the endgame in chess. In short, Beckett uses such artists as storytellers, actors, clowns, game-players, etc., to represent allegorically the self-creating artist called man. Like man, the Beckettian artist is always inventing stories of his own significance, assuming heroic roles, making mess of life, and enjoying himself as a player in the game of life. Witnessing a tragic adventure in the hands of a clown, we realize how the cosmic clown called Man, who was brought on the stage just to fill time, has been exploiting that position of no-specific-role to dominate the stage like a protagonist.

To depict human situation in its totality on the primary, secondary and tertiary level, Beckett employed yet another strategy—the multiplicity of time-scales. While a traditional writer would be content to place his 'action' within the bounds of one level of time, Beckett shows his protagonists living on many levels of time simultaneously. Cosmic time which makes the entire history of man look an infinitesimally small moment is not something that can be experienced in terms of events; it is something that one can at best perceive as an intuitive flash. It is brought to mind through the protagonists' obsession with such irrational numbers as the decimal rendering of $1/3, 1/7, \sqrt{2}, \pi$. Biological time that relates man as a species to other animals and natural processes is suggested through references to birth, growth, decay and death. That, in a way, explains Beckett's obsession with old age. Man-made chronological time, measured objectively on clocks, is reflected through references to schedules, and in the themes of habit and routine. Finally, subjective time, which is measured emotively and psychologically, accounts for memories in Beckett's works.[1]

Cosmic, biological, chronological and subjective times not only mould the thematic tenor of Beckett's plays but also determine their structures. For example, *Waiting for Godot, Endgame* and *Happy Days* have the cosmic pattern of an asymptote: as the length approaches infinity, content approaches zero. In plays like *Krapp's Last Tape* and 'That Time', biological time assumes the shape of a broken cycle—a cyclic movement that goes back to the starting point but is discontinuous here and there. The pendulum-movement so characteristic of chronological time is to be found in the patterns of 'All that Fall', 'Footfalls', and 'Act Without Words I'. 'Not I', 'Embers', and 'Eh Joe' emulate the chaotic patternlessness of the subjective time of memory.

Perhaps nothing in Beckett is marked more by the experimental spirit than language. In fact, there is in Beckett the dethronement of both language and logic. The linguistic travesty does not, however, imply a return to meaninglessness. Instead, it facilitates the perception of a deeper reality. Thus, to depict a life that is inexplicable and humanity that is incapacitated by the lack of any dependable faculties of communication, Beckett evolved patterns of such a language as explains nothing—in fact, communicates nothing. The monotonously entangled nature of its words and sounds suggests the very insipid but intricate pattern of human life. Hence, too, the inverted syntax for the disjointed quality of life. Likewise, scraps of life are depicted through fragmented phrases and splintered bits. In a way, the very tenor of language suggests the decadence of life. Also its meaningless reiterations epitomize the absurd flux of life. The ignorance and impotence of non-knowing and non-caning man is felt in the irrational and weak construction of the language. For this purpose, Beckett broke syntactic order, exploited the emptiness of cliches, detached words from their meanings, or replaced dialogues by monologues. He also roped in soliloquies to convey the alienation of individuals in the isolated islands of their egos.

In the same way, Beckett relied heavily on dissonant repetition or dreamlike aural patterns. This was done with a view to foiling the expectation of objective ideas and logical sequence because those should go only with an ordered and rational existence. In fact, one often gets the impression that Beckett's language is for its own sake rather than for any meaning. That is as it should be because his aim was to prompt the reader to be content with life for life's sake instead of hankering too much after the meaning of life. That is why it has been suggested that for sense in Beckett, one must look not at the words, or between the words, but within the words.[2] Firmly believing that howsoever meaningless, life is better than death, Beckett used language, howsoever hollow, to kill silence which is a form of suicide. Another trick that Beckett plays in this connection is to break one sentence into many parts and to let several characters mouth what would be just one speech in the traditional drama. Thus multiple voices, all cohabiting in the same sentence, enable us to see multiple selves in the same personality. Thanks to such verbal devices, the impact of Beckett's plays lies not in what they say or mean but in what they do to the spectators—arousing a direct sensuous response and thus affording an experience rather than an argument.

A work of literature that merely seeks to express nothing and that raises questions only to beg them recalls to mind that notorious definition of philosophy—a blind man's search in a dark room for a black cat that is not there. That is also something one could say on the one hand about the efforts of man to evolve and on the other about the struggle of a reader/spectator to look for meaning in Beckett's work. In any case, uncanny is this situation in which the artist's vision, the work of art, and the impact tend to yield the same experience—a rare achievement in itself. But, then, what kind of experience is this search in the dark for a non-existent black cat—comic or tragic? Surely, it can be both hilarious and devastating. Beckett's plays, too, are at once macabre and farcical. We leave his theatre profoundly disturbed, thinking about the depressing facts of life, the world without end, the intriguing nature of man, the multi-pronged progress of time, the inevitable mortality, and so on. And yet during the performance we have had everything associated with comicality—clowning, slapstick, ludicrous inhering deformity, grotesque exaggeration, Rabelaisian smut, punning, parodies, paradoxes, mockery, and what not. Great is the art of Beckett that accommodates at once vaudeville fun, music hall cross-talk, commedia dell'arte, physical humour as well as tragic paraphernalia. No wonder critics hail Beckett as a stoic comedian or comedian of impasse, and suggest for his plays such labels as absurd, grotesque, dark comedy, black comedy, macabre puppet show, etc. For at least *Godot*, Beckett's own preference was for 'tragicomedy'. But that is a genre that has had such a long tradition that it has acquired definite and fixed parameters both thematically and formally. No wonder Richard Dutton adds a prefix and calls Beckett's masterpiece 'still-born tragicomedy'.[3] True, as the title of one of Ruby Cohn's articles has it, Beckett's comedy is 'something old, something new'. According to her, to begin with, comedy rises from the rhythm alone, 'then we seize fragments of sense, lift veil after veil, beat our brains upon fiction upon fiction and arrive full circle at laughter—hysterical perhaps at our plight. If it were not so pathetic, it might well be tragic.'[4]

Indeed, Beckett's plays are funny but only to a point. Suddenly we stop laughing, the non-funny comes to dominate, and man is seen heroically confronting the cosmic forces. Then, perceiving some kind of anarchy in the cosmos itself, we burst into irreverent laughter which subsides again as suddenly as it had blown up. This goes on and on—this perception of alternating layers of comedy and tragedy beneath each other—until we discover in man an actor in the cosmic farce. Now we find ourselves in the position of a clown who laughs to suppress his tears at the horrible joke of life. It is laughter born not of a sense of superiority but in self-defence. In *Watt*, a character distinguishes among three kinds of laughter—bitter, ethical satire that laughs at that which is not good; hollow, intellectual irony that laughs at that which is not true; and macabre ***risus purus*** that laughs at that which is not happy. As Vivian Mercier suggests, Beckett's own laughter is a category apart—an aesthetic brand of comicality that goads one into laughing at that which is not beautiful. Proceeding from the grotesque, it is a defence mechanism against what is traditionally regarded as holy.[5] J L Styan compares such desiccated humour to the impulse to laugh in a church.[6] This sacred profanity at once disturbs and pleases because, while we are amused by man's antics, we feel sorry for his plight.[7]

Alec Reid is intrigued by the fact that the near-clowns of Beckett bring a clearer knowledge of ourselves and increase our capacity to live fully, almost like the heroes of Aeschylus and Sophocles.[8] However, that compassionate understanding does not precipitate into catharsis, intellectual or emotional. Instead, more often than not, we come away totally exhausted, as at the end of a nightmare. In fact, at the end of a play, a reader's emotional note corresponds to that of the hero's—silent and immobile. Proposing to go, Vladimir and Estragon don't move; Clov is silent, and Ham motionless; Krapp lies still with his tape running on in silence; Winnie and Willie just look at each other. For Beckett this correspondence at the end is what matters the most because now, our participation reduced to zero-degree, we are restored to our real selves.

This is a totally different impact from what a tragedy does to us. There Apollonian and Dionysian are reconciled; here the gap remains unbridgeable. While the tragic hero would struggle for meaning and significance, the Beckettian hero fights for survival; the former is true to his essence, the latter to existence. If tragic crisis precipitates into the birth of a new value, in Beckett there is no value before or after the crisis. Denied the natural gifts of survival, here is man determined to wrest not glory but the gift of mere existence. Right in the beginning of his career, Beckett had produced in Belacqua his prototype of a protagonist—an anti-hero who would do nothing to realize his potential but only lie dreaming. Or waiting, as it were, for things to turn up—for Godot to come.

4 Ending the Unendable

Endgame (1956) caused Beckett's critics no less of a headache than *Waiting for Godot.* Coming at a time when people were not yet attuned to the avant-gardism of the fifties, its unusual theme and technique made it look, on the one hand, deliberately opaque and on the other, pregnant with the possibility of too many meanings. Some saw in it what was only too obvious: the disintegration of the family, master-slave relationship, or the death of a rich man; others discovered, on the other hand, the themes of the emptiness of life, the unending search for the self and the struggle with death. Accordingly, the set of the play came to be interpreted variously as a Jewish temple, the soul's dark cottage, a skull, a giant uterus in the womb, a hideout during a nuclear explosion, and so on. Likewise, if Hamm appeared to some as an artist, a blind story-teller like Homer or James Joyce, for others he was a psychotic, a sadistic maniac, a senile creature, or the dying God of Nietzsche. If one took his name for a pointer, he could be a modern Hamlet, Noah's son, a ham-actor, or a hammer; by the same token, Clov might be an abbreviation signifying clown, clow (French for nail), clove-spice, or a clover-footed animal.

In 1957, when *Endgame* was published as well as premiered, *Godot* was still an unsolved riddle. Reading the two plays together, people were quick to note that both Pozzo and Hamm are blind masters dependent for their existence on their slaves. Also, towards the close of each play a boy appears. Although he signifies the future, he is far from welcome to the protagonists. Similarly, if *Godot* had recalled the Gestapo, World War II came to mind in *Endgame*, in the form of a nuclear shelter. Thus did the theme in both the plays appear to be the same—waiting for death. Indeed, those who were convinced that Godot stood for death claimed vindication of their stand in *Endgame*. On the other hand, those who saw *Godot* as having more to do with leaving than with waiting concluded that both the plays had the same refrain—to leave or not to leave. And if the essential vision of *Godot* lay in being born astride of a grave, *Endgame* also seemed to say that when we begin to die, we begin to live, and vice-versa. In any case, here again, action lay in non-action.

Beckett himself, however, took pains to highlight the fundamental difference between the two plays. According to him, while in *Godot* the audience keeps wondering if Godot will ever come, in *Endgame* the point is whether or not Clov will ever leave.[1] He is also on record as having declared that *Endgame* is more elliptic and inhuman than *Godot*.[2] Once this difference is grasped, one can see why, instead of the phenomenal world, we have here a stark setting. That should also explain the ring-like circular plot of *Endgame*, against the open-ended chain-like progress of *Godot*. Indeed, here is, in the words of Ihab Hassan, 'Beckett's purest apocalyptic play'[3] that projects humanity in terms of broken down old creatures—bereft of everything, neither deserving any kind of pity, nor having any piety. Here the Cartesian dictum, 'I think, therefore I am', stands changed into 'I cry, therefore I am'. Thus, when Clov reports that Nagg is crying, Hamm deduces immediately, 'Then he's alive' (*Endgame*, 42).

One can perhaps reconcile the similarity as well as the diversity between the two plays if one follows Ruby Cohn's suggestion that in *Endgame* the paraphernalia of *Godot* has been reworked to create an entirely new play—like the use of the same pieces of chess to play an entirely new game. True, having seen one game does not mean having seen all the games; each game does offer a new kind of experience. Anyway, howsoever different, each game would nevertheless be called a chess-game. In other words, the different experiences of these two plays represent only different aspects of the game called life. In short, *Endgame* is neither a repetition nor an antithesis of *Godot*, but only a complement. Read in the context of the preceding chapters, it is an expression of the same old tragicomic vision, viz., man's heroic but foredoomed effort to reach the Godot stage—an effort that shall never end. Even as Man has been waiting to reach the superman-stage, generations have come and gone, civilizations have risen and fallen, hope and despair have alternated. All this has yielded a series of twilight phases when life and earth have tended to pass from one into the other but the process of death has never become the act of death. As the proposal to go is not followed by the act of going and Man has always escaped by the skin of his teeth, the scenario has been one of an endgame. In that stalemate-situation, the king is constantly checkmated but never killed. Such a game can go on and on monotonously sans dramatic turns—without any hope of victory or fear of defeat. Exactly in the same way, with scores resolutely at zero, the action of *Endgame* continues. Nobody feels like playing and yet they keep playing, for the show must go on. No wonder when Clov suggests, 'Let's stop playing', Hamm exclaims emphatically, 'Never' (*Endgame*, 49). Even at the end, Clov does not really leave but remains lurking at the door. That, in a way, leaves open the scope of continuing the game somehow. Anyway, even if he does leave, there is that boy outside who might come in to take his place and continue the game. The chances are that the next morning either Clov or the boy would do what was done by Clov in the beginning of the play, i.e. arrange things before the handkerchief is removed. That opening situation in itself is a symbolic way of setting the stage for the chess-game of life. It is like removing the cover from the chess-board where it is supposed to be lying to signify the suspension of the game. To indicate that the action starts towards the closing stages of the game and closes when again it is far from ended, the play begins with 'Finished' and ends with 'remain'. No wonder, too, Hamm observes, 'The end is in the beginning and yet you go on' (*Endgame*, 44). And that is what one can say about *Godot*—and about life.

Beckett once tried to explain his vision in *Endgame* to Ernst Schroder who played Hamm in the 1967 Berlin production directed by Beckett himself:

> [Hamm] is a king in the chessgame lost from the start. From the start he knows that he is making loud senseless moves. That he will make no progress at all with the gaff. Now at the last he makes a few senseless moves as only a bad player would. A good one would have given up long ago. He is only trying to delay the inevitable end. Each of his gestures is one of the last useless moves which put off the end. He's a bad player.[4]

Very terse though this statement is, it deserves a closer look. Beckett compares Hamm to a king in chess—a chess-piece, so to say; but soon thereafter he is referred to as a player. Does this identification of pawn with the player, puppet with the puppeteer, signify confusion or mixing of metaphors? Possibly, here is a most characteristic trick of Beckett's. In this trick of inverted allegory, we have the myth of man playing a man in such a manner that one can interpret the action in terms of neither symbolism nor pure mimesis.

Obviously some of the things are so very improbable—for example, old people in ash bins—that insistence on strict realism is bound to raise all kinds of unanswerable questions. And yet looking for symbolic meaning is so frustrating. Traditionally, a symbol signifies something different from itself throughout and consistently. But, in Beckett, in the same play, a character may stand for himself, for a certain aspect of human personality, for all the men in an age, for man as a species, or for the entire Life. No wonder when a critic approaches a Beckettian play, he finds himself playing with the author a kind of chess-game. Whatever his moves or interpretive strategies—naturalistic, expressionistic, symbolic, Cartesian, Jungian, Freudian—he is constantly checkmated. This goes on and on until the realization dawns that such is the experience of man in his game with the world—in his search for the meaning of life. Perhaps, instead of insisting on any realistic or symbolic interpretations for any consistent meaning, we are expected to grab the essence of the experience that a work affords. In *Godot*, it was the experience of not giving up despite utmost hopelessness so that we may feel man's endless effort at evolution when his very survival is not guaranteed. In *Endgame*, it is the experience of continuing to play a game that is over so as to feel what it means for man to be condemned to exist in a world in which he has been foiled in every effort of his to play a significant role. In a way, taken together, the two plays seem to say that, apart from marking time, man's existence has no meaning whatsoever.

On a realistic level, *Endgame* is the story of a blind, tyrannical rancher confined to a wheelchair in a room cut off from the world, while his aged parents are confined to ashbins. They are all attended upon faithfully by a younger but temperamental servant. Even as the master is frustrated because of his total dependence, the servant is frustrated because of the master's tyrannical ways. They are fed up with each other and yet they cannot change the situation: the master has no one else to attend on him and the servant has nowhere else to go. Even at the end, the position is unchanged; in fact, the start and the close are interchangeable. And this despite so much of activity, so much talking, both serious and funny. There is also a great variety in terms of emotions—love, compassion, indifference, humiliation, impatience, anguish, contempt, anger, violence, derisive laughter, etc.—and yet nothing crystallizes as a result of incessant churning.

To lend to this experience the mystery of life, Beckett makes this simple plot intricately complex. For that, the texture of the text is enriched through innumerable suggestions. For example, to represent the human situation of preserving what is almost dead, as in the pickles, the characters are named so as to suggest ingredients of pickles such as ham and clove. This suggestion is reinforced visually when Nagg and Nell peep from bins as if they were pickled in jars. Likewise, when we realize that in addition to putrefied Nagg, old Nell, middle-aged Hamm and a much younger Clov, there is a child on the threshold of entry into this family, we think on the one hand of several generations and on the other of so many stages of degeneration. This idea of identifying generation with degeneration is endorsed further when the decomposing Hamm takes to composing his chronicle and brings in another father. To cap it all, through the joke about the tailor (*Endgame*, 21-2), we are reminded of yet another father—the Father of us all, i.e. God. All this adds up to one impression that the story of Hamm is the story of Man—the story of many generations piled together like grain upon grain. In fact, the idea of piled grains is implanted in our mind right in the opening speech when there is a reference to Zeno's 'impossible heap'.

To hammer home the idea that the eternally unchangeable story of man will never finish or receive the 'finishing' touch (of Godot-stage), the word 'finish' is used on twenty occasions—at times in one sense and at times in the other. Though himself incomplete like the three-legged toy-dog, man has the temerity to find fault with the universe and to boast of his own achievements. In this he is like the tailor in the story who keeps tampering with one part of the trousers or the other but cannot complete them and yet is conceited enough to compare his handiwork with God's creation. Man's claim to be at the very centre of the world is visually concretized when Hamm insists on his chair being placed exactly in the centre of the room. That this room represents the closed world of man is brought home by the declaration that Flora, Pomona and Ceres are outside its walls (*Endgame*, 30). Confined to its claustrophobic limits, Hamm is driven to the wall and brought back. That is an allegorical way of hinting at the apocalyptic experiences of man—facing extinction but being saved by the skin of his teeth. In this room, Hamm has managed to live on through tonics and sedatives, stimulants in the mornings and tranquilizers at night (*Endgame*, 23). This is an implicit reference to the survival of man through innumerable strategies. Man's insistence on orderliness and the rise and fall of civilizations is represented through Clov's arranging curtains, furniture, etc., and his going up and down the ladder. That he has always bungled this is conveyed in Clov's being sometime without glass, sometime without ladder, sometime with both and sometime with neither. Only from the height of the evolutionary ladder it is possible to gain insight into the real situation—that the world outside is zero, the earth is corpsed, and the ocean is sunk in grey light. In concrete terms it means what is repeated more than once—'something is taking its course' (*Endgame*, 17, 26), even though it amounts to nothing. Conversely, light is sunk and yet it is not night; it is finished, nearly finished and yet not exactly over. Perhaps it will never be over because it is the situation of Zeno's millet grain. Indeed, 'The bigger a man is, the fuller he is.... And the emptier' (*Endgame*, 12). In other words, like the play, Man too is stretched over the two ends of 'finished' and 'remain'.

In interpreting *Godot*, I had suggested that standing for the mental and physical aspects of the human personality, Vladimir and Estragon stood for composite man waiting for the Godot-stage. Accordingly, the two Acts of that play presented the story of man's encounter with a civilization (Pozzo) and its companion culture (Lucky) at the stages of its zenith and its nadir. *Endgame*, I suggest, presents the story of that stage of human existence when man is fed up with a certain civilization after it has failed to yield the desired results. The play thus depicts a dark and stagnant phase in human history when one civilization is dying but the other is not yet in. Thus seen, Hamm is Homo, the genus of man, Clov being the civilization that sustains him. Indeed, Clov speaks for every civilization when he says, 'I love order. It's my dream. A world where all would be silent and still and each thing in its last place under the last dust' (*Endgame*, 39). Later, too, he refers to what is expected of a typical civilization—love, friendship, beauty, order, and compassionate attention for the suffering (*Endgame*, 50, 51).

Now, man cannot survive without civilization and a civilization is an orphan without man. Their relationship is akin to the adoption of an orphan by an old, crippled rich man. The adopting one gives enough to ensure survival but no more; on the other hand, the orphan's service is marked more by obedience than by willingness. Hamm has been such a father to Clov; obliged to each other, they do just enough not to end the game in their own interests. The boy outside could possibly be another adopted son—a younger civilization, so to say—to take the position of Clov, if he leaves. It is possible that he too would get fed up and quit, only to be replaced by yet another boy, and so on. As Nagg and Nell have engendered Hamm and not just adopted him, they stand for the Nature-oriented stages of the human species. Now reduced to fossils, they are confined to ashbins. Their talk of kissing and loving is a measure of the never-dying pagan urge for life within man. Nell's dying wish to go to the 'desert' (*Endgame*, 22) also betokens a preference for the wilderness of nature to the closed though cosy world of man.

Basically concerned with the dialectical relationship between man's Being and Becoming, Beckett is invariably representing allegorically how man's efforts at evolving himself just sustain him without ensuring any growth. However, if in *Godot* the focus was primarily on the quality of Being unaffected by Becoming, in *Endgame* it is on the hope of Becoming preventing a regression into non-Being. No wonder when Clov asks Hamm if he believed in the life to come, the latter replies, 'Mine was always that' (*Endgame*, 35). Cut off from the world of nature where he would be a doomed species, man restricts his activities to a small world of his own where he is sustained by civilizations that come and go. This is represented by placing Hamm in a small, curtained room where nature remains unperceived except from the two windows—one opening on the desert (symbolizing death) and the other on the ocean (symbolizing life). This is as good as saying that, despite his efforts to cut himself off from nature, man is still related imperceptibly to the natural forces of life and death; that the natural in man persists in his mortality as implied in Hamm's observation, 'But we breathe, we change! We lose our hair, our teeth!' (*Endgame*, 16).

Man's mortality as well as creativity makes him a 'rancher' in senses more than one—a breeder of cattle as well as a bleeding one. The blood-stained handkerchief underlines the latter sense even as we think of a feeding house when we see Clov returning so often to the unseen kitchen. Closed and small, it has limited resources which are getting constantly depleted. This epitomizes the lessness of the world of man—in contrast to the vast realm of limitless resources available to those leading a purely natural existence. That we are witnessing things from the 'other' end is implied in the fact that the hanging picture has its face to the wall. Placed in such a situation, the rancher here is feeling pulled between the opposing forces of life and death. And that amounts to asking that ancient, existential question—to be or not to be. No wonder this Hamlet-like rancher is named as Hamm. As he lies bleeding helplessly, he has to depend on some one to run his farm, to keep everything in order and to ensure his sustenance. Such a depended one is Clov. Any adopted son, when required to serve the foster-father like this, is bound to feel fed up and leave. He would then be succeeded by another who too might fare the same fate until the master himself would feel equally fed up with the arrangement. Such is the thematic implication of the situation dramatized. Hamm here is Man served by civilizations, Clov representing one of them.

Thanks to the rise and fall of civilizations, man has managed to survive, but his patience is gradually getting exhausted. Whether it would reach the breaking point or else crystallize into a real evolution is anybody's guess. Since the exact position would be known only at the end of time, the present situation is at best like the addition of one more millet grain in that 'impossible heap' of Zeno. Zeno did talk about a quarrel between mortal microcosm and immortal macrocosm but never was the concept of millet grains applied to that conflict. Beckett applied the concept to Time in relation to Man and visualized that the task of man becoming a superman was as impossible as his giving up the evolutionary process. Measured in terms of decades, centuries or even millennia, man's evolution would inevitably amount to stasis—like the arrow that Zeno proved to be always stationary. In another paradox, Zeno pursued this logic to declare that Achilles could never overtake a tortoise. To move means to be in this place and at the same time not to be in it. Such, indeed, is the movement of Man in his evolutionary progress.

That Clov represents not the starting situation in human evolution but quite a late civilization is underlined by his opening speech, 'Finished, it's finished, nearly finished, it must be nearly finished.' This is reiterated by the fact that Hamm asks Clov to put him to bed. However, it is by no means the closing stage either—a fact brought home visually when, getting up, Hamm punctures the word 'absolute' with a yawn (*Endgame*, 12). This age too is one such yawn in the eternally long series of breaths. Hamm's charging Clov with the polluting of air suggests that the latter stands for an industrial age, perhaps even the modern age, its visionlessness and mechanical mobility having been hinted at in Clov's defective eyesight and awkward gait. Perhaps the difference between the ages is minimal—'All life long the same questions, the same answers' (*Endgame*, 13). Anyway, in Clov's age, there are no painkillers nor any bicycles. The references are probably to the painkillers of transcendental values and the Cartesian bicycle. Equally exhausted is the stock of pap and sugarplums—life-sustaining, sweet illusions. The only thing that the Clov-civilization can offer are the hard biscuits of reality. All this points to an age of disillusionment and nausea. In this age of the wasteland, nature is as good as dead for seeds cannot sprout. And the only writing on the wall that the modern civilization can read is 'light dying' (*Endgame*, 17). It looks like an eschaton but it might not actually end up in another Deluge or Ice Age—as implied in Hamm's reference to tonics: 'In the morning they brace you up and in the evening they calm you down. Unless it's the other way round' (*Endgame*, 23). And that accounts for Man's being eternally incomplete, like the three-legged dog that Clov has made.

Hamm insists on the dog's being placed in such a position that it might appear to implore him—his way of deriving psychological satisfaction from an illusion of god-like importance. Another source of much psychological satisfaction is his 'chronicle' (*Endgame*, 35-7) which is an allegory of Man on earth, with Life Force as the narrator. Here is an account of how Adam came crawling on the earth in a zero-situation and implored for bread for his starving brat. Life Force could have said 'No' and that would have meant the end of it all—man's extinction as a species. But 'he' took pity on Adam and employed him as a gardener—a nature-taming cultivator. But not content with mere survival, egotistic man must have more. Thus, he started asserting and glaring with mad eyes in defiance of the wishes of his benefactor. The narrator (Life Force) is disgusted and feels tempted to end this story. But he has not done that so far because this story can be ended only by bringing in some more characters—that is, if Life Force patronizes some other species. Interestingly, since father in the narrative has left the child behind unattended, it tends to be the story of yet another failing father.

The finale of Hamm's narrative, the end of the story of interdependence between Clov and Hamm, and the finishing touches in the tale about the tailor—all tend to assume the same format. And it is the format of the endgame in chess—slow, self-erasing but endless. Each story can be ended, and there is no dearth of characters for starting new stories—'the place was crawling with them' (*Endgame*, 44). But any new story would also be so like the old one. If so, why end this one? That is what the ambiguity of Clov's lurking at the door after leave-taking signifies. If it is not Clov, it would be the boy, but Hamm would continue to be served and the story go along.

Godot has two Acts to underline the fact that, despite the passage of time, essentials do not change. *Endgame* has only one Act because here Beckett has achieved that effect through a multiplicity of 'fathers' and 'sons'. Had there been a second Act, Clov would have still been there—possibly a little more fed up and in a situation of even greater 'lessness'. Else, Hamm would have been in Nell's ashbin, Clov being the master served by the boy outside and trying to complete the chronicle, even as another boy would be on the threshold. In that unwritten scenario, Clov would be as indifferent to Hamm as Hamm is to Nagg in the present situation; on the other hand, he would be as hostile to the new boy as Hamm is now to the boy outside. In short, it will always remain the story of failed fathers and failing light. Yet, thanks to the hope that 'something is taking its course', it would always seem that 'it's a day like any other day' (*Endgame*, 33) and that therefore 'there's no reason for it to change' (*Endgame*, 13). With generations countering degeneration, composition setting off decomposition, the impasse-situation would always justify 'grey light'. Not surprisingly, at the close, even though Hamm exclaims vehemently and repetitively, 'You cried for night; it comes— ... It FALLS: now cry in darkness' (*Endgame*, 52), yet there is no dimming of light. That this vision is as apocalyptic as it is eschatological is implied in the fact that the set is so like a womb as well as like a skull. Also civilization bears the name of Clov to suggest at once splitting (as in cleaving) and knotting (as in clove-hitch). In the evolution of man, breaking a relationship can also be a step towards a new relationship. Perhaps the salvation of man lies in ending the human history—to facilitate its restart. Man's progress is, after all, like the labour of Sisyphus in which the important thing is not just the unending ordeal but also the scope of a restart. That is what makes the boy outside so important, even though, at the same time, no effort is made to save him from death which he would inevitably meet if he does not come in.

Anyway, the final curtain comes down on Hamm lying in the same position as at the start of the play. We know that he is not dead—not yet, at least. We know, too, that death is outside; Hamm was never there and is not there yet. Indeed, death is the painkiller that has not been made available to the species called Man. The possible departure of Clov signifies the close of Hamm's reckoning with him—the end of a particular civilization. But that need not necessarily mean the end of evolution. Of course, Clov's possible departure also breeds insecurity in Hamm who now talks of 'moments for nothing'; but, then, this is not happening for the first time. No wonder Hamm adds, 'now as always' (*Endgame*, 52). He knows that he will continue to live—a fact reflected in the resumption of his narrative. True, fictionalizers in Beckett tell stories only to escape the pain of living. After all, what really matters is neither the story nor the storyteller but the act of telling. It is an allegorical way of saying that what really matters is not Man or his history but the fact that he exists. Now, the act of living might be an unending sequence of breaths, but living is more than breathing. Just as inhaling a breath cannot be regarded as life nor its exhaling as the end of life, similarly the coming and going of Clov is no more than a breath in the eternal life of Hamm. It must not be forgotten that it is not Hamm but Clov who talks about finishing in the opening speech; Hamm talks about remaining even at the end. To put it differently, civilizations come and go but Man remains. Thus seen, in *Endgame*, as in *Godot*, beginning and end, birth and death, survival and extinction, tend to become interchangeable. Indeed, even when a civilization passes away, man remains waiting for his fulfilment—whatever it is—possibly at the end of time.

5 Allotropes of Atrophy

Placed beside *Waiting for Godot* and *Endgame*, *All That Fall* (1956) appears somewhat atypical. Far from leaning towards abstraction with life frozen into stasis or reduced to a box, there is an almost naturalistic imitation of life. In respect of ever-changing locales, multiplicity of characters and variety in sounds, here is, indeed, God's plenty. The passing of time is no longer a problem; what is more, everyone is on the move. But all this notwithstanding, a closer look reveals that this atypicality is more apparent than real. In fact, the play paints yet another apocalyptic picture depicted through characters who have so much in common with the metaphysical tramps of *Godot* and the charismatic cripples of *Endgame*. Blind like Hamm, Dan Rooney too is a chronicler; and here, again, towards the close, comes Jerry with a message, like the boy from *Godot*.

Typical or otherwise, *All That Fall* proved equally intriguing with regard to the numerality of possible interpretations. Does 'Fall' in the title refer to Adam's Fall, God's promise in the psalms about lifting up the fallen, or simply the child's falling from the train? For quite a few critics, it signified the fall-season, autumn—the period between summer and winter to represent the link between life and death. That is why it is argued that most of the characters are middle-aged—passing through the autumn of their lives. Generally the fall of the child from the train is attributed to Dan who had thus possibly fulfilled his obsessive desire to nip a young life in the bud. His hostility, it is averred, stemmed from his perceiving in children a threat to his own child-like security in Maddy's care. Some critics even go to the extent of suggesting that because of this hostility Dan himself might have killed Minnie. According to yet another view, this hostility is the cause of Maddy's childlessness; as for Minnie, she is possibly an imaginary child who was supposed to have 'lived without being born'—as Jung described a patient of his. If so, the carrying of a ball by Dan could mean his carrying castrated testicles. On the other hand, we have an equally plausible suggestion that the ball belonged to Minnie and he has been carrying it around secretly, out of his affection for the departed soul. A natural corollary to such an assumption would be that the child in the train fell accidentally and that Dan would not share this fact with Maddy only to save the sentimental woman from mourning again the loss of Minnie. The latter interpretation makes Dan a warm-hearted creature despite his cold exterior. Likewise, the suggestion that Dan wants to kill children out of compassion to save them from the misery of human existence appears only as valid as the argument that he wants to avenge the loss of Minnie by killing other children. Masterly, indeed, is Beckett's art which makes Dan look as much a heartless monster as a sensitive soul—a proponent of life as well as of death. Of course, there is also that very simple but no less viable view that the child in the train might have fallen out of fright on suddenly seeing blind Dan in the corridor.

Be that as it may, Dan's entire conduct is marked by ambivalence. When Jerry is asked by Maddy the reason for the late arrival of the train, Dan exclaims, 'Leave the boy alone, he knows nothing; come on!' (39) In this, is he betraying his guilt or trying to save Maddy from the pain the news would release? And when Jerry blurts out the shocking news, Dan's only response is a groan! Earlier, when Maddy had asked him about the delay, he had begun with a simple exclamation of exasperation, 'Good God !' (30), but soon he lost his temper and started giving his own version. His adopting the narrative tone makes his role ambiguous and he is possibly devising a mask that can accommodate imaginative modifications to defend himself. It also paves the way for the diversionary digression regarding retirement from business—to make Maddy forget the real issue. Maybe, by wrapping the child's fall and Dan's role in such layers of ambiguity, Beckett was actually trying to create a situation of mutually cancelling possibilities. In any case, this ambiguity facilitates our proceeding from the arbitrary fall to the ironic indictment of God's ways, as implied in the incongruity between the psalmist's promise and the obtaining actuality. Indeed, never has God fulfilled his promise of upholding all that fall. Instead, whatever fell has never risen again—be it Man from the Paradise or autumn leaves, Minnie or the child from the train. No wonder then that, when the text of the sermon is mentioned, it provokes blasphemous laughter (38).

The balancing of mutually cancelling suggestions is important insofar as it serves to accommodate the thematic counterpointing—a balance between creation and decreation resulting from the interplay of Eros and Thanatos, animus and anima. Indeed, here is once again the same old Godot theme of possibilities sans certainties, potential sans achievement, evolution sans progress. No wonder, too, in this play also action winds itself back to the starting point.

The naturalistic details prompt one to treat the action as a simple story of an old and fat woman's dragsome journey to and from a railway station to receive her blind husband on his birthday. But such a reading is aborted by the patently questionable fact that, going to the station, she encounters only such persons as are going in her own direction, while, during the return journey with Dan, she doesn't meet anyone at all, either coming or going. In fact all this—plus the fact that the place is ominously called 'boghill'—makes me feel that we must look beneath the surface realism. To perceive that deeper meaning, one should receive the action of this radio play through the ears. Once one subjects the play to that kind of auricular reception, the play tends to sound like a history of man's existence on earth since his fall. Thus may one 'hear' Humanity starting from its pastoral surroundings, passing by the ruinous house of primitivism, experiencing numerous encounters, and traversing up and then down the stairs of civilization. Alas, however, the long-awaited Godot turns out to be a monomaniac murderer, an iceman rather than the bridegroom—a situation that inevitably facilitates a return to primitivism. Going only by sounds, it is not difficult to surmise imaginatively what difference the presence of mankind has made to existence on this earth. But for man, all would have been the silence of the void, broken occasionally by animal noises. Even though all the human voices in the play do not really amount to anything very dramatic, yet whatever activity there is, is because of man. In other words, the human drama may not be good enough, but it is the only one there is.

The pity, however, is that, despite so much of travail and effort, man's advancement is by no means solid because each stage has been marked by evolutionary flaws. This is suggested by the graded modes of conveyance as well as by the fact that the effectiveness of all of them is impeded in one way or the other. Thus we have a cart driven by a donkey that won't budge, a cycle with flat tyres, a car that has to be choked to start it, a train that comes too late. These hitches are mechanical counterparts of the biological rot in human existence—

the death-in-life that manifests itself in the numerous references to ailments, paralysis, blindness, lingering dissolution, etc. Indeed, the saga of stupendous effort notwithstanding, human life is neither better nor worse than what it was initially. And this primarily because Eros is countred by Thanatos.[1]

As if to strike the keynote of the play, Schubert's *Death and the Maiden* is heard right in the beginning. It is heard again towards the close as a kind of summing up. Possibly this is to underline the fact that the curse that came with Adam's 'Fall' implied the subjecting of human existence to the tyranny of the senses—as the source of both fertility and mortality. As life and death came together, man's efforts to undo the curse by creating opportunities of evolution out of the Fall were foredoomed. If God Himself cannot uphold all that fall, how can man reverse the vertical, downward direction for an upward growth? His effort could at best effect horizontal movement. That is why, in the play, the journey is horizontal and the little rise up the stairs is followed by a journey that brings Maddy back to the starting point. This is, as it were, a way of endorsing the Viconian vision regarding man's cyclical return to primitivism.

Of course, mortality dominates the play so much that the play has been called a litany of death. Besides Schubert's music, death makes its presence felt in Minnie's demise, in the hen's being crushed under the car, in the little child's falling on the line under the wheels of the train, and as an associate of the various forms of decay such as old age, ailments, paralysis, senility, rotting leaves, autumn, etc. Nevertheless, the 'maiden' is never far behind as is clear from such frequent references to sex and fertility as dung-manure, lewd laughter, the bawdy angle of the signal, the suggestive echo of the sex-act in Maddy's being pushed into Slocum's car, and so on. Indeed, if rain and wind are present, there is a clear sky, too. This is like saying that if one cannot depend on the promise of a clear sky, one need not fear excessively the wind and rain also. It is again like the parable of the two thieves in *Godot* which urged one neither to despair too much nor to presume too much. Who can depend on the goodness of God, on the truth of His mercy, on resurrection, the Second Coming, or renewed vitality, when Christ himself came riding on such a sterile beast as a hinny? On the other hand, what hopes can one pin on man whose 'busyness' is so purposeless that retirement from, and engagement in, the business yield the same result? Both ends of the alley are extremely narrow though not exactly blind. In short, dust returns to dust, and in this circuitous journey from and to the ruinous house one keeps hovering around the boghill. If it is suicidal to move out, it is a lingering dissolution inside. And thus, after the shocking epiphany of the close, Maddy and Dan continue dragging their feet. It is like falling asleep again after a nightmare. It is a typically Beckettian ending that signifies yet another start in the process of eternal recurrence.

In short, *All That Fall* is the story of humanity dragging its feet through the stages of the cart, the cycle, the car and the train. It has been attracting sympathy and frittering it away until the train of modern civilization has brought a visionless, vampire-brained monster who uses the train of organ-grinding civilization to crush the very hope of future-progress. That brings humanity back to primitivism. This does not, of course, imply a no-change situation because, in the process, the physical aspect has weakened and the intellectual aspect gone more sinister. In a way, the close tends to be an ironic comment on the change which was supposed to signify progress but has in fact spelt decay and disaster. With such Sisyphus-like labour, never can man hope to undo his fall and evolve into Superman-Godot.

In 1956, when Beckett received from the BBC a tape of his first radio play, *All That Fall*, it served as an introduction to the marvel of tape-recording. He was fascinated to hear Patrick Magee's voice as Slocum reproduced with life-like authenticity. It did not take Beckett long to think of exploiting the retentive properties of the tape as an instrument of recollection. In fact, by 1958, he had already written his piece called *Magee's Monologue* which, with the passage of time, became *Krapp's Last Tape*. In the process, the monodrama acquired two voices—one live, the other taped. He used the tape as mechanical memory—as against the voluntary and involuntary memories which he had discussed twenty-seven years ago in his dissertation on Proust.

According to Proust, while all animals live in space and are victims of biological time, man is the only creature that lives in time. He alone is conscious of chronological time. What is more, he creates subjective time by bringing the memory of the past into his present, consciously, subconsciously, or unconsciously. It is the complex functioning of memory which keeps transforming man's personality almost continuously. Indeed, in the absence of an enduring ego, an individual can never be approached as a consistent whole. Instead, he may be perceived as a succession of individuals. Consequently, a man's life tends to become a series of events on which we can throw no light, or a series of problems that cannot be solved. No wonder Proust talked of multiple 'selves'—a new 'I' for each new moment.

Krapp's Last Tape is Proustian in its assumption of multiple selves but Beckett wouldn't be Beckett if he subscribed to others' views without effecting alchemic transmutations. To me it appears that he has drawn typically Beckettian conclusions by applying the laws governing individual memory to the working of racial memory. In fact, even in *Proust*, Beckett could not help projecting some of his own perceptions. Now, in *Krapp's Last Tape*, he has gone far beyond Proust. No wonder then that while Arthur K Oberg calls the play Proustian,[2] according to Rosette Lamont, it is anti-Proustian,[3] even as Frederick Hoffman regards it as a parody of Proust.[4] If an individual's self is a collage of 'selves' changing every moment, how can, Beckett seems to have asked, any individual be known by others, or even by himself? After all, with every ticking second, all the earlier selves become archaic. And what an interesting dramatic confrontation it would be, Beckett might have wondered, if he brought together two or three such 'selves' separated by spells of time. Maybe, such a juxtaposition had been visualized by him earlier, too; but he had never attempted it for one obvious reason. At least one of these selves had to be a memory of the old self; and memory being something subjective, he could not possibly construct it in its totality. Now, the tape made it possible to record a 'self' at a given moment and to reproduce it with scientific exactitude later. This facilitated the possibility of handling changes wrought by time in a man's identity and bringing together an individual's varied versions at different stages. What is more, the tape-recording facilities brought home to Beckett the distinction between an event recorded on a machine and its subjective recollection by the man himself. After all, not only is the recollecting mind changeable in itself but may also be subjected to nostalgia or any other emotional reaction. Toying with the idea, Beckett seems to have discovered that he could use the tape also for an interplay between memory, memory-within-memory and even memory of a memory. In *Krapp's Last Tape*, Beckett has not only used the tape-recorder as a kind of oral mirror reflecting the protagonist's 'self' at the time of recording but also made the tape-recording self recollect an even earlier self. Thus has Beckett been able to capture three Krapps concurrently—K-69 (the wearisome, 69-year old Krapp in his own person), K-39 (the middle-aged Krapp whose voice on tape we hear), and K-29 (the young Krapp about whom K-39 is talking). Seeing at a glance these different selves, we perceive not only the changes in the texture of the protagonist's growth but also the fact that essentially he has remained unchanged in many aspects. Thus the addiction to bananas, alcohol and sex, and moral indignation at his past self, are factors common to all the stages; and yet there are clear variations in respect of the capacity to eat, the venues of drinking, the frequency and manner of sex, the nature of memories, and the depth of hypocrisy.

Here is, so to say, yet another case of having changed but not changed enough—something that applies, in fact, to all Beckett protagonists. After all, they represent the same mankind. Indeed, it is possible to say that Krapp is Everyman and his different 'selves' represent Man in different ages. Thus viewed, Man emerges as a chronic lecher who cannot help peeling the symbolic banana of sex despite his tall, hypocritical claim of transcending the natural urges. In fact, the assertion of moral superiority by every new age only implies growing sexual perversity—as in the case of Krapp. K-69 plays and replays the sex episode but skips the vision part on the tape. This preference for sensory experiences, as opposed to intellectual insights, is typical of Man too. Sensory experiences yield insights but, instead of accumulating or assimilating them into a vision, man prefers to retain only the memory of the sensuous thrill. It is because of this incapacity to learn enough from experience that his evolution is not linear; instead, it tends to be repetitive, almost circular. Man's refusal to learn from the past is borne out by history which, like Krapp taped at intervals, records the experiences of man.

Indeed, once this identification between Krapp and Man is established, one can easily see that Krapp's three stages correspond to the series of growth, maturity and decline in human evolution. Like Krapp, Man too has never lived; he has only avoided living life. Thus viewed, Krapp's actions are more symbolic than realistic. For example, his consulting his watch again and again signifies Man's obsession with time. Likewise, Krapp's eating a banana, his vacuous stare, his fiddling with the keys and drawers, and his withdrawal to darkness could represent, respectively, Man's preoccupation with sex, unproductive brooding, material possessions, and clandestine indulgence in sensuous pleasures. This way, Krapp's lying paralyzed after hearing the old tape stands for the existential shock of self-recognition. In the same way, when K-69 claims, 'What is a year now?

The sour cud and the iron stool' (62), he possibly represents the desublimated existence of man today. That also explains why Krapp finds nothing significant to record on his last tape. Indeed, modern man can no longer talk of high moments, the golden ages.

In this context, Krapp's forgetting his earlier selves and feeling a stranger to himself is a telling comment on the nature of man's evolution. What hope of superman or Godot can there be in the future of a species which always keeps changing and has such a flawed racial memory that it cannot recognize even its own past self? In a situation like this, when there is no definite identity, there cannot possibly be any definite gain from experiences of the past. Like the 'selves' of Krapp, the generations of mankind fail to communicate and the result is at once horrible and comic. That makes Man a grotesque buffoon in his own tragedy. The trouble with him is that he never had the will to redeem the situation; he always thought that the real time for action was in the past. It is to be noted that it is not K-69 but K-39 who declares 'Perhaps my best years are gone. When there was a chance of happiness. But I wouldn't want them back. Not with the fire in me now. No, I wouldn't want them back' (63). No such despair is mouthed by K-69 but it is implied in his final motionless stare as the tape runs on in silence. In that silence, the audience might hear mankind echoing the song which Krapp was trying to sing:

> Now the day is over
> Night is drawing nigh-igh
> Shadows . . . of the evening
> Steal across the sky (62)

And when it is recalled that, according to the opening stage direction, all this takes place in a 'late evening in the future' (55), the whole play acquires the depth and power of an apocalyptic vision.

Indeed, here is again an eschatological situation in which the final glimmer affords an epiphanic insight into the fate of man at the hands of the double-headed monster called Time. The continuous process of creation and decreation has resulted, and will continue to result, in incessant activity without producing any worthwhile action—total stasis despite unending movement. It is not for nothing that the play is littered with references to time. The idea is to trace the impact of time on Man through its impact on an individual. Thus Krapp's age (be it 39 or 69) tends to represent an Age in the progress of mankind. It is, of course, the same Krapp but, at different moments of his life, he appears as three different persons. Likewise, mankind too looks different in different ages but is the same species nevertheless. Like Krapp claiming new perceptions at different stages of his life, Man too claims to have a new outlook with every new age; but in either case, the change is more imaginary than real. What a bizarre contrast the juxtaposition of two ages of the human race would create is suggested by the coalescing of the twin laughters of K-69 and K-39.

Thus seen, *Krapp's Last Tape* becomes a reworking of the Godot theme—man's failure to evolve despite incessant changes brought by time. The changes are there and apparently so complete that a later generation may refuse to recognize the earlier one—like K-39 wondering if he was such a young whelp at 29, or K-69 referring to K-39 as 'that stupid bastard' (62). Krapp's declaration of his own self as 'Not-I' does not, however, signify man's acquiring a moral superiority or forward evolution. On the contrary, he continues to be the silly clown that he always was. If he cannot see the unchanging characteristic of his, it is because he can always see the fool that he was but not the fool that he is. It is in his very nature that the source of human failure lies—in his permanent inability to accept himself for what he is. Though congenitally impotent, Krapp has been deluding himself with the notion that he is wilfully avoiding sexual dissipation because he has to canalize his energies into his magnum opus. Thus he is seen as deciding in favour of a less engrossing sexual life at 29 and bidding farewell to love at 39. At 69, it is too late and he can only talk of love, the actual performance (with Fanny) being so grotesque. When all this is taken together, it only means that in his craze to create a story of grand passion, he has forfeited love itself. This is as good as saying that Man, in his obsession to evolve, has never really lived.

Of course, the question is still open. Is Krapp's masturbation the cause of impotence or its result? In the case of man, has the realization of having lost his opportunity come too late, or was it a case of congenital incapability? Indeed, failure of man's evolutionary efforts can be traced as much to the fundamental incompatibility between man's physical and intellectual aspects as to his refusal to live a full-blooded life in the name of creative evolution. To put it differently, while man's 'becoming' was spurred by his mortal condition, his failure to 'become' is rooted in the very condition of his 'being' itself. That brings death so close to life that love and death appear as the two obverse sides of the same coin. It is, so to say, the case of identifying

Death with the Maiden—a vision concretized towards the close when Krapp, listening to the tape, puts his arms on the table to assume the position he had during that 'memorable equinox' (57). As he lies in that position, the tape goes silent; so does Krapp's heart-beat. And as he lies dead, he is in the position of love-making in the punt. Now, of course, it is death that he embraces. The ambivalence of this image recalls the identification of tomb and womb in *Godot* in the talk about giving birth astride of a grave!

Like *Krapp's Last Tape*, 'Embers' (1959) too is a kind of memory play in which we have one character plus voices. Here, too, the passions have lost their once-flaming quality; however, their recording and reproduction is not mechanical. Instead, Henry carries his people in his mind like gramophone records which he can play as and when he wishes. Indeed, he can summon them, make them speak louder and have a sound or speech repeated or rejected at will. One could even say that in this radio play, the protagonist is living a radio-drama—hearing voices without seeing the dramatic personae. That makes the inner world of Henry's skull the locale where the past is relived and thus embers rekindled. Embers thus become what rotting leaves were in the earlier radio play, *All That Fall*—dying but not dead. In that sense, 'Embers' may be yet another version of *Endgame*—so close to the end and yet somehow continuing. The inability of the embers to die out completely and their lingering potential for igniting a flame are felt to be as real as the decline of their original power. In fact, the decline as a necessary stage or precondition of rekindling corresponds to the ebbing of a tide before its rise. No wonder, at one stage, Beckett thought of 'Ebb' as the title of this play.

Perhaps 'Ebb' would have been a less intriguing title for a play in which the sea is heard in the background from the beginning till the end. What is more, it has become an integral part of the protagonist's aural imagination. The sea it was that devoured Henry's father; it haunts him still. Above all, drowning its roar through endless talking has become the sole obsession of Henry. However, eventually Beckett opted for 'Embers' as the title. In this connection, it is worth noting that even though both the sea and embers represent life as well as death, quintessentially they are inverted images of each other. Embers have ash outside and fire within; sea is Eros on the surface and Thanatos at the core. In fact, associated with infinity, timelessness, sound and fury as the sea is, it represents better the macrocosmic Life of the Universe; on the contrary, signifying time-bound, mortal existence and silence, embers should be the right metaphor for the microcosmic life of man's world. Thus, in finally opting for 'embers' as the title, Beckett has indirectly indicated that the drama here is about the futile but heroic effort of the puny microcosm to defy the gigantic macrocosm.

'Embers' is the story of man's ambivalence towards the Life Force as reflected in the relationship between life and Life. Since Henry associates the sea on the one hand with his father who has become a part of it and on the other with Ada to whom he made love for the first time on its shores, he feels both fascinated and repelled by it. No wonder he cannot get away from it and yet he dare not go into it. Indeed, man would love to partake of the divinity and eternity of Life but he does not want to become a part of its formlessness. He is afraid to be sucked in by its infinity as that would mean losing his own identity. He prefers a less chaotic existence in a world of his own making even if it means being subjected to mortality. Indeed, he creates his own sounds by talking and walking on the shingles of life, even though he knows that these are too feeble to drown the roar of the sea.

By choosing to live on the shore, rather than on the sea, man has denied himself the right to eternity and thus he stands subjected to the tyranny of Time—living in time and dying in time. This fate he had accepted in the hope of creating a story in which he could be a creator instead of mere creature, but the actual outcome has been very different. Man has been creating civilization after civilization but each time he has failed. Of course, he would start again out of the ruins of the previous civilization, like the rebirth of phoenix out of ashes—out of embers, so to say. A phoenix dies to be reborn to die again to be reborn again; ditto for human civilization. The rise and fall of civilization has been so frequent and this has been going on for such a long time that at times it is difficult to tell whether, at a given moment, the jaegers of civilization are on or off.

If we approach the play with these assumptions, it affords a fairly sustained allegory. As Heinrich in German means head of the family, Henry is possibly the head of the human family, i.e. Adam. He was forsaken by his father when he made love to Ada—precisely like Adam's punishment for a similar disobedience. That Ada is Eve is confirmed by her name—literally, a part of Adam, to signify her creation out of Adam's rib. Henry's father also remains invisible, like

God, even though his presence is felt. The father's description of Henry as a 'washout' (96) is an apt expression of God's disappointment in Adam. It could as well signify the prophecy of God about what man would be in the world. Henry's not entering the sea but continuing to live on its shore and making feeble sounds on the shingles against the roaring sea signifies man's alienation from the universe and continuing with an insignificant existence. Henry and Ada have engendered Addie (mankind) whose life is marked by rigorous training in music and riding (culture and civilization). That Henry is as much disappointed in Addie as his own father was in him signifies man's failure to afford an alternative to the macrocosm. Against the roar of Life, human life is no more than a thudding sound produced by striking two stones against each other. Indeed, as in the play, microcosmic existence comprises only fragments of narratives, snatches of sound, memories, projections of imagined glory. This life is by no means any more significant than the one he would have lived if he had not opted out of the eternal sea of Life.

However, Henry cannot accept this shocking reality; instead, he would rather indulge in illusion-mongering through endless chatter and invention of stories of self-projection. This is as good as saying that, by developing fresh strategies of survival, man continues to deceive himself into believing that he can perpetuate himself. This business of inventing stories might be a psychological need, a kind of defense mechanism; but, in effect, it is as ineffectual as Henry's trying to drown the sea through incessant talking. Indeed, when Henry says that every syllable is a second gained (102), he is referring to the desperate effort of Man to wrest from inevitable mortality a little more time through the imagined stories of human significance. That is also what is implied in Henry's wish that the horses could be trained to mark time (97), the reference being to the horse of Time. However, Henry knows that, despite all his efforts, nothing has been gained. No wonder he keeps repeating 'No good' when narrating the story of his alter-ego, Bolton. This is in marked contrast to what God had exclaimed after the creation of the universe—that it was good.

If Henry is Adam, who is the protagonist of his story, Bolton? Generally he is treated as a fictionalized version of Henry's father or even of Henry himself. Since the name Bolt-on can mean the nailed one, he could be Christ. However, as a closer look will reveal, Beckett has employed a parodic inversion. The idea probably is that man too is being crucified, though without the redemptive recompense enjoyed by Christ. Christ died quick and returned to life after death; Man is taking so long to die. In fact, his is a case of dying even when alive. Being divine, Christ represented eternal life and was thus like the sea; man is mortal but still alive, like the embers. Now embers may be rekindled by blowing through a hollow pipe; here, too, a doctor called Holloway tries to fan up the embers of Bolton's life through an injection. Hollow, indeed, are the strategies of survival!

If the sea represents Life, the room in the story is the microcosm that man has created. It is bitterly cold because the fire is out, but it does have some embers still buried in its ashes. That makes it more congenial than the world of nature outside. No wonder then that, when Bolton plays with the curtain, Dr Holloway shouts at him not to do so because the draught from outside could kill him. This is as good as saying that in man's microcosm life might have been reduced to embers but the world outside is even worse—completely dead. In the room there is at least some warmth, some life. In other words, the futile existence of Man in the microcosm is better than his certain extinction in nature. No wonder, at the close, Henry once again goes no farther than the edge of water. And this when he knows that he is doomed to lead an empty life. Aptly enough, his diary records nothing for him to do on Saturday or Sunday—or on any day except the plumber's visit on Friday. Is this plumbing at nine a counterpart of the panhysterectomy at nine to be performed by Dr Holloway in the story? If so, it would mean, naturally, the end of (pro)creation—a most ironic counterpart of crucifixion which also took place at nine on a Friday. In the present case at least there won't be any resurrection.

The play has no second Act but there is ample suggestion that the action here is happening neither for the first time nor for the last. That is why Holloway says, 'We've had this before, Bolton, don't ask me to go through it again' (104). Indeed, if there were more Acts, in each one, Henry would be still on the sea-shore, haunted by its roar, feeling tempted to move towards it but stopping short at the water's edge. This ambivalence will persist because Life Force, despite its divinity and eternity, operates through the disgusting act of sexuality. Perhaps that explains why we have so much talk about sterility, abortions, washouts, hysterectomy, etc. That brings us back to the import of the crucial scene in the Bolton-Holloway story.

Dr Holloway is prepared to give Bolton a shot, a sedative or painkiller, but Bolton wants something different which is not spelt out. Henry appears to behave like a chronic drug-addict insisting on another dose which the doctor is not willing to give. Perhaps this refusal of a mere sedative and beseeching for a stimulant implies man's desire for another chance to live, howsoever miserable. On the other hand, it is possible that Bolton being desperately fed up with life, is asking his doctor not to prolong it through sedatives but to put an end to it through mercy-killing—a request that not even the friendliest doctor would accede to. If this is the case, it should mean Man's having decided to commit suicide. That the twin interpretations look equally plausible is not a matter of chance but the result of a deliberate effort on the part of Beckett to create a balance between the equally powerful human instincts to live and to die. To put it differently, having forfeited the choice to enter or not to enter the sea of life long ago, now the only alternative before man is to end or not to end the microcosm. He has realized, as it were, that Godot is unlikely to come; but he knows too that it is too late for suicide also. And that is what justifies the metaphor of embers for human existence—at once dying and living.

Or could it be that the doctor in the story refuses to oblige because he is in favour of a more radical remedy—something like panhysterectomy that would destroy at source the very possibility of breeding life? This would mean the total annihilation of the race instead of merely tinkering with the ever-recurring cancer of human civilization. This interpretation makes Beckett look a deeper-dyed pessimist than Heine who had said:

> Lo, sleep is good, better is death; in sooth,
> The best of all were never to be born.

Indeed, as Beckett has always believed in the possibility of living without being born, he might as well go a step farther than the end of the human species—the destruction of all life. That was, it would be recalled, the problem in *Endgame* too where not even a flea was to be allowed to survive. Anyway, as in *Endgame*, in 'Embers' also that end is never reached and at the close we are swung back to the starting point. What remains is the murmur of the sea and Henry still on its shore. With Bolton still pleading and Holloway equally adamant, the narrative also remains where it was. This is Beckett's way of declaring that the story of ending being unendable, the wait for Godot shall have to continue.

When asked to sum up a typically Beckettian play, what are the phrases or images that throng one's mind?

> Waiting.—Endless persistence. Infinite resignation.—Hopeless hope. Incorrigible optimism.—Tomb and womb. Death and the Maiden.—Tyranny of time. Old age and mortality.—Progressive dissolution.—Endgame.—Eschaton.—Existence on the stage. Existentialist monodrama.—Escape from the void through verbiage. Endless chatter.—Churning of stale words.—Glory of the trivial. Mystery of the inane. Sensuality of the impotent.—Fiction as strategy of survival.—Eternal incompatibility.—Cartesian bicycle.—Viconian cycles.—Proustian habit and memory.

Interestingly enough, all these phrases/images apply to *Happy Days* (1961). Indeed, here is epitome of Beckett's vision—*Godot* and *Endgame* rolled into one.

As in *Godot*, in *Happy Days* too, filling time with waiting for the end is presented in such a manner that, seeing in the two Acts just two steps in the process of eternity, one can visualize what the preceding and the succeeding stages would be like. The pull between hope and despair over the arrival of Godot comes to mind in the ambiguous ending of *Happy Days.* Is Willie leaving in despair or getting ready to respond to the advertisements? Is he here to kiss or to kill? Is he just back or on the point of departure? Is he trying to reach Winnie, or her revolver—to kill her, or to kill himself? If in *Godot* Biblical references come in for parodic ridicule, so do literary quotations here. Even the title is an ironic dig at the Gloria Prayer—'days without end'. Of course, echoes of *Endgame* are also heard continually. After all, this too is a study in survival on the verge of nothingness. Thus, in Willie's limited mobility we have Clov's handicap, just as Winnie's burial in sand approximates to Nagg and Nell's confinement in ashbins. Clov's preparing to leave at the end is so like Willie's dressing for a journey. Like Hamm's fear of life starting again from a flea, here formication has the dreaded potential of fornication. Once again, things are getting exhausted progressively. In fact, in this play too one hears the echoes of Beckett's previous plays. For example, the song *Death and the Maiden* appears to have come from *All That Fall* reframed as *The Merry Widow*. Likewise, the bell here is a veritable reincarnation of both the whistle in 'Act Without Words I' and the goad in 'Act Without Words II'. With the former, this play further shares the blazing light of the desert, while, as the contrasted studies of introvertism and extrovertism, Willie and Winnie have come straight from the latter mime. *Krapp's Last Tape* also comes to mind when we see here a similar quasi-monologue that forms, deforms and reforms the past. What is more, the face of Willie here and the face of O in *Film* are seen for the first time only at the end.

Does the commonality of these features signify Beckett's limited stock of tricks? Perhaps it would be equally valid to argue that, instead of telling different stories, Beckett is communicating the same view of life in different ways. Indeed, here, as everywhere else, Beckett's concern is with an ever-new shape for the same 'mess', a fresh way of expressing the inexpressible, a new allegory for the same basic story about the progress of man in this world. Therefore, as in the other plays, in *Happy Days* too we must resist the temptation of insisting on one meaning and discovering a one-to-one correspondence for each detail. Instead, we must learn to be content with the semi-symbolic, mutually cancelling suggestions inhering in the subtext. Of course, when fused together, these suggestions yield an intriguingly incoherent and therefore incomprehensible pattern until we realize that such indeed is life.

Right from the beginning, we are prompted not to perceive the action here only on the realistic plane, as an imitation of life. After all, in which desert on our planet can we hope to see a woman buried in sand up to her breast or neck and talking incessantly of happy days? That makes us realize instantly that Winnie is more than a woman—standing for something or someone else. Gradually, what gets imprinted on one's mind is her physical charm, her endless chatter, her dull routine, her incorrigible optimism, her renewable possessions, her incompatibility as well as her indispensability with regard to the other character, Willie. Buried in the earth as she is, she has something 'earthy' about her—something vulgar as well as possessive. In fact, the way the set makes her charming face appear to be an integral part of the vast expanse, one immediately thinks of her as Mother Earth. And the way Willie is prowling around, the tableau appears to represent Earth in relation to Man. All this makes *Happy Days* a play about Man's life on the Earth and the gradual exhaustion of resources, despite the never-ending process of natural renewal.

That Winnie is to be treated as more than a woman and identified with Earth/Nature is suggested by the fact that she wakes up with the ringing of a bell—like Earth awakened to life by the birds' chirping. Earth's beauty is at its best at dawn as if freshly rouged up, like Winnie here. That the Earth's resources are running out to the point of exhaustion is represented by the nearly empty tube of toothpaste. However, as nature automatically replenishes its stock, Winnie has a new mirror, a new bottle of medicine, a new parasol in Act II. If Winnie's vanity bag stands for the beauties of nature, her revolver might signify the terrible aspects of Nature in tooth and claw. The bag also contains Willie's 'marvellous gift' (*HD*, 11) which turns out to be a toothbrush made of hog's setae. This is, indeed, a telling comment on the triviality of man's role on the Earth!

Now, man has been aspiring to survive on the strength of his puny intellect, but his effort has yielded an existence marked by an all-too-slow evolution. This is represented by Willie's bald head, brooding tendency, infantile eating of excreta, and turtle-like slow pace. Since Man has been refusing to submit to nature and exerting his will, understandably enough, he has been called Willie; Winnie, on the other hand, has been so named because of the fact that, in the long run, it is nature that has its way and thus wins.

Between Earth/Nature and Man, there has not been much understanding. The reason for their alienation lies in man's selfish absorption in his own petty projects. No wonder Willie is too lost in his newspaper to respond to the overtures of Winnie. The newspaper symbolizes, as it were, man's unquenchable thirst for useless knowledge. All that this newspaper-oriented intellectualism yields is the promise of a job for a 'smart youth' (*HD*, 14)—a reference possibly to man's eternal immaturity with regard to his illusive ambitions in respect of evolution. In any case, whenever man has responded and held communion with nature, it has marked a spell of joyful co-existence—the so-called 'happy days'.

That Earth's relationship with Man has passed through many stages is implicit in Winnie's reminiscences. Her first ball was with John*stone* (italics Beckett's own—*HD*, 15) who had a bushy, tawny moustache—a clear reference to Man living in bushes during the Stone Age. No wonder her first kiss is associated with the toolshed, piles of pots, etc. (*HD*, 15). That man essentially continues to be a hairy ape is brought home when Willie's forearm appears with a card. This disgusts Winnie, signifying Earth's impatience with the ugliness brought by Man. Of course, despite this disgust, she wants Willie to be near her; she needs him. After all, it is through man that life on the Earth has some significance. Besides, whenever in doubt, Winnie wants Willie's verdict and explication. This peculiar dependence has made her not only excessively solicitous but also over-protective, as her painstaking instructions during his crawling (*HD*, 21) signify. She wishes him to come to her and live by her side but he is totally indifferent. Such indeed is the relationship between Man and Nature. No wonder the relationship has not yielded anything worthwhile. It is a case of 'No better, no worse, no change' (*HD*, 12)—a situation akin to what we had in *Godot*. Anyway, like Vladimir there, Winnie won't give up.

Act II represents further the alienation of Man and Nature but things continue, still caught in ambivalence. As Winnie is buried deeper and looks older, we understand that Nature is exhausted and human existence is becoming even more painful under the burden of time. In this Act, since Willie is even more silent, Winnie is frightened at the prospect of his leaving her. And when he does appear, he is dressed to 'kill'. As he tries to climb up to her, Winnie, thinking that he is coming to kiss her, exclaims, 'Oh, this is a happy day, this will have been another happy day!' (*HD*, 47). But he either slips or slinks away. Indeed, Man's return to nature can signify a return to barbarism; man would not possibly wish that. No wonder we start suspecting his motives: is he trying to reach her just to kill her? Or is he trying to reach the revolver instead? If so, does he want to use it for killing Winnie, or else for killing himself? Caught in this ambivalence, Winnie's admiration mixes with nagging and the two stand simply locked in each other's gaze. Beckett leaves the situation wrapped in ambiguity with all possibilities equally open. This is as good as saying that Beckett refuses to anticipate what form the impending end might take—death of man, death of Nature, or return to savagery. It might mean as much a return to the happy days of nature as a movement towards the happy days of doom. After all, there is scope for optimism even in the latter prospect. Indeed, if in the process of evolution there is degeneration, there might also be some chance of regeneration in the process of decay.

Now the interaction between Man and Earth has failed to yield a heaven on earth but it has by no means been an exercise in futility. Man's evolution being an interplay of the forces of Eros and Thanatos, the resultant endgame is marked as much by dissolution as by persistence. In this framework, dreary and cheery sound as interchangeable expressions. As hope tends to mean despair and vice-versa, gloom, defeat and impotence serve as the fabric of 'happy' days. Thus, incurable optimism gets interwoven into the substructure of chronic pathos and undercurrents of existentialist philosophy run beneath the surface of cheerfulness. No wonder, most characteristically, in the face of annihilation, Winnie takes to nail-filing and tooth-brushing; likewise her metaphysical commentary is interrupted to find what is pure in the toothbrush. And when it is discovered to be merely hog's setae, this addition to her knowledge is treated as a great discovery of historical significance (*HD*, 16)!

Telling, indeed, is the contrast between the triviality of Winnie's mindless chatter on the one hand, and her optimistic persistence on the other. In fact, the play attempts to equate the glory of her persistence with the banality of her existence. It is not surprising, therefore, that Winnie's inadvertent, inexact and incomplete quotations tend to evoke tragic associations even with the most trivial situations. For example, along with the discovery of hog's setae on the brush comes Ophelia's anguished cry (*HD*, 11), the colours of the rouge get linked to Romeo's description of 'dying' Juliet (*HD*, 14), and the scorched earth is projected as the realization of Omar Khayyam's dream of 'Paradise enow' (*HD*, 25). In fact, throughout the play, inanity approximates profundity, cliches carry twisted truths, endless chatter proves less communicative than dead silence. Indeed, here, routine habit serves as an alternative to the suffering of being, and vulgar conditioning becomes indistinguishable from the deep mystery of life. What all this implies is that the tenor of life on the earth is marked as much by repetitious routine and churning of stale words as by the laws of mortality. In short, here is a clown enacting a tragedy. Thus seen, the play brings home the realization that if man's expecting to become Superman via these existential inanities is foolish, his giving up in despair would be an inglorious betrayal of the evolutionary efforts of mankind spread over millions of years.

In *Happy Days*, there is no third Act, but one can surmise about the possibilities. Maybe, Winnie would be completely buried and Willie left alone; possibly, Willie would rescue her from burial and start a new life. More likely, the situation would be the same: 'no interest—in life—poor dear Willie—sleep for ever . . .' (*HD*, 11). One thing alone is sure: there would be no real life for Winnie without Willie. 'I used to think that I would learn to talk alone . . . (*Smile.*) But no. (*Smile broader.*) No, no (*Smile off.*) Ergo you are there' (*HD*, 37-8). Man is there just to ensure life on the Earth. In other words, howsoever absurd his existence, man's living is justification in itself. Marked by want of communication and warmth, such an existence may be full of routine and meaningless activity and its ironies may be blasphemous sniggers at God's little jokes (*HD*, 24), yet man will have to live, ever-waiting for happy days which may never come. But wait he must, for this hope against hope is the essence of human life.

In *Happy Days*, Winnie is buried in sand but she is still alive—noticing things around her and commenting on them. *Play* (1963) marks a further stage in desiccation. Here, the situations has worsened: not only is it the head alone that is visible but even its function stands reduced to just one activity, viz., speaking. And this in respect of not one but all the three characters. Even otherwise, the stage of happy days has been passed as the characters are parts of the urns signifying a postmortem existence. In later Beckett, we have disembodied heads. Anyway, the characters here are already incapable of action, gestures or facial expression; even their voices are toneless. And as should be expected in a typical Beckett play, narration is at the heart of drama and full of memories about 'that time'. What is more, here is yet another variation on the old theme of endgame, i.e. the inability to end—in this case, to end one of the two relationships. Equally characteristic is the strategy to round the end back to the starting point and thus suggest through repetition a touch of never-ending, eternal progression.

It is customary to interpret *Play* as Beckett's version of *No Exit*—a play about the inability to escape the pervasiveness of bad faith even after death. The locale of the present action is supposed to be the no-man's land of the after-life, possibly in the lower circle of the hell. The characters are presumably damned to talk endlessly about their petty lies and vices in the love triangle that they had comprised on the earth. Maybe it is possible to say that, like Sartre, Beckett also assumes that one's consciousness survives after death. But, surely, the situation here is qualitatively different. While Sartre's characters debate their situation, here we have a collage of three monologues. Since the speakers appear to be unaware of their presence or even of the deaths of one another, at best they represent three isolated egos. Each being a void, no communication is possible. Thus seen, the 'triangle' epitomizes the quintessence of all human relations—a mode of relatedness that yields neither conflict nor communication. Even what is intelligible in isolation tends to become opaque in the process of interplay. In fact, the same facts may even lead to different kinds of conclusions, even different values. Although M, W1 and W2 meant well and were faithful in their own respective ways, they all appear to have deceived one another and even themselves. Indeed, the line separating the value-scales by which man lives is so very thin that one's moving from one to the other may be as imperceptible as a spectator's rocking on the twin planes of illusion and reality while viewing a play. Perhaps that is why the play has been called *Play*.[5]

In a play, one is in the eyes of others what one is not—precisely what is happening in the views of M, Wl and W2 about one another. Again one is supposed to be 'playing' when one is not being oneself but projecting an image of oneself—at times to deceive others, at times to deceive even one's own self. That kind of 'playing' is at the heart of the stories told by the three characters here. Even otherwise, the reality of a play lies in relationships. Here, too, at the core of the action is a network of interactions—for example, between characters and light, light and darkness, sound and silence. The most conspicuous, however, is the interaction among different versions of their relationships. In fact, so intricate is the pattern thus created that it is difficult to tell whether these are three different plays comprising one trilogy or three short plays created out of one. Perhaps it is a reworking of the familiar belief that the world is a stage on which we all play our own roles. Beckett appears to add that although each character believes that his life is a full play, actually it is only a part of the big play that never ends. Or, maybe, it illustrates how an archetypal myth (say, a love triangle) may yield different plays just by changing the focus.

Depending on how one interprets the play, light has been invested with different meanings—a torturing inquisitor, a recording angel, a spectator's 'eye', a playful god enacting a drama for his own amusement, a bored spectator interrupting the action mid-sentence or even mid-word. On one thing at least there has been unanimity: it is more than a theatrical lighting effect—almost a character. It is not without significance that, instead of talking among themselves, M, Wl and W2 all address this light throughout. Another conspicuous aspect of the light here is that it is not what light usually signifies—a source of enlightenment and therefore something sacrosanct. Instead, it has about it something sadistic, almost imperious. Could it be Time, the double-headed monster that kills as well as creates?[6]

For me, the key to the identity of the light—as also to the theme of the play—lies not in the action but in its tenor. The broken bits of the three versions are felt to be inter-related but, in the absence of a clear perspective, it all looks an intriguing mystery. In human evolution, too, the stories of progress in different areas might yield coherent accounts but any effort to relate them to an overall picture leaves one simply bewildered. It is not difficult to imagine what Man would report to Life Force if he were to give up his present efforts at evolution.

His troubles arise from the fact that he has to reconcile the needs of nature and the requirements of civilization. For complete fulfillment he needs both, but even as civilization resents the natural beast in him, nature regards his fascination for civilization as a kind of betrayal. In other words, Man, Nature and Civilization comprise a triangle and inevitably the process of evolution involves tension, risk, compromises, deception, self-deception, inauthenticity, etc. As the situation is getting on his nerves with increasing intensity, Man might abandon both. *Play* depicts Man's departure as a disaster for all of them. In short, for us, M, Wl and W2 stand for Man, Nature and Civilization, even as the light is the Life Force before which the three are rendering their respective accounts of what had happened. Of course, none of them knows the whole truth. Missing him, Nature is convinced that Man deserted her in favour of Civilization, even as Civilization believes that the beast in Man triumphed at long last. Man is, of course, the greatest loser because for him it implies the threat of extinction. His consolation is that his place might be taken by some other species and that common loss might bring Nature and Civilization together.

Of course, that shall not be; it cannot be—because Nature and Civilization are too incompatible to adjust. Even if the Life Force were to facilitate another effort—as implied in the close when the spotlight effects a resumption of the opening speeches—it would only be a repeat-situation. In fact, having no other choice, the Life Force would keep playing this game again and again, possibly till eternity. And the chances are that the result would be ever the same. The pull from Nature would always be countered by one from Civilization, thus balancing any progress with a matching atrophy. Indeed, in each replay, Man would be as assiduous as ever, Nature would always be vulgar and possessive, and Civilization ever and ever a fascinating vamp. Thus would this low comedy of existence continue to be full of lies, pettiness, jealousies, trivialities—dragging, stopping, and starting again, exactly the way it is in *Play*.

That there is not going to be any radical change in life is hinted at by the fact that this drama of banality is not only without action but also without any emotion. The near-static progress of mankind is suggested through the immobility of urns. In the absence of plot, character and crisis, everything is reduced to its verbal essence—another peculiarly human attribute. Indeed, here, too, as in human affairs, language is both refuge and imprisonment. No wonder all speeches are toneless, impassive, full of cliches and free from poetic imagery—to match the thematic banality. The underplaying of such dramatic strategies as conflict, climax and denouement is a way of declaring that on the stage of the world what is being played out is not a tense drama but a piece of dull comedy. Here, as in life, sights, sounds and pauses have their own special inter-related rhythms. Resulting from the contradictory pulls of nature and civilization, these rhythms on the one hand obviate any chance of dramatic progress and on the other prevent the end of activity. Indeed, neither will Godot come, nor will there be a finale for this endgame.

6 It Goes Without Saying

Beckett's chronic problem being how to express the inexpressible, he had to perform all kinds of experiments. He discovered, for example, that it was necessary for him to liberate the artist from himself, art from the work, theme from experience, content from form, mind from the senses, spirit from matter, and so on. Finding the traditional media unhelpful in this exercise, he had to undo the straitjacket of tradition by divorcing plot from character, character from dialogue, dialogue from words, words from gestures, gestures from action, action from significance, and so on. Normally these things go together because they supplement one another. To stall habitual responses, Beckett felt that he had to rework the elements of theatre, or dispense with one or some of them, so as to concentrate on selected elements. Thus, in certain plays, he has used pure narrators, whose whole being is contained in the act of trying to tell the story; such plays have words without action. On the other hand, in some plays we have pure actors whose whole being is contained in the act of acting with the help of very few words. The underlying idea was that if language was inadequate or redundant, it should be dispensed with completely so that the essence of man could be perceived intuitively rather than cognitively.

In theatrical terms it meant resorting to the 'motion poetry' of pantomime. After all, miming is not only a language universally understood but also a form of auto-symbolism. Thus may an actor represent all mankind, a solitary place signify the whole universe, and a single day encapsulate all the ages. Indeed, facilitating minimalism, reductionism and therefore abstractionism, the skeletal structuring of a pantomime can easily telescope a whole life and even epitomize the essence of the human condition. Even otherwise, nothing could better express the tragicomic failure of man than a tramp's silent clowning. At least in 'Act Without Words I' and 'Act without words

II', Beckett has so transmuted chaplinesque miming into philosophical buffoonery that one could call these pieces metaphysical comedies.

Most critics have seen in 'Act Without Words I' (1956) gods' sportive malice and irresponsible sadism towards man who is condemned to suffer eternally like Sisyphus. Others see instead a similarity with Tantalus who was offered comforts only to be denied them. Still others would see in the effort a Pavlovian pattern of repetitive movements and deduce that man's learning is all-too-slow or else that he is totally incapable of learning anything. Or, possibly, man is using nature's gifts for suicide. The pessimistic conclusions regarding the futility of human existence are sought to be justified by a reference to the close where the performer looks at his hand fatalistically. Linda Ben-Zvi goes to the extent of seeing in this mime a modern version of the age-old rites of survival at the will of a superior intelligence.[1] But, then, there are those who interpret this hand-gazing as an indication that man is learning to depend upon himself. Anyway, it is possible to deduce that here, once again, we have the story of the unavailing and yet unending evolution of man. It is to be noted that, unlike the Tantalus-situation in which water was in the stream below, here it is in a carafe above; thus the mime has not to bend down but to strive upward. Likewise, he is being teased not with any ready fruit but merely with a tuft of palm leaves. The important thing here is that his failure indicates his imperfect thinking rather than total helplessness. The man here does bungle but learns the right lessons; and yet he does not pursue things to their logical end. Indeed, both logic and enterprise fail to help this Tantalus but he would not give up. He continues to play this game even when there is no longer either any hope of victory or fear of defeat—as in an endgame.

In fact, we have in this mime more or less what we have in both *Waiting for Godot* and *Endgame*—infinite endurance, endless repetition, possibilities without achievement, effort sans progress, aborted attempts at suicide, a return to the original situation, absolute inability to continue and an equally absolute inability to give up. Here is, indeed, the paradoxical situation of man who uses his intellect to convert handicaps into opportunities but misses solid opportunities because of the imperfectness of that very intellect. Consequently, his needs are always within his reach but never within his grasp.

As the curtain goes up, we see a desert ablaze with dazzling light;

a man is flung 'backwards'. He gets up, dusts himself and starts brooding. This, I suggest, is a depiction of the way Adam unwillingly landed on the barren earth where nothing but discomforts awaited him. If being flung corresponds to Heidegger's vision of 'dasein', brooding is the Cartesian characteristic of man: 'I think, therefore I am'. To begin with, Adam must have responded to nature the way this man does when he hears whistles from the right and left wings. Who is there in the wings we do not know, nor why this man is flung back. But most probably it is an allegorical depiction of man's interaction with nature in a realm where only the fittest survive. Being ill-equipped to survive on the basis of physical strength, man is beaten back—presumably by the other species. This is something like what happens to Estragon off-stage when he reportedly spends the night in a ditch. This makes man beware of nature—as represented by the mime's refusing to respond to the whistle the next time. At this stage Life Force intervenes to breed in him the hope of evolution. Gradually this becomes a game between nature (whistle from right and left) and the Life Force (whistle from above), the point of wager being whether or not a species can survive without the help of nature—on the strength of his mind. Life Force offers Man the means of evolution but, thanks to his imperfect mind, he takes too long to learn his lessons. He bungles in such a manner that not only does he fail to avail of the opportunities but also at times makes those very means of survival the instruments of suicide. Annoyed, the Life Force feels like withdrawing its patronage; but there being no one else to play the game with, it has to persist with its support of man. It renews its munificence and even increases its offerings, but in its keenness to ensure that man does not depend too much on external help, it gives only as much as would suffice, if exploited intelligently. Result: Man neither evolves nor goes extinct. In the process, he has become a kind of cosmic clown—to the amusement of Nature and dismay of the Life Force.

At the close, we return to the initial situation but things are poised to start again. It naturally prompts one to believe that the action would continue to be repeated more or less along the same pattern. The Life Force would continue to patronize man who in turn would keep disappointing it despite his best efforts. Never would man vanish from the scene, nor grow into a superman. The stasis would go on and on like the stalemate of an endgame in chess. Always would man keep looking at his hands as if to attribute his failure to his fate, little realizing that the trouble in fact lies in the imperfection of his mind.

Of course, it is possible to put another construction on this ending if we assume that whenever man looks at his hand it is for a different purpose. For example, to begin with, he might have been wondering if his soft hands without claws were strong enough to overcome the wildness of nature. Next, he might have gazed at his palm to wonder what was in store for him. Finally it could as well signify a measure of confidence—a determination to depend on his own hands for his progress, to play his own game, so to say. In other words, the close has the usual Beckettian ambiguity suggesting at once his giving up the game and his making up his mind to use his hands as well as his mind. Most characteristic, indeed, would be the creation of an illusion of balance in which the chances of things going either way would be equally strong. It is, as it were, the end of *Godot* and *Endgame* fused into one: fed up with each other, Life Force and man propose to go their own ways but don't—and cannot.[2]

In 'Act Without Words II' (1956) the role of the whistle is taken by the goad which signifies evolutionary agency. That assumption is underlined by the fact that it acquires more and more wheels—the symbols of science and technology. Here, instead of Heidegger, Descartes and Tantalus, we think of Jung, Vico or Sisyphus. Both A and B, who come out of the sacks, eat carrots, put on and take off clothes, and crawl back into sacks; otherwise, they are studies in contrast—typically Jungian types, viz., the introvert and the extrovert. At every step, the former broods and acts in a sloppy and sickly manner, while the latter is quick, slick and precise. In a way, we have here a typical Beckettian pair, resembling Vladimir and Estragon, Pozzo and Lucky, Hamm and Clov, Winnie and Willie; their lying in sacks is akin to ashbins in *Endgame* and sand-dunes in *Happy Days*. The pattern of repetition suggests that what we have here is the endless recurrence of labour a la Sisyphus. Since in Beckett repetition invariably signifies Viconian cycle, we would not be totally off the track if we treat A and B as alternating civilizations. Of course, despite a lot of delectable activity, there is little change in the essential situation. Indeed, human history is not only littered with the rise and fall of civilizations but also marked by the alternations of antithetical ages—spiritual and materialistic, classical and romantic, Eastern and Western, oriented in mind and in body, etc. The sacks at the end of Position III have exactly the same order as in Position I—a progress so akin to the shifting of milkcans from one end of the platform to another. Indeed, this piece of mime seems to declare that no worthwhile evolution has been possible in man's progress because, in civilization after civilization, his thinking and acting have continued to be polarized—between actionless thinking (as in A) and thoughtless routine (as in B). Still, even though nothing significant can accrue as a cumulative result of such an alternation, the promptings of Life Force (the goad) have to be responded to. In other words, despite the unending process of futile repetition, man must continue to wait for Godot.

The exploration of silence as a new medium of expression in the twin 'Acts Without Words' was only one of the numerous experiments launched by Beckett. His aim was to assess the potential and relevance of the various elements/aspects of the performing arts for his themes. Immediately after the mimes, Beckett tried his hand at such lavishly verbose plays as 'Embers', and *Happy Days.* Then came experiments with sounds in 'Theatre' I & II, 'Radio' I & II, 'Cascando', 'Words and Music'—pieces marked more by novelty than artistic beauty. In this quest, to exploit the quintessential elements one by one, he turned to cinema, too. In his first cinematic venture, 'Film' (1963), he concentrated on the elements of action and movements—as in the silent movies.[3] Of course, it did not necessarily imply a return to the soundless cinematic world of the 1920s—a fact that he indicated by letting a single 'ssh!' (165) pierce the silence. It was as good as announcing that the sound-track *was* available and that dead silence was only a matter of deliberate choice.

Now, what exactly is 'Film' about? The script does refer to Berkeley's '*esse est percipi*' (to be is to be perceived), but then Beckett adds immediately that no truth value attaches to this statement (163). Perhaps Beckett wanted to state that the film is not an elaboration of Berkeley's dictum but its extension, refutation or application in different contexts. Most probably Beckett was tickled to note that this axiom sums up what happens in the cinematic medium. Only such objects and characters exist in a film as are captured by the camera. That is to say, they owe their being to their being perceived by the eye of the camera. This idea, it appears, prompted Beckett to make a film about filmmaking—by turning the medium into a vision. The camera is a character here. What is more, the piece is titled 'Film'—probably to signify that filmmaking itself is the subject.

A film, Beckett realized, is a peculiar mode of perception—not a direct viewing of reality per se or its 'imitation' but what is perceived by the lens of the camera. The camera, of course sees all—objectively, closely, from within and without, collectively, or one by one. But the very process of recording and reproduction involves the business of illusion-making which naturally distorts reality. In recording action, for example, it is the camera that moves; but in the action reproduced, the movement is transferred to the recorded image. Likewise, innumerable images reproduced in quick succession create the illusion of stillness or normal movement. This realization opened up a fascinating possibility—the intriguing possibility of recording the reality pertaining to the illusion that lies in the very process of perceiving the reality. In a way, it amounted to asking: can the eye of the camera see itself? That is precisely what Beckett's 'Film' tries to realize. No wonder once Beckett thought of calling it 'The Eye'.[4]

The concern with cinematic medium might have been the starting point but Beckett seems to have gone as much beyond filmmaking as beyond Berkeley. In the process, focus shifts from perception to self-perception. When Bishop Berkeley talked of perception, his concern was with God's eyeview. According to him, the universe is maintained in existence only by virtue of God's continued perception of it. Berkeley is happy that God perceives us all because our very being depends on His perception. Berkeley never meant to say that man's being depends on his own perception; that is the twist Beckett seems to give. Accordingly, afraid of being perceived by God, man would rather not be; but as he seeks to escape from being itself, he ends up with self-perception—with the realization that we exist because we perceive ourselves. Since all perceptions require a perceiver as well as the perceived, man's 'being' entails his being both. That makes him at once a hunter and his own quarry. That is the implication of the chase in 'Film'—between the pursuing perceiving self (E) who desires to perceive and the pursued perceived one (O) who tries to hide. That makes the relationship between '*esse*' and '*percipi*' rather paradoxical. It demands one's being conscious of such consciousness as one is seeking to escape.

Indeed, Beckett's concern is not with the Berkeleyan glory of divine perceivedness but with the agony of perceivedness—an agony peculiar to man. Afraid of being perceived, O would like to abolish all eyes—animal, human and divine. But he cannot escape one eye—'I'. Only when isolated from the rest, he sees himself for what he is and realizes that the menacing eye was not God's but his own. Agonizing indeed is this perception about self-perception as an inescapable form of perceivedness. This is, as it were, a Beckettian variation of the existentialist dialectics. To escape the absurdity of existence, man had turned to 'others' but that has made living equally absurd in a different way. Of course, to say this, Beckett operates within his pet context of the Godot theme. In brief, what 'Film' seems to say is that man's struggle to evolve with the help of his intellect has ended up in his realizing that his much-bruited intellectual 'eye' has a distorted vision.

Thus seen, the progress of O is an allegorical depiction of the progress of man. First of all, he is in the Street of Nature, where he mixes with other species who are shocked at his conceited, egoistic airs. Next he is seen on the Stairs of Civilization where his climbing is paralleled by the decline of others. Reaching the Room of Modernism, he destroys the image of God and shuts out the eyes of 'others' only to face the shocking fact about his unseeing eye. The street, it may be noted, is dead straight, with no side-streets or intersections. That is as it should be in the situation of nature where laws are universal, uncomplicated and inexorable. No wonder, too, all of them are going in the same direction (of mortality) and in pairs. These are all different species, O (man) being only one of them. At this natural stage of existence, man's effort to escape shocks the other species, as represented by the jostled couple. On the stairs, O encounters a flower-woman—a way of saying that the idea of climbing the stair of civilization was a romantic illusion. Anyway, the stairs lead O to the room—the modern age of disillusionment, of facing reality. The pugnacious hostility and promiscuity of the age are represented by cat and dog. Parrot and goldfish also stand for two other typically modern attributes—mindless vociferation and purposeless but incessant mobility. If earlier progress was marked by illusions, now O takes to delusions. He ejects or occludes all the reflecting eyes and even covers up the self-reflecting mirror. Having created this fortress of unrelatedness, he finds himself alone—with nothing but the story of his own life as represented by the seven photographs. As he recalls this story—the history of man unrelated to other species—he finds it totally uneventful. In disgust, he destroys all those images of his own one by one.

This backward stripping brings him back to his original quintessential self. At this moment, he is shocked to realize that he has been his own victim and that, being one-eyed, his vision is hopelessly limited. Anyway, the shock of recognition makes O close his eyes, cover his face, hold his head in his hand—attempts to shut out the knowledge about himself. Before the curtain comes down, O sits rocking in the chair—to represent his vacillation and uncertainty about future. Even otherwise, too, man's progress has been so like a rocking chair, going up and down but not forward—in motion and yet not moving!

The dramaticule 'Come and Go' (1965) is not exactly a mime but it certainly is what Hugh Kenner called it, 'a play made of . . . silences'.[5] It begins with silence and ends with silence. Of course, 121 words are uttered but they all repeat just a single pattern of conversation. What is more, the speeches are so sandwiched between long silences that they only serve to heighten the impression that the inaudible is more important than what is heard. In fact, this breeds in us a tendency not to rely too much on what we see or hear but to build our understanding of the play on what is not there. As each of the three women sitting on a single bench leaves one by one to return after a while, the interim is used by those left behind to whisper something about the absent one. Their tone is scandalous but not catty, sympathetic but not complimentary. Since the core-content of the whispers is left to our imagination, the goings-on acquire a touch of mystery. The more we try to relate what we perceive through the eye with what we couldn't hear, the more are the patterns of possibilities we create—like every new shake of a kaleidoscope.

Of course, on one level, it is a very simple stage business. However, as the silences impinge themselves on our consciousness, after every enactment of come-and-go, we cannot help looking for something beneath the surface. Once that exercise starts, everything appears a question-mark. What or who are those women? Are they widows or old spinsters? Why are they called by half-names? Do their names signify any individual traits? Why do they go out, and where? What is the shocking aspect of the whisper in each case? Is it different every time or something common? Does it pertain to some scandal or a misfortune? Why isn't the person concerned aware of it? What is its connection with the rings? And so on.

Finding in the opening speech an echo of the opening line of *Macbeth*, some critics have felt tempted to regard these women as witches. But, then, it has been noted by others that the reference is to a meeting in the past rather than in the future. Besides, far from making ambiguous predictions about the glory to come, they appear to throw dark hints regarding the misfortunes that have been. In any case, they are concerned with the fortunes of one another, not gloatingly but prayerfully. No wonder there have been suggestions that they are not three witches but three Graces. Likewise, while the title recalls to mind T S Eliot's modernistic young ladies talking of Michelangelo, their dresses underline their being Victorian old wives indulging in prudish whispers. The whispers might be about the presence of rings—claiming nonexistent happiness; but they might as well be about their absence—their not having lived full life (Hence: half-names). Possibly it is a reference to the rings of old-age wrinkles and their impending death—the common fate of all. Putting of such possibilities together tends to self-cancellation. Such, indeed, we realize, is the pattern of human life and therefore the progress of mankind—just coming and going, and no more.

In a situation in which future is duplication of the past, when scandals about others are in fact our own misfortunes, and where life-sustaining illusions come so close to life-denying delusions, the story of life will always remain the same. There is no need to tell it; silence will be equally eloquent. In short, in the drama of life, as in this play, characters will come and go; nothing will happen, nothing will change. No wonder all the things that the women here do cancel one another—scandal-mongering and pity, hypocrisy and guilt, confidence and suspicion, charity and malice, illusive fantasy and delusive reconstruction, social intercourse and evasion of reality. It is an impasse in which the potential of continuance is as high as the possibility of evolution is low. Thus seen, 'Come and Go' is yet another reworking of the human situation in which mankind is projected through a trinity of creator, destroyer and preserver, as suggested by the half-names—Vi(tality), Ru(ins), and Flo(w).

Sent to Kenneth Tynan on the back of a picture postcard, 'Breath' (1969) was less a play than a happening. Calling a piece which needs no more than thirty-five seconds to enact 'a farce in five acts' sounds like a joke. Indeed, it is only to be wondered if people would have taken 'Breath' seriously if it had not borne the name of Samuel Beckett. Now, of course, it has been hailed as the last word in ultra-compression. In any case, marking the very acme of the experimental spirit of Beckett, here is a piece that dispenses with all such dramatic elements as action, words, even protagonist. Their places have been taken by such theatrical elements as light, sound and set. Indeed, one could say that here the set is the only character, increase and decrease of light the only action, and breathing the only dialogue.

Surely a traditional theatre-goer feels baffled, even cheated, by what happens on the stage. A cry accompanied by inspiration (the sound of inhaling a breath) is followed by another cry accompanying expiration (exhaling). But Beckett fans know that it always pays to look deeper for some latent meaning. No wonder, quite a few critics have discovered in the 'breath' profoundly metaphysical significance. For example, it has been suggested that the piece is a dramatization of T S Eliot's declaration that when it comes to brass-tacks, life comprises 'birth and copulation and death'. More often it is assumed that the breathing here encapsulates the entire existence of an individual and that the play depicts simple continuity of a man's life. Thus seen, the first cry possibly echoes Lear's exclamation, 'When we are born, we cry that we are come/To this great stage of fools'. The second cry, on the other hand, might signify an individual's sorrow at departure from the world. Indeed, man is as reluctant to come as he is hesitant to go. Rung in by life and rung out by death, neither his arrival is of his own seeking nor his exit. Since he cries at being expelled from the warmth and safety of the womb as much as at having to re-enter the darkness of non-being, birth-cry and death-rattle are almost identical.

Of course, there are some other critics who insist on relating this play to Beckett's vision in the other plays. For example, the piece is supposed to dramatize Pozzo's lament: 'They give birth astride of a grave; the light gleams an instant, then it's night once more.' Indeed, in the context of eternity, an individual's existence is so short that death seems to come at the very instant of birth; consequently, a whole life time may sound no more than a breath. Possibly one could extend the scope of this epiphany and say that the breath stands for a generation, an age, a civilization, or even mankind. Thus seen, the stage littered with miscellaneous rubbish possibly stands for the universe with all its chaos, even as the absence of any vertical dimension in the set possibly implies the absence of any upward growth. In this context, the role of light is also worth noting. Its increase and decrease synchronize with the inspiration and expiration, respectively; the period between the cries is the spell when the stage looks brighter. It is possible to deduce from this that though the absurd dominates the universe eternally and Man's short-lived efforts at evolution are foredoomed, yet it is he alone who has brought some life as a relief to the absolute void, some voice to disturb the eternal silence, some light to pierce through existential darkness. In other words, let man continue his efforts even in full knowledge of the fact that the essentials never change and that Godot will never come.

In 1963, still pursuing his interest in wordless expression, Beckett not only worked on his almost-silent 'Film' but also started writing 'J M Mime'—a mime for Jack McGowarn. In that, two pairs (a son and his father, and a son and his mother) were to carry each other and describe through quick movements the greatest number of paths that can be traversed along the quarters of a square to arrive back at the starting point, i.e. the centre of the square. The big idea was to effect gradually greater and greater complication in what might appear something quite simple to begin with. Although that mime was never pursued to completion, it is popularly believed to have served as the seed-idea of 'Quad' that Beckett wrote in 1982. Here, too, we have wordless series of movements with a square of four players, but the overweening concern here is not a return to the centre but to avoid the centre at all costs. Surely, had Beckett completed the mime in 1960s, it could not have had the geometrical format and symmetrical polyphonic beat 'Quad' has now. Besides, since Beckett had acquired in the 70s an obsession with voices, faces, and paces, 'Quad' is full of visual and aural rhythms inhering percussion, colour-scheme, footfall, etc.[6]

As the players scurry around like rodents, it might be fun to begin with. The way the fixed courses are repeated with slight variations, even monotony starts sounding feverishly exciting and hilarious. But, soon, the fact that the centre is constantly avoided injects an element of terror in our mind. If the opening movements are like the flickering lights on an animated sign-board, the subsequent business appears so sinister and hypnotic that one cannot help brooding over the possible deeper implications. Of course, my suggestion, as usual, is that the scurrying players represent humanity which is ever on the move. However, coming and going, repeating the same course with variations, they may be not just men as individuals but generations, ages or civilizations, too. The underlying idea possibly is that man has managed to go on and on by experimenting with different combinations in respect of collaboration among individuals or ages. This is dramatized in the unbroken movement on the stage by creating such formations as solos, duos, trios, even quadros, through the joining and jettisoning of players. That each player in 'Quad' is associated with his own colour in respect of gown and 'light', his own sound of footfall and percussion instrument, is as good as saying that in the hurly-burly of human intercourse, each individual—and each age or civilization, for that matter—sees things in his own light, beats his own respective trumpet, and tries to leave his own brand of footprint on the sands of time. Likewise, the players' covering the same courses in different series signifies variation in the tenor of human progress despite seeming distinctness and individuality. Again, each player begins in darkness, moves into light, is seen busy running about, fulfills his predetermined course, and returns to darkness. Here is, indeed, a series of activities that correspond to the fate of every individual as well as every civilization.

While working on 'Quad', Beckett again appears to have been bowled over by the fascinating potential of wordless performance. More so, because he saw in it a way out of the problem that he found himself confronting then. With growing old age, he was getting more and more interested in the mystery of the soul, the life beyond, and the world of spirits. To express these, he felt, words were too helpless. Possibly he could steer clear of ideas if he concentrated exclusively on music. Likewise, he could abort the search for meaning if he concerned himself solely with images, and dispense with arguments if he remained content with inferences alone. It might be possible to capture the essence of dreams, spirits, and illusions by substituting the representational episodes and verbal rhetoric with purely formal action and cinematic images, respectively. That is the strategy followed in the video-mime called 'Nacht and Traume' (1982). That Beckett's concerns during the early eighties hovered round mysticism is clear from the fact that he invariably turned to W B Yeats for inspiration. In this frame of mind, the so-called reality of the universe appeared no more concrete than the world of dreams. Being such stuff as dreams are made on, man is born to live a dream. Since that makes living a kind of 'dark night of the soul', man's death implies the end of the dream as well as of the dreamer. This is the vision dramatized in 'Nacht and Traume' (Night and Dream) in which Beckett has effected the interplay of the waking world and the dream world—like two mirrors reflecting each other.

Minimally lit and grey-haired, A sits in right profile with head bowed and hands resting on a table. The humming of Schubert's 'Lied' called 'Nacht and Traume' by some male voice puts him to sleep and thus A dreams a dream about himself in a dream. In the dream, A becomes B sitting in the same posture but in left profile and some four feet above the floor-level. The simultaneity of the dreamer and the dream, the dreamer's dreaming of himself as dreaming, then the presentation of the same with a difference and making the dream look the reality itself, and finally the disintegration of both the real and the dream worlds—all these inevitably intrigue one to ask numerous questions. For example, what is real and what is imaginary; whether the fuller reality is encountered in life or in dreams? No attempt is made to answer the questions verbally because no words are used. However, one might infer from the empty screen at the close that the only reality is Nothingness. Without saying a word, the play has said a lot about life.

Perhaps equally significant is the wordlessness of the dream—offering of a cup of water and gentle wiping of the brow by a hand that belongs to someone invisible. Could it signify divine help from the invisible God through humming angels? Or does it imply that the desire of A (Man) about B (Man's self-image) receiving help from R (an agent of the invisible Life Force) is fulfilled not in real life but only in a dream? Or, maybe, all this is aimed at prompting us to ask whether man's ambition about his evolution is a sweet dream or a horrid nightmare. It is worth noting that while the succour brought by R brings comfort, its repetition in slow motion turns it into a nerve-wracking nightmare. Possibly it is a way of saying that, in his effort to realize his dream about becoming Superman (Godot), man has repeated his experiments in civilization so often and so slowly that the very experience of living has become a nightmare.

7 Voice, Face and Pace

For giving shape to the mess and expressing the inexpressible and aiming at pure experience rather than the imitation of an action, Beckett had to free his drama from naturalism, social setting and external plot. Therefore, in certain plays he dispensed with words; in some others, he did without action or without physical presence. Thus, there is total immobility in some plays and unceasing movement in the others. Hence, too, speakers without listeners, and vice-versa. Of course, a composite art like drama or theatre cannot be reduced to its basics alone and thus, for the subtracted element(s), there had to be some kind of substitution. For example, in the plays that I am going to discuss in this chapter, the action is substituted by the mechanics of sound, light and movement—by evolving, as it were, a choreography of voice, face and pace. The visual rhythms of shades, the verbal rhythms of voices, and the kinetic rhythms of walking or rocking, all coalesce into one another. Thus is built a unified image on which our attention is so riveted that those rhythms cease to be disparate aspects of perception. By freeing the image of all nonessentials and by transmuting it into 'animated hieroglyphic', Beckett goes, as it were, beyond minimalism. In the context of the Godot-theme, one could add that, in the human evolution also, of utmost importance are man's face (identity as species), pace (his up-and-down progress) and voice (his articulated will to continue).

Is 'Words and Music' (1961) really just a 'virtuoso arabesque' that makes no statement, as Ronald Hayman declares,[1] or a kind of symbolist poem without any analytical meaning, as Hugh Kenner would have us believe?[2] Knowing that Beckett's surface inanity is invariably misleading, critics have been at pains to discover some allegorical or philosophical level of meaning.[3] As usual, critics have seen in the play diametrically opposed situations.[4] Indeed, sometimes, it is hard to tell whether abstraction is in the play or in the interpretations.

Whatever the semantic or symbolic significance, 'Words and Music' is a typically Beckettian experiment with the quintessential components of a radio play, words and music serving as characters and comprising its radiophonic vision. They yield yet another allegory about man's existential situation in which he has to reconcile the incompatibles—the animal and the angel, Caliban and Ariel. For want of Prospero's magic, man cannot but fail. Caliban feels that he can express himself in words, but that is by right the medium for intellection. On the other hand, music, the language of the heart, has gone to Ariel who thinks. Thus condemned to etherealize his thoughts or theorize about his passions, man has become a croak. He can either create, like a raven, a music that is jarring, or pour, like a frog, words that mean nothing.

Now, there are three themes which Words and Music are asked to express—Love, Age and Face. Being a passion involving the heart at its intensest and therefore excluding the mind, Love belongs to the realm of music. No wonder, while we have great expression from Music here, Words sounds too rhetorical and pompous. In fact, in terms of verbal expression, passions so diverse as Love and Sloth tend to lose distinction and sound alike. As regards Age, it is a stage that signifies the weakening of passion as well as of thought—that is, the disintegration of both heart and mind. Consequently, when Words and Music perform 'Age' disparately, they falter and fail to give adequate expression and that exasperates Croak into calling them 'dogs' (129). However, when they collaborate—with Words contributing diction and Music rhythm—the result is poetry which is neither purely cognitive nor purely emotive. As regards the theme of Face, its recollection implies evocation of passion through the mind rather than through the heart. That is why, Words resents the accompaniment of Music and succeeds independently. He creates the right sentiment, so much so that Croak is truly overwhelmed and cries, 'Lily' (132). Later, however, when Music joins and poetry emerges, the collaborative result is too cloying to be satisfactory. No wonder, disgusted, Croak leaves in a huff. All this amounts to saying that it is disastrous to yoke Words and Music together in every situation as Croak has been insisting. What is more, the process of synthesizing the two leads to their losing their characteristic essence. Thus, while the once-gentle Music becomes rude and starts retorting, the once-insolent Words feels humbled enough to sigh.

Seen closely, what has been said earlier is a telling comment on the nature of Man. In his effort to synthesize Caliban and Ariel, he has become a croak. When he feels, he takes to rhetoric; when he recollects, he grows sentimental; and when he can neither think clearly nor feel passionately, he poeticizes! If we substitute Music by Culture and Words by Civilization, the frustration of Croak's creativity becomes an allegorical comment on the labour of Man. Harmonizing of culture and civilization might succeed in mediocre ages that are strong in neither, but otherwise the two undo the work of each other. At times they end up acquiring the negative qualities of each other. That accounts for the perversity of man's evolution—always in motion and yet not moving at all. Indeed, Caliban and Ariel may add up to a Croak but cannot yield a Godot.[5]

Like 'Words and Music', 'Cascando' (1962) is also a sort of invisible opera. Here, too, music is so important that the script is more of a libretto than a play. However, while Words and Music are in conflict, Voice and Music in 'Cascando' are not; instead they link arms, as observed by Opener. No wonder he does not leave in a huff like Croak. Also, the theme is no longer the memory of a woman, nor is there any effort to fuse voice and music into poetry. In short, despite some similarities, the two pairs are different. Certainly, Beckett was not the one to repeat his experiments.

It is possible so to interpret 'Cascando' as to treat Opener as an artist obsessed with the desire to complete a story—despite overwhelming drowsiness represented by Music. When half-awake, he starts urging himself to complete the story. Only when fully awake does he tell some story until he loses consciousness once again—to awaken in a few moments to make another determined effort to continue the story. Of course, he drifts from the conscious again into the subconscious and then into the unconscious states, but only to be jolted back into consciousness. Such, indeed, is the tenor of human evolution—repetition in the form of rise and fall. That the overall progression inhering the sequence of gradual change is downward is indicated in the title, Cascando, which means decrescendo, diminishing volume, decreasing tempo, faltering progress, etc. In fact, cascando-tenor marks the progression of all—the story of Voice, the game of Opener, the journey of Woburn.

Since Woburn is the only character with a name, it is reasonable to regard him as the protagonist. His name is a characteristic trick of Beckett's, for it can mean at once woe-born and woe-burnt. In the

French version he is called Maunu, which means evil-born or ill-begotten. As that sounds remarkably like Manu, the Sanskrit word for man, probably Beckett meant to imply that Man had been subjected to woes right from the start. The Fall is implied in the references to a few misfortunes before Woburn's birth—man's arrival on the earth. Here was Man, called upon to make a choice between the hill on the right and the sea on the left. That could mean a choice between regaining Paradise (from where he had been thrown out) and the ever-changing world. Since he opts for the latter, man moves downwards stage by stage, in the direction of the sea. First of all, he is seen in the lap of nature on the bank of a river amid trees, then on the sand dunes, later on the stones (shingles), and finally by the sea. Even while traversing this overall decline along the slope, level by level, he has been falling and rising again and again. This tortuous progress towards the unknown ship signifies Man's fall after the Fall.

Woburn is, indeed, yet another allegorical representation of man. In fact, he subsumes all the aged derelicts of Beckett. No wonder he too wears on old coat and hat, wields a stick, flees from home, stumbles through several landscapes, falls in the cruciform position, sprawls in mud, face down, rises to seek a shelter, runs through sand and stone or up and down the slopes, urges himself to continue, staggers on and on despite exhaustion, and finally drifts rudderlessly in a boat or ship. Even the words that form the refrain are familiar Beckettian echoes—'finish', 'rest', 'sleep', 'this time', 'the right one', 'same old', 'no more stories', 'come on'. After all Beckett is only concerned with man as an existential artist busy creating his microcosm. Ever urging himself to go on with his effort, man's sole aim is to discover the right clue to his own evolution which would spell the end of his ordeal. Even though the rise and fall of human civilizations amounts to man having created a thousand and one stories, the story is not yet over. Of course, each time he feels that he has at long last got the right hunch and that he is approaching the finishing point—got him 'nearly'—yet he always ends up discovering that the story has assumed once again the same old pattern. As it signifies man's not having changed enough, it inevitably necessitates a restart in the belief that the best is yet to come. The real problem is not finishing the story but of finding the right story which, when finished, would free the narrator from the obligation of going on and on. The irony is that the story which would end all stories itself knows no end!

If Woburn is Man, who is Opener and what is he 'opening'—and 'closing'?[6] To us it appears that he is Life Force that has been opening (and closing) the accounts of so many species and is now fiddling with the cassettes of man's story rather wantonly. At times, getting impatient, it decides to 'close' but only to open again. That is why man has often found himself escaping extinction by the skin of his teeth. As for Voice, it is the radiophonic version of that component of human mind which represents verbalized thought, as against intuition represented by Music. Under prompting from the intuitive will to live, man has allowed his rational faculties to evolve the strategies of survival. But his intellection being imperfect, his plans have backfired. Music, when alone, stands for the pure evolutionary urge; its combination with Voice signifies divine stimulation of the human mind, even as Voice alone implies prolonging of the story through renewed effort of the human thought. As man's progress has invariably been countered by retrogression, he remains practically where he was. If anything, he is even less secure and therefore on a lower note of the decrescendo. Anyway, since Life Force keeps stimulating the will to live—like Opener opening the channel of Music—the effort is always revived.

Now, man's existence being a sort of art, it is marked by all the laws of creation. Art being a form of divine madness, the artist creates in spite of himself; to be an artist is to fail; no artist can ever reach the end. In a situation like this, as an existential artist, man too cannot, and shall not, be silent even when he knows for certain that he is bound to fail in his effort to evolve. Let him rise and fall as many times as he might, he shall never give up, nor become superman. In other words, Man as Woburn is doomed to fall and rise till eternity and Life Force as Opener has to keep opening and closing for ever and for ever. Voice and Music will link arms again and again only to end in silence which, in any case, will never be permanent. The important thing in this process is not the end, nor the rise, but the fall which gives birth to another rise. After all, without a fall, there cannot be a rise. No wonder one of the refrains is 'He's down—that is what counts' (140). Since man lost the right to immortality along with Paradise, the only alternative to doom lies in a series of apocalypses—in cascandoes, so to say. That is why Woburn, Voice-and-Music, and Opener—all move down the scale by stages, following the pattern of decrescendo. It is like the ebbing tide. Anyway, just as the tide is bound to rise again, sooner or later, there will again be the tide of creation involving Life Force and Man. The silence at the end might be a comma-situation between the tide that has broken and the one that is about to start again.

The multiple patterns of rise-and-fall at the levels of Opener, Voice-and-Music, and Woburn imply an overall process which communicates the vision of the play. That is what makes 'Cascando' a play of impact rather than one of argument. The image that haunts one is that of Woburn in the bilge on a ship heading nowhere and yet moving on and on. That epitomizes the fate of Man: 'I can't go on; I'll go on'. Who knows whither man's evolution would lead him? He invariably finds himself having moved either too far or too late, but he is moving nevertheless. This situation is bound to continue till eternity before cascando freezes into silence—like the last digit in a recurring decimal.

On first reading, 'Eh Joe' (1965) appears to be a simple play with the trivial, almost banal, theme of a wanton womanizer haunted by his guilt-ridden memory. What is more, for a curious reader of Beckett, there may be nothing new here, because much in the play is either a muffled echo or an ominous portent of some of his other plays, before or after.[7] To see the unusual and profounder aspects, it is necessary to remember that this was Beckett's first television play.

Sound-track plus camera being specifically televisual paraphernalia, Beckett uses both but in his own typically experimental vein of reducing the medium to its elements. While other writers would make the twin elements of voice and image synchronize, Beckett treats them as disparate entities. Consequently, we have here the speech of one and the face of the other—the dominating visual presence of the one who does not speak or the captivating aural presence of the one who is invisible. Likewise, while normally we expect the focus to be on the speaker, here that pride of place goes to the passive listener. What is more, it is not the story of the speaker but that of the auditor. That makes 'Eh Joe' an inversion of the dramatic monologue: it is the listener who is seen when the speaker's presence is assumed. This inversion surely is not for its own sake; it is very much related to the theme. The basic idea is to concentrate on the expression on the face of the person whose story is being told to himself. Every movement of the camera is like one step deeper into Joe's mind and thus we notice his reactions more and more closely.

And what is it that we do see? The critics who interpret the play as a play of guilt have declared that, thanks to the pricks of conscience, the face tends to become more and more like a mask of sorrow. But, in saying this, they forget that, according to the stage directions, the face of Joe is impassive from the beginning till the end. There is no sorrow but only the tension of listening. Had Beckett meant to portray guilt, the voice should have been that of the victim. Joe is, in fact, without any conscience; he has been killing its voice all his life. A hardened criminal, he does not feel any guilt; he cannot feel anything at all. Let his face or eye be seen as closely as one wishes, let it grow bigger and bigger till it is as huge as the screen itself, but never does one discover even a single trace of guilt there. Even in the intensest moments of self-perception, there isn't anything akin to the creative suffering of tragedy. His trouble is psychological not spiritual. His life is a saga of espousals and betrayals that cancel one another and leave him unfulfilled, unredeemed. Unlike Jesus who gave without taking and suffered to redeem mankind from mortality, Joe takes without giving and drives the humans around him to death. If Christ represents the pinnacle of perfection, Joe is an imperfectible and irredeemable antimessiah who shall never regain Paradise. To put it differently, Joe is Everyman who shall never become superman.

So, the story of Joe is akin to the history of mankind. Like Joe, since his birth, man too has resented the fact that his father (God) threw him out on the earth mercilessly and his mother (Nature) let him down by not affording adequate protection against the ferocity of the universe around him. Forced to struggle for existence, he has managed to survive but lost his humanity in the process. Becoming utterly callous, Man has turned against his parents, God and Nature, and killed them in his mind; worse, he has learnt to exploit his associates in a most selfish manner. He has flirted with one civilization after the other but each time, feeling that the best was yet to come, he has switched over to the next. That is precisely what is implied in Joe's affairs with women—in his taking without giving. Like Joe, man too has convinced himself that in his conduct he is emulating his parents, God and Nature. This practice of self-deception enables him to quell the disturbing voices; this is what Joe calls 'mental thuggee' (203). Disgusted with such heartless jilting of civilizations, Life Force is bound to transfer its patronage to some other species. The voice in the play could, indeed, be that of Life Force upbraiding man for his wantonness. In severing the link, the loss is going to be man's and not that of the Life Force. 'But I found a better. . . . As I hope you heard. . . . Preferable in all respects. . . . Kinder. . . . Stronger. . . . More intelligent . . . Better looking. . . . Cleaner. . . . Truthful. . . .

Faithful. . . . Sane. . . . Yes. . . . I did all right' (204). Life Force cannot forgive man for deserting everyone after exploiting them; it is particularly sore at the way man's indifference has been forcing suicides on civilization after civilization. Most touching is the reference to the fate of one such victim called 'spirit made light' (205). That should be culture which Matthew Arnold had described as 'sweetness and light'. Culture being an exclusively human attribute, it could not have survived after man's desertion. No wonder 'she' tried multiple devices to end herself. In the climactic moment, her tender hands and soft breasts broke against the hard stones. That could imply the role of stony, scientific temper in facilitating the end of culture. Even though Life Force is moved by this tragic end of culture, man (Joe) feels no scruple. The accusation makes him tense but by no means repentant.

After trying Voice as a character in radio and television plays, Beckett seems to have wondered if he could extend his experiment to theatre as well. After all, if Eye (E) could be the protagonist of *Film*, why can't Mouth be that of a stage play? Mouth, in any case, appeared the next logical step—after Winnie's head—in his journey from person to face to ultimate absence. Could he repeat on stage what he had done on the small screen in 'Eh Joe'—voice directed at a listener's face? And, maybe, like the three levels of narration in 'Cascando', he could try three levels of listening, too—the audience in the auditorium, an auditor on the stage, and the mouth hearing voices in the head. The result of the experiment was 'Not I' (1972). Of course, there is no Croak or Opener here; if anything, the voice of Mouth is completely out of control. The breathless verbosity resulting from the breakneck speed produces three levels of tedium as well—for the protagonist, for the actress, and for the audience.

This experiment is a very characteristic Beckettian trick to turn dramaturgical paraphernalia inside out—to effect radical displacement, so to say. In traditional theatre, situations, characters and dialogues help the development of one another. Dispensing with all these, Beckett has depended primarily on words to create the entire dramatic edifice. No wonder the play resembles so much the typically Beckettian voluble fiction—a monologue in stylized but broken prose. As in the novels, here, too, the narrative moves back and forth in time, and thus do past and present get fused. Instead of a linear pattern, we have cyclical progression effected through repetition, variation, ad-libbing, verbal diarrhea, etc. Drawing inspiration from Caravaggio's portrayal of the scene of St John's beheading, and from intense waiting writ large on the face of an Arab woman in a djellaba, Beckett has added verbiage to the visual of a silent witness to create a most haunting image. Indeed, one feels a deep impact in spite of oneself, even without grasping anything cognitively.

'Not I' is one of the densest masterpieces of Beckett. Through maximum minimalism Beckett has succeeded in creating in just 15 minutes what a novelist would need many volumes to communicate. Even otherwise, it sums up most succinctly the entire history, geography and topography of Beckett-land. In fact, it is possible to say that one hears here the voices of all Beckett heroes since Belacqua—the voices that have been reverberating since 'Echo's Bones'.[8]

But, then, who is this Mouth and how is it related to 'She' on the one hand and to Auditor on the other? The fact that it is made deliberately conspicuous on the stage through a pinpointed spotlight speaks for its pivotal significance.[9] As Auditor and Mouth appear at a higher level, as if hanging in the air, one thinks of a soul rendering its account before a recording angel. Angels with sex indeterminate are compassionate yet helpless and so is Auditor. This possibility prompts me to suggest that Auditor is Life Force to whom humanity, represented by Mouth, is trying to explain the reason of its flawed evolution—man's acquiring knowledge too late when he was too old, almost senile. When the body was sound and the mind was healthy, knowledge was denied to him; but when he had already built the world along the most irrational lines, knowledge exploded. It is worth noting that, in order to reflect the growing indifference of Life Force, Auditor gradually loses compassion and finally shrugs shoulder out of helplessness. Equally noteworthy is the fact that, like man, Mouth is a meeting point of body and mind. In short, if in 'Eh Joe' Life Force was accusing Man, here is Man offering his defence.

The narrative pertains to the story of a little girl who was born prematurely. Having lost her parents soon after birth, she grew up in a God-forsaken hole without receiving any love at any stage. Leading a mechanical Life, she never got to speak a word till she was old enough to be 60 or 70. She couldn't speak even in moments of intense private agony—for example, when she was raped in the field, or when physical ailments made her rush around. Her extreme penury made her do her sparse shopping quickly and silently, and even when summoned to the court to clear herself of a charge, she failed to utter a word. Brought up in the Protestant faith, she believed that she was born to suffer as a punishment for the sin of being born! In old age, one day, she lost her eyesight, her hearing ability and even the power to feel. However, she felt something buzzing in her head and lo, suddenly words started pouring from her mouth. And here she is talking incessantly—all inane, senile talk. She feels that she has something to tell about her life, about her past suffering; but since she has lost the power of feeling, it appears to her that the person talked about is someone other than herself. Hence her insistence on the third person—'Not I'.

If we substitute 'dumb humanity' for the little girl, the play becomes an allegorical version of the problems pertaining to human evolution—identity, communication and perception. Created as a freak and having lost the love of Father God and Mother Nature, Man has been living on this God-forsaken earth since God knows when. Convinced that he is being punished for his disobedience in Paradise, he has been leading a mechanical life with no interaction with other creatures in the universe. He did once believe in God's being merciful until he realized that He was instead more like Jehovah. Having led this dumb, mindless existence for too long and having accepted suffering as a way of life, he stopped thinking about his existential agon. He won't talk about his deprivation as a species, about his being violated by nature in tooth and claw, or about his mortality; he won't even answer to the charge of Original Sin. In the process he has lost his power of feeling. However, after he lost all his powers of perception and grew senile, he acquired the power to express himself. Now he has found words but it is too late. Having lost the key to feeling, his outburst is heartless as well as mindless. Ironically, when he had a lot to say, he had no words; now when he has words, he has nothing to say. As man's quintessence lay in his thinking—'I think, therefore I am'—the present state of mindless verbosity signifies loss of man's identity. Hence the 'Not-I' situation.

As Man has been patronized by Life Force because of his thinking faculty, the loss of that very faculty has rendered Life Force gradually indifferent to Man's fate. Maybe, the only chance of man's regaining sanity lies in his return to Nature, but that would inevitably mean his pursuing the old course and repeating the cycle. In a situation like this, when mind and body fail to work in unison, when there has to be rotation between mindless passion and heartless knowledge, or between total dumbness and inane verbosity, how can man reach the Godot stage? It only means that man is eternally doomed to produce only fundamental sounds in each sense of the word, for his logic would be either rudimentary or else a mere fizzle. In other words, man's art in respect of creating a world of his own is at best ***arse rhetorica***. In this connection, it is easy to see that like the protagonist spouting forth cataracts of words when he has nothing to say, Man is proposing a plethora of thoughtless strategies of survival when he has no basic material to ensure his evolution. This futile, grotesque effort is concretized in the mesmeric dance of tongue, lips and teeth in the cavern of the Mouth. The grotesque has, of course, its own aesthetics—absurd and yet haunting. This is precisely what one could say about the human existence in the universe—totally meaningless and yet powerful in impact.

In 'That Time' (1975), too, there is an auditor called Listener whose disembodied head, like one in a Dali painting, hangs in the air like Mouth in 'Not I'. In fact, the resemblance between the two sets is so close that Beckett once referred to 'That Time' as brother to 'Not I'. What is more, he disallowed a double bill comprising these twin plays on the plea that they were of the same texture. In either play, one's experiences are no longer felt to be one's own and therefore the use of the first person singular is eschewed most stubbornly. Concerned with solitude, desolation and distress, both the plays distil the theme to its concentrated essence and thus in just a few moments the full experience of the totality of life is crystallized. However, our concentrating on the listener's face rather than on the speaker's mouth makes all the difference. Indeed, if action in 'Not I' could be summed up as 'She talks', in this case it would be 'He listens', and whereas Mouth's outpourings are live sounds, A, B and C here are all reproductions of prerecorded voices.[10]

It is worth noting that Listener is not merely a character but also the set itself. That implants the idea that the entire stage stands for the head and that the voices emanating from different parts of the stage signify voices in the head. Speakers placed to the right, left, and above the stage enabled Beckett to transform language into a kind of scenic space. This was Beckett's strategy to create a visual existence for inner consciousness. By projecting from outside such voices as are in fact inside the head, Beckett has succeeded in effecting an integral unity between what is inside and what is outside, the first and the second 'persons', the eyes and the ears, the listener and the speaker, the fragment and the whole. That is what facilitates the flow of scenes from the past into one another to form the present. What is more, experiences pertaining to distinct stages of life get so closely related in spirit as to forge themselves into one long experience. This suggestion is reinforced not only through unpunctuated paragraphs but also through the intercalation of fragmented experiences into a single, three-strand soliloquy. To grasp the deeper meaning, therefore, it is necessary not only to put the fragmented parts of A, B, C together but also to treat what all of them say as a single narrative split into parts.

Taken individually, A describes his bafflement in recalling what had happened when he visited in old age Folley's Folly, where he used to seek shelter in his childhood whenever he ran away from home. The nostalgic old-age revisit proved abortive because the entire locality had undergone a sea-change. However, the memories of that revisit tend to complicate the memories of the visits in childhood. Of course, even otherwise, the recollection of childhood visits is bewilderingly vague because he had visited the place so often that he finds the details of the memory of any particular visit mixed up with those of several others. In a situation like this, he cannot but ask again and again: 'When was that' (228) or 'was that another time all that another time was there ever any other time but that time . . .' (235).

An equally baffled B asks in the same vein, 'When was that an earlier time a later time before she came after she went or both before she came after she was gone . . . soon after long after' (233). B's situation pertains to innocent youth when he would lie stock-still beside 'her' on a stone in a wheat field or on sand—not making love or even touching each other but just vowing love every now and then. Though apparently a radically different, blissful, summer situation, it was in fact an inverted image of the childhood situation itself. Company to himself in childhood, in youth he was lonely even in the company of the beloved. What links this youth on the other hand to the old-age situation is his chronic impotence. As in old age later, in youth also, when he tried and tried, he couldn't do it. No wonder his memories of youth get mixed up with old-age sexual situations.

The memories of C belong to middle age when, as a derelict, or possibly as an outlaw, he struggled to seek shelter at night from winter rain in deserted public places like the portrait gallery, the post office, and the library. These series of flights represent yet another facet of solitude. As he had visited these places hundreds of time, now he cannot draw from memory a single, continuous thread of any one particular visit to these places also. Each place is, however, associated with some event that has left a haunting memory. For example, he cannot forget his seeing his own likeness in one of the portraits in the portrait gallery. Likewise, in the post office, he had once a feeling that people around him were looking through him, as if he were no more than air. Similar, indeed, was a certain visit to a library to find it filled with dust from floor to ceiling. As his efforts to reconstruct in isolation any one of these high moments prove slippery, he asks, 'was that the time or was that another time another place another time' (234). In fact, being connected with hiding places, all the memories tend to get fused into one another.

Despite all these confounding links and correspondences, A is a veritable Paradiso, B a Purgatory, and C an Inferno. This transforms 'That Time' into Beckett's version of *The Divine Comedy*. Of course, it is an ironic version of the way an individual progresses from the Paradise of childhood to the Inferno of old age. But lest a reader should stop short at that kind of conclusion, Beckett has deliberately fragmented the memories to break the chronological order. In the present arrangement, one cannot help deducing that in all the stages of life we have attributes of hell, heaven and purgatory. Silence and solitude are common to all—the child's hiding place, the lovers' tryst and the deserted public places at night. This is as good as saying that, quintessentially, man's loveless existence on the earth has been a millennia-long saga of solitude. Since this is the result of the interaction between man and Time, the title prompts the reader to realize the role in man's life of that double-headed monster who has been operating both as generator and destroyer since Adam's fall. The childhood of humanity was so like its present old age of senility that it appears as if evolution had come full circle. At best one could say that all the effort had resulted only in breaking the stone (common to all stages) into dust.

My suggestion might appal those who have convinced themselves that these are no more than the memories of an individual, Listener. I suggest that the play is a kind of periscope. Although we peep through the lens of individual memory, what we actually see is a refracted image created by the other lens of racial memory—aged humanity ruminating over its past, historical events, which are so akin to one another that the recollections are repetitive, imprecise and confusing. Memory A suggests that in the infancy of civilization, Man was like a typical child—seeking refuge in the isolated but lovely surroundings of nature whenever he was annoyed with his divine father over such issues as the Tree of Knowledge. The revisit in old age refers to modern man's futile hankering after old innocence. In between there have been moments of either togetherness or else of humdrum pursuits. The former made Man feel that he could communicate while the latter deluded him into believing that he had perfected the cultural aspects of his existence. Unfortunately, however, the activities of neither the head nor the heart have yielded any real advance. The quality of his intellectual preoccupations is epitomized in the dust that covers the receptacles of all knowledge, books. In the other fields, his life has been a series of exercises in aimless wandering, escapist games of hiding from others, sentimental nostalgia, public postures, etc.

Of course, Beckett is not unequivocally cynical in his vision. When the closing speech of C refers to dust filling the whole place, Listener gives a toothless smile (235). This could be an ironic, impish or derisive smile; but, seen in the context of the dust, it could as well be a proof of the fact that he is not just dust. At least not yet—that is, so long as he is alive. This is as good as saying that life may be absurd but it is not as bad as death—not, in any case, so long as Man is around. Man's vision may be imperfect and his capacity to articulate may be marked by fragmentation, but whatever activity there is in the universe, it is because of him. The rest is silence.

'Footfalls' (1975) is yet another exercise in minimal movement for maximal impact. Once again, Beckett concentrates on the essentials and creates such an elliptical, grotesque dramaticule as tends to sound like man's 'graffiti on the walls of time'.[11] True, coming after 'That Time', it seems like a step back, towards traditional theatre : it has a character with a name, a whole body and normal English syntax. Nevertheless, in respect of meaning, it is perhaps as elusive, opaque and impenetrable as 'Not I' and 'That Time'.[12] Still interlacing sound and silence, movement and stillness, light and darkness, Beckett continues to experiment with multimedia choreography in voices, faces and paces. What is more, typically Beckettian is the use of repetition, reiteration, variation and circularity. Equally characteristic is the art of fictionalization in May's soliloquy—creating a subtle collage through a pile of fragments.

To grasp Beckett's real intention, perhaps it would be helpful to recall the rehearsal notes for the German premiere of the play as reproduced in *Journal of Beckett Studies*, Summer 1977. When Ms Hildegard Schmahl, the actress playing May, asked Beckett how the figure of May was to be understood, he recalled Carl Jung's lecture in London. The great psychologist had declared that once he could not help a certain female patient because she wasn't *living*: she existed but didn't actually live! Obsessed as Beckett was with that story, perhaps he saw in that girl the potentiality of being without the being proper. Possibly it is this potential (= maybe) that the name May signifies, and a possibility without real substance points to a ghost-existence. Wrapped in a worn grey gown, her grey dishevelled hair flowing, and walking softly and slowly, May does have the looks and bearings of a ghost. To complete the effect, the light is at the fullest at floor-level. What is more, one hears the feet although these are otherwise invisible. While the image captures one's attention like any piece of ghost fiction, the mystery is intensified when May starts speaking to an invisible addressee—another ghost, so to say. As these visible and invisible ghosts converse, the sense of mystery is sustained not only by the soft footfalls and slow voices but also by the echoing chimes. In this eery atmosphere, one cannot but wonder about the identities of the ghosts—about 'it all'. As Amy sounds like 'Am I', the play becomes 'it all' about 'I'—the mystery of 'my' story, i.e. Man's identity. Indeed, man is also a veritable ghost in the universe—always moving, generation after generation, and insisting on making his presence felt through his footfalls, even though he is utterly incapable of leaving any footprints. Like May, Man (dropped from Paradise) also just began (on the earth), without being born. Indeed, Man too is existing, not living. No wonder his story (= history) is a collage of fragmentary truths piled up in a spirit of random improvisation. Since his is not a case of work in progress, it will never be completed; rather it will always remain work-in-process.

As I look at it, Mother, May and Amy represent humanity in three generations. Each human generation, too, paces forward in regular movement only to wheel back to touch the starting point where, instead of stopping, it keeps moving on and on till it wheels back again. This is, so to say, yet another way of representing the unending ordeal of Man moving up and down the ladders of civilizations. The image of May pacing back and forth on a stageboard represents, as it were, Man in the world leading a pedestrian life which, though futile and repetitive, is rhythmic and cyclic in its progression. 'It all' is repeated at the end of every episode, and the hollowness of mouth when uttering this phrase is a visual depiction of the hollowness of 'it all' of human existence. Significantly, Beckett insisted on the phrase being mouthed in such a manner that no sound might be heard at all. Anyway, as the theme is contained not in the words alone but communicated through the stage-image of pacing, the mode of speaking, the correspondence between word-rhythm and step-rhythm, and the ghost-like mystery of 'it all', one might say that content resonates through form.

Of particular significance in this connection is the pattern of May's pacing—a variation of the pendulum but forming ∝ (infinity). This is as good as epitomizing the tenor of Man's eternally long odyssey created through a series of short episodes about individual men's encounter with time, as they come and go in this world. The fact that the passage of time is important in this dramaticule is brought home through chimes in the beginning, at the close, and between the episodes. Not surprisingly, stage directions insist on the chiming growing fainter and fainter progressively. The echoes of the chime could be representatives of the past in the present. Or, maybe, that is only a way of universalizing the theme, as if to say that the suffering here is not confined to these characters but encompasses everyone—the entire mankind, each generation being an echo of the preceding one. This suggestion is reinforced when we see the girl-in-the-mother and the mother-in-the-girl alternating with each other. As the sufferings of each daughter make the mother feel guilty, the latter appears again as the former's daughter for atonement and thus perpetuates the cyclic process. The sportive May grows into Mrs Winter only to give birth to an Amy who, as another version of May, would grow into some kind of Winter to give birth to yet another Amy, and so on. This would go on and on till eternity.

This 'ghost trio' is, so to say, an image of the process of eternal recurrence in the human situation. Not surprisingly, V at the end of episode I (240) and May towards the close of the play (243) repeat the same question—'Will you never have done . . . revolving it all?' In a situation like this, man's evolution is bound to remain a series of 'movements in a spiral of perpetual change', as Enoch Brater would put it. Godot, the Superman, will, so to say, never come even though his presence will always be felt in his absence. In short, it is possible to regard 'Footfalls' as *Waiting for Godot* reworked on a miniature scale.

Yet another 'ghost' play with soft, even inaudible, footfalls is 'Ghost Trio' (1975). If May had grey dress and grey hair, in this play it is 'all grey'—multiple shades of grey in floor, door, pallet, sheet, etc.[13] Perhaps it is possible to say that here Godot is transmuted into an abstract frame of painting for television.

True to the tradition of abstract art, we have simple shapes here. But gradually the beauty of the images is so concentrated that an intriguing sense of mystery is built up, because what is absent tends to be more important than what is present. As with abstract art, the play starts with V stating the obvious and yet within a few minutes our mind is filled with hosts of questions and suggestions. We seem to follow everything and still we grasp nothing. That is why, while the play appears totally inane at one level, at another it affords more possibilities of meaning than many a full-length play.[14] Just as an abstract painting is usually built around some basic form like a triangle, square, or cube, here too we have rectangles galore in mutual interaction. And the way these concrete rectangles are manipulated to create not only trios[15] but also a ghost atmosphere[16] is simply mind-boggling. But, then, the all-important question is: what do these ghosts and trios communicate? Surely, Beckett was not the one to just play with rectangles or sounds for their own sake.

If we forget the shapes and echoes and try to absorb the action in its intrinsic essence, it appears to be a situation in a studio, complete with camera, cassette, director (V) and hero (F). Everything is ready and yet nothing is happening because of the absence of the long-awaited heroine who sends instead an errand boy with the message that she won't come. The association with studio is brought home indirectly, too. The three parts of the stage business correspond to the recording process in a studio—introduction (Pre-Action), trial run (Action) and takes/retakes (Re-Action). Perhaps, Beckett implies that the world is not a stage, as the Bard of Avon had declared, but a studio in which nothing gets done because the chief performer is absent. But, then, who could be this elusive, long-awaited, absent one? My answer, as usual, would be Godot, the Superman.

For a clearer understanding of this allegory, let us look more closely at the action. That the chamber set is a miniature version of the world at large becomes clear if we manage to get on Beckett's minimalist wavelength. In Pre-Action, as we are taken around the room to see the Floor, V observes, 'Dust (*Pause*). Having seen that specimen of floor you have seen it all'. So it is 'it all' once again—the earth encapsulated in a rectangle of about one square metre. This world may be viewed telescopically or microscopically, expanding or receding. This appears to be the implication of using the camera for taking a general view, medium or near shots, or close-ups. The 'sole sign of life' (249), F represents Man in the world. His receiving directions from V should signify Man receiving commands from the Life Force.

Perhaps that is why V is audible but not visible—a situation that makes him a kind of ghost. There is also something ghost-like about the person who is constantly expected but never arrives. Such a ghost is Godot, the Superman. Of course, the third one in this ghost-trio is F himself because, even though seen, his presence is without any substance. Incapable of doing anything tangible, Man on the earth is also such an insubstantial being. Of course, he is the source of all the music (harmony) that is there in the world, and yet it is he who creates through his purposeless activities such sounds as cause creeps. Of great significance in this context is the use of Beethoven's symphony which was written for an opera based on *Macbeth*. It obviously signifies that man's ambitions have not only raised ghosts but also turned himself into a walking dream. Ever on the move, man has always been keen to make his presence felt through his footfalls. He has been repeating his efforts with ever-changing strategies but he has never succeeded in producing anything more than creating a crescendo or decrescendo of a civilization. No wonder Pre-Action, Action and Re-Action add up to No-Action. Far from leaving any footprints on the sands of time, Man has failed to create anything even as evanescent as a reflection in a mirror. Not surprisingly that shocks even his director-patron, the Life Force. F's resuming the opening position at the end signifies his being poised for a restart. It is as good as saying that Man will continue his effort for ever and for ever—with the selfsame result of frustration, of course.

In short, 'Ghost Trio' projects human life as a nightmarish drama enacted by three ghosts—the visible but insubstantial ghost called Man being goaded by the invisible ghost called Life Force to wait for the most elusive ghost of all—Godot, the Superman. Man is doomed to fail eternally in this wait and the reason is hinted at in the profusion of rectangles. Everything visible is rectangular except Man—a Beckettian way of declaring that man is a round peg in a square hole.

'Ghost Trio' has a twin in another TV play, '. . . but the clouds . . .' (1975) and invariably they comprise a double bill under the common title of 'The Shades'.[17] True, there is no ghost-like footfall here, yet the way V evokes the image of his beloved, there is something very akin to the raising of ghosts. In both these TV pieces, emotions arise from seeming abstractions so much so that critics are often reminded of modernist paintings—those of limbs and drapery by artists like La Tour, and the ones by David in the case of '. . . but the clouds . . .'. V here is also a disembodied voice but the person to whom this voice belongs is very much present. This exercise of a mute figure listening to a voice (his own, or someone else's) helps underline something so peculiar to television technology, viz., the separation of visual image and narrative voice on video and audio cassettes. The camera may no longer be a character in '. . . but the clouds . . .' but its presence is very consciously perceived. V directs his instructions about retakes and replays as in a TV studio, the descriptions are followed by silent depictions, and action proceeds only when okayed with a 'Right'.

If 'Ghost Trio' had accommodated its source of inspiration, viz., Beethoven's Ghost-symphony, '. . . but the clouds . . .' is similarly related to 'The Tower' by W B Yeats. Thematically too the two pieces have a kinship because in both there is an obsession with an absent woman. In each, an old man is keen to see his beloved, but while in 'Ghost Trio' waiting is at once interrupted and sustained by a messenger boy, in '. . . but the clouds . . .', the awaited one does visit. Of course, it is only in imagination—in the form of a nostalgic image. This fact has prompted critics to treat the play as a comment on age and memory—as if the play were a translation of Yeats's verbal symbology into a visual image.[18]

But, surely, Beckett was too experienced a writer not to realize that every viewer would not be familiar with Yeats's poem. Certainly the play would fail to communicate anything to those who are not sufficiently well-read. Being essentially antiacademic, Beckett would surely give a periodic or distortive twist to it. Therefore, one should take the play as it is—reading the quoted lines literally as they figure in the present context and not as an echo of Yeats's vision. Seen thus, it is the story of a man who spends his days on the roads in the West and returns at night to change his clothes in the eastern closet before settling down in the northern sanctum to think of his beloved. This oft-indulged nocturnal exercise proves mostly futile though occasionally her face does appear, either to disappear immediately or else to linger for a while murmuring, '. . . but the clouds. . . of the sky'. Obviously, western roads, eastern closet and northern sanctum signify more than meets the eye. Traditionally, the west is associated with materialism, the north with romanticism, and the east with spiritualism in general and the cycles of birth and death in particular. Thus interpreted, the action on the screen should amount to saying that, busy with materialistic pursuit, Man has been passing through the Viconian cycles. He has been hoping to see the much-desired

Superman, but that Godot-stage has always eluded him. Occasionally a genius or some advanced civilization might create an illusion of a passing glimpse but that illusion is not only rare but also flitting. The only thing that the 'visitation' communicates is that life and its realization in the form of evolution is an airy nothing—'but the clouds' on the fading horizon. Indeed, a glimpse of the Superman-Godot is as evanescent as the sleepy cry of a bird at evensong!

In 'Rockaby', the dominant voice offstage is prerecorded but there is also the live voice of the same speaker. The latter not only joins the former in uttering simultaneously 'Time she stopped' seven times, but also butts in with four independent 'mores' in a manner that divides V's monologue into four 'acts'. Indeed, this makes the play a mosaic of several experiments tried earlier—in 'Not I' (disowning the first person stubbornly), 'That Time' (process of listening to a recorded voice), 'Cascando' (speaker as a goad in the verbal pyrotechnics), and 'Krapp's Last Tape' (mixing the recorded and live voices of the same person). What is more, in the tradition of 'Ghost Trio' and '. . . but the clouds . . .', here is 'a performance poem' as Enoch Brater would call it.[19]

The rocking chair is, nothing new in Beckett; it is as old as *Murphy*. The play concerns V, the recorded voice of a woman (W) rocking in a chair, talking about a woman who, tired of looking at other windows and waiting for their blinds to go up, went down the steep stairs to rock in her mother's chair and talk about a woman in a rocking chair looking at windows and waiting for the blinds to go up before she went down to rock in her mother's chair and talk about a rocking and talking woman who . . . On the surface it appears to be a case of simple repetition as in a roundelay. But gradually one starts feeling intrigued enough to wonder about the way W is related to the woman in V's story—'another like herself', 'another living soul' (277). It is worth noting that W is doing exactly what the woman in the story does—sitting in a rocking chair, feeling like her, talking to herself like her, trying to get out of herself, coming back 'in', looking out of the window for another like herself, and so on. Is the woman in the story W herself ('saying to herself/whom else'), her mother, or her daughter? Mother being m+other, it could mean, as it has been suggested, *another* version of *m*(am)—another version of 'me'. Perhaps it means that the daughter takes the place of the mother until, becoming herself a mother, she continues in her daughter. That process reminds one of

May, Mrs Winter and Amy in 'Footfalls' and of Nagg, Hamm, Clov and the boy outside in *Endgame*. This is a situation comparable to a mirror-within-a-mirror or song-within-a-song—like the dog-in-the-kitchen story. Anyway, in the seesawing of mother-in-daughter and daughter-in-mother, as one end goes up and the other comes down, it is all so much like swinging in a rocker.

In the Beckettian world, life is a cradle in which one is rocked to the sleep of death. As an old woman in a cradle brings to mind the twin ends of life—the child just born and the old one about to die—the up-and-down movement of the rocking chair tends to become a visual realization of man's coming and going. Or else one might see in the return to childhood rocking the completion of a cyclic movement that lets lullaby and threnody dissolve into each other. Thus seen, 'Rockaby' becomes an illustration of Beckett's seminal vision regarding man's giving birth astride of a grave. Indeed, the more one concentrates on the rocking, the more is one convinced that it has something ontological about it. The similarity between the movements of a rocking cradle and a pendulum might induce the suggestion that the play has something to do with the ups and downs of time. I suggest that W is humanity in the rocker of Life Force, V being the voice of humanity narrating man's history, viz., the rocking tenor of the rise and fall of civilizations. Thus the four 'acts' of the play (similar but not the same) may be treated as Viconian cycles. That W stands for humanity is reinforced by her shimmering costumes—jet sequins and flamboyant headgear which symbolize Man's bruiting claims about dazzling significance in the universe and the uniqueness of his intellectual glory.

Now, in rocking itself, either the chair is a self-propelling machine or else the perpetuation of its movements is contingent on the will of the seated person. Besides, a rocker can mean not only the rocking chair but also the person who lends the necessary force to stimulate or sustain the rocking movement. If the seated person supplies that force, he too becomes a rocker. Such indeed is the relationship between humanity and Life Force. This identification between the player and the prop, the instrument and the instrumentalist, gets crystallized in the narrator becoming the story when the speaker in 'Rockaby' relives the fate of the protagonist. Again, in rockaby, the movement goes on and on, up and down, until the seated person either goes to sleep or wills its stopping. Similarly, in the rockaby of life, the day Man goes to sleep through extinction, or himself wills to end this rocking, Life

Force will find it difficult to operate. So far, Humanity has continued because, she has invariably given the movement a fillip by asking Life Force for 'more'.[20] Since her tone has been growing progressively fainter and softer and she has started feeling that it is '*time she stopped*' (italics Beckett's own), humanity can any day decide to 'fuck life' (282) and thus bring the rockaby of existence to a dead-stop. After all, Man is not only the rocked one but also the rocker.

8 Odds, Discards and Fagends

Beckett's silence during the last years of the seventies resulted in his overcoming his obsession with disembodied voices. In 'A Piece of Monologue' (1980), the live voice is back along with the whole body—in the place of a mere face. In fact, it is possible to say that we have here body without the face because, the figure being only dimly lit, the face is barely visible. What is more, along with the face, the pace has also gone out. Thus, we have a starkly static situation in which there is no movement—not even the minimal motion of the closing and opening of eyes. Yet, far from signifying a return to traditional dramaturgy, the play is marked by a typically Beckettian experimental spirit. In a dramatic monologue, the passive presence of an unseen listener is assumed; here is a piece in which the speaker himself turns out to be the addressee, too! Besides, by making the recital itself the action, Beckett has transferred the dramatic conflict from the character to the language which thus acquires the position of a protagonist. This is as it should be in a play which projects speech, 'lip lipping lip' (268), as a synonym for life.

Structurally, the play is quite close to 'Not I', but the play that comes closest to it thematically is *Waiting for Godot*. The very opening line here—'Birth was the death of him'—is a veritable paraphrase of Pozzo's parting philosophy: 'They give birth astride of a grave, the light gleams an instant, then it's night once more'. Significantly, after uttering these words, Pozzo exclaims 'On!' and goes away. 'A Piece of Monologue' is also concerned with such an exclamatory *going*.[1] Indeed, right from birth (with the word 'go') till death ('going away'), life is a form of going. That is to say, 'begun' and 'begone' not only sound alike but also mean the same thing. That makes life—the process of 'going on'—a process of 'gong to go', much like the lighting of a lamp which, at the very moment its wick is lit, starts dying—'going out'. This binary link between birth and death is hammered home when the opening line is repeated and is followed by phrases referring to 'born dead of night', or an infant's ghastly (death-like) grinning (265). True, there is something funereal in the play throughout and death comes to mind again and again in the reiterative references to nights, funerals, burials and ghosts. But, references to birth are no less frequent. Even the ghost imagery does not tilt the balance in favour of death. After all, ghosts are associated not with death per se but with *life*-after-death—a return from death into life. What is more, every night, darkness is dispelled when the lamp is lit. The binary core of the play is epitomized in the dim light on the stage. In a twilight, it is difficult to say whether darkness pierces light or vice-versa. In short, we are expected not only to feel the creepy movement of death in life but also to perceive death paving the way for life.

Significantly, the lamp that is lit is a standard skull-sized white globe. If the skull is associated with death, it also brings to mind a 'head'—the head of man who is the prime mover of everything around. The kinship between man and lamp is reinforced by the similarity in the tenors of the lamp and the speaker's narrative—reduction *sans* annihilation, declining and yet going on. Once this kinship is rooted in the mind, one feels that the routine of lighting the lamp has symbolic power of a ritual. Indeed, in the long night of eternity, Man has been keeping the lamp of life lit. That there was nothing but silent darkness before Man's arrival in the world and that it might be equally dark after him is suggested through the stage business—silence for 10 seconds before the monologue begins and a similar silence for 10 seconds after the monologue, before the curtain comes down. Thus seen, Speaker ceases to be an individual and comes to be identified as Mankind who is reviewing in this swan-song the tenor of its existence. In his precarious start as a freak in nature, Man appeared doomed to extinction—grinning in the crib 'up at the lid to come' (265). During his life, he ravaged the fellow-species that he loved—tearing to shreds the pictures of those 'he all but said of loved ones' (266). He invited, as it were, his end by resisting nature—burial in pelting rain under umbrellas. Nevertheless, he has maintained a sort of survival through the strategies of civilizations—lighting with extravagant matches the lamp which is snuffed out to be lit again. In a situation like this, Man is protected but his life is bleak and cheerless. Hence empty room, blank wall, dim light, pallet bed, etc.

This room being like a grave signifies the universe being a graveyard of the different species. But Man is content to remain buried here; he might even prefer to be a ghost living after his death. Hence the profusion of ghosts here—ghost light, ghost room, ghost grave, ghost loved ones, etc. That makes Man a ghost attending his own funeral Anyway, although a mere ghost, Man is the only one moving in the graveyard of the universe. Whatever activity is there in the universe, it is of his making. In thus being solely responsible for whatever activity there is, Man is enacting, as it were, a monodrama. That makes his life the biography of the world even though it amounts to a solo performance—a monologue, so to say. In short, human life is a piece of monologue in which the chronicle of Man's birth, death and rebirth make it a ghost story.

Now ghost is a ghost and it cannot act; the ghosts may interact but that cannot yield any solid gain. No wonder, Mankind has no real achievement to its credit despite all its unending pursuits. Inevitably, the effort of Man to assert 'No such thing as none' (266) is doomed to be countered by 'No such thing as whole' (269). In other words, if Man is not going to be extinct, he shall not become a complete whole either. He shall continue to oscillate between the twin poles of birth and death without ever becoming Superman.

Can one attend one's own funeral or be haunted by one's own ghost? The titillating possibilities could not but fascinate Beckett. In this frame of mind, he seems to have thought of some other equally outlandish possibilities—for example, a dreamer dreaming about himself dreaming, a rocker rocking a rocker, an artistic catastrophe resulting in the act of building a catastrophic scene, torturers taking turns as the tortured. Such, indeed, are Beckett's obsessions in his last plays. While in such a state of mind, Beckett received an invitation from the Ohio State University, Columbus, to present a play on the occasion of an international seminar. Called 'Samuel Beckett: Humanistic Perspectives' (7-9 May 1981), it was being organized to celebrate his seventy-fifth birthday. The thought of his listening to 450 literary critics' 'readings' of his own plays must have afforded him one more of those intriguing situations—listening to a tale about listening to a tale. Beckett possibly imagined how mystified he would be when the mystery of life, as experienced by him and transmuted into the mystique of art by himself, would be interpreted to him by those mystified readers! Wasn't that situation itself a piece of drama, he seems to have asked himself. Result: he wrote 'Ohio Impromptu' (1981).

In his younger days, an invitation like this might have prompted him to play a prank on the critics—like that celebrated lecture on 'La Concentrisme'. But, then, one cannot play such tricks at 75. However, since the imp in him was not yet dead, he seems to have thought of a subtler ruse. He gave his piece a title that would seem to honour the host city as well as modestly claim that it was only an improvisatory bit; but, in actual effect, the play was to have a dig at both the city and the assembled critics. Now, traditionally, among American children, 'Ohio' is the answer to a popular riddle which asks what is high in the middle and nothing at the ends. Ohio is thus O (= zero) + hi (= high) + O (= zero). That, Beckett wanted to imply, was going to be the tenor of the Ohio seminar—nothing before and after the high rhetoric of the critical verbiage. That is to say, starting in baffled darkness, it will end in a similar darkness, despite all the dazzling brilliance of the learned academicians in between. Thinking of all this, Beckett might as well have chuckled to himself, 'But isn't that true of life itself—so much of sound and fury sandwiched between nothingness?' The very utterance of the word 'Ohio' suggests this progress from void to void with empty action in between. After all, the mouth in uttering 'O', 'hi' and 'O' is always open and empty—a nevoid.[2]

The reading of a story in the narrative being read is a familiar Beckettian trick—like a play-within-play or a story-within-story. But is Listener really the subject of the story he is listening to and is he himself the Reader, too? If there are any clues to point to the sameness and interrelationship, there is also a lot that tends to underline the diversity and separation.[3] Perhaps the emphasis is not on the details but the general pattern. Here that basic common pattern is one of strange meetings interspersed with sad partings in the case of those who are essentially doomed to experience the terror of solitude again and again—as against the eddies that flow and conflow. The important thing is the potential of repetition ad infinitum—like the dog-in-the-kitchen song. Of course, at the end of time, some day, the end of the story-within-story will be reached and there will be nothing left to tell. But even at that snapping moment, the situation would be akin to the starting point. Indeed, even an infinitely long yawn of 'hi' cannot fill the mouth and change a sigh into anything other than a sigh, an 'O'.

That gives each story the shape of O-hi-O. And that makes me believe that the theme of 'Impromptu' is also the same old, sad tale of Man's impromptu evolution in which he is always moving, Ohio-like, from nothing to nothing with a lot of sound and fury in between.

Why he had parted from his dear one (Life Force), or who had deserted whom—there is nothing to indicate for certain. But even when he chose to move into the unfamiliar room of the 'microcosm' against the wishes of the Life Force, the latter continued to take care of him by offering him comfort through one civilization or the other. However, whenever Man and a civilization came to grow as one, it ordered the snapping of that connection—to the bewilderment of both. This has happened time and again. In every succeeding age, Man has reviewed the progress of his own evolutionary creativity ('read' his 'story') to find the reason of his failure. Each time he has tried to move into yet another civilization ('unfamiliar room') only to repeat almost the same stages—acquaintance, parting and bafflement. Indeed, even when the sad tale appears to be over, the resolution is found to have resolved nothing. The story continues to repeat itself; the book is not closed. That makes the history of man a kind of ghost story which continues even when it is over. In fact, it is like that story which, haunting the reader, becomes a part of his life.

'Catastrophe' (1982) was yet another impromptu piece written in response to a request—this time from the Committee of Artists Defending Other Artists to protest against the jailing of a dissident Czech playwright, Vaclav Havel, for his outspokenness on human rights issue. The format, too, corresponds to that of an impromptu work—a play-within-a-play in the form of a rehearsal in progress. Surely, the theme of the rehearsed inner piece is tyranny, the protagonist (P) representing the victimized, wretched proletariat. In the best traditions of agit-prop tableaux, P was not to speak anything but sit silently like a lifeless object—a miserable posture that is universally associated with the dispossessed and dehumanized sections of humanity. But, Beckett being Beckett, he could not be content with just one level of tyranny. He must multiply the layers so that in P the audience might see the victim of diverse forms of tyranny. Since the invitation had come from artists defending other artists, Beckett thought of referring to the tyranny in the field of arts itself. That was a very shrewd decision because, while the organizers might be duped by the surface tyranny, Beckett could have an equally scathing dig at the tyrannical ways of the organizers of agitational plays. Thus, while the one-actor rehearsed-piece is a political miracle play, it is studded within such a three-character frame-play as is clearly a parodic indictment of agit-prop theatre.[4]

Parallel to the schema of torturing, we have a catastrophe about a

Catastrophe. What D and A are trying to create is called 'catastrophe'—the final event in a tragedy signifying disaster. They have almost completed their creative process and feel elated at the result obtained; but, suddenly, P raises his head. As this undoes the whole effect, it proves a catastrophic change in the artistic creation itself. Thus, there emerge three pictures of catastrophe. The one visualized by A is a purely mechanical, calculated exercise in which there is no definite vision; D is after a spectacular effect via hit and trial. Both these are feudal in concept because they tend to ignore the artist's will. P's concept has an emotional base, being born of tragic defiance. Here is the true spirit, the earlier ones being mere trappings. Only the final catastrophe has a truly tragic core. In tragedy, the protagonist must act even if it means inviting disaster. In the 'catastrophe' created by A and D, the protagonist was expected to stand quietly without any action or even a single line of speech. P's raising his head, contrary to D's wishes, implies defiance for which he shall have to pay the heavy price of replacement.[5]

Once the idea of tyranny beneath tyranny gets rooted in one's mind, it is not difficult to perceive yet another level of meaning in which a different kind of artistic creativity is involved. The clue for that lies in the fact that the final image which keeps haunting us after the show is over is that of a man who refuses to be manipulated. Perhaps this play is a dramatization of the catastrophe created in the universe by Man who asserted his will against that of the director God and His assistant, Nature. Nature had visualized for Man the usual kind of catastrophe—extinction like that of other species; God, however, wanted a more spectacular end for his favourite creature who was, after all, the best of creations. Since this want of harmony between God (D) and Nature (A) tended to make him a freakish being, man would not let them have their way but must decide his own fate. This wilful assertion to create himself has resulted, of course, in a veritable catastrophe. The microcosm created by man is puny, insecure and vulnerable; but, insofar as it is a monument to his free will, it is a masterpiece, too.[6]

If Beckett's last plays are concerned with artistic creativity, it is by no means surprising. Approaching eighty, any writer would find himself brooding over his life and art and analyzing the relationship between his experiences, the life around him, and his works. Not surprisingly, in 'Catastrophe', art and politics tend to become mirror images of each other. In this frame of mind, it was but natural for him to recall the German totalitarianism he had experienced in his younger days and to see in the tormentor-interrogator a reflection of the way he himself had been pursuing a similar search for meaning in his work, novel after novel, play after play. Perhaps he felt that this was true of every artist trying to get at the secret of life. In every work an artist feels he is about to grasp the secret of life that had eluded him in the previous ones; but, alas, his confidence once again ends in a sense of shame: entering head haught, each work exits head bowed. Thus seen, each creation tends to be an exercise in a self-imposed tyranny in which the artist ends up being a victim as well as a victimizer. Now, in his late seventies and feeling all the time that he might be writing some of his last works, Beckett could not but feel tormented by the fact that he had failed in his life-long search to perceive the quintessence of life and to discover a shape for the mess of existence. Anyway, as he extended his broodings over his own failure to the failure of artists in general, he probably realized that it was equally true of the failure of the existential artist, Man. In life as well as in art, the curious and tyrannical search continues until the inquisitor not only realizes the futility of it all but discovers himself to be the one guilty of the crime. Indeed, each new generation torments the older one to be tormented by the next. In the case of man also, Beckett discovered the action to form a cyclic whole. And that is what we have in 'What Where' (1983).

Like a catastrophe in a catastrophe, or a dream within a dream, in 'What Where' we see torturers being tortured. Bam, an archetypal inquisitor, is not satisfied when Bom reports his failure to extract the requisite secret from his victim whom he has given the works. Feeling that Bom is trying to keep the secret to himself, Bam puts Bim on Bom to give him the works and thus get the secret out of him. Bim is confident that he will succeed but returns to report a failure. At this, Bem is asked to take over as tormentor of Bim, but he too fares no better. Since there is no one else left, Bam, the inquisitor, himself assumes the role of giving the works to Bem. Even he returns head bowed, thus deserving the same fate as his predecessors because the basic question remains unanswered. Of course, time has been moving along its own cycle—from spring to summer to winter and possibly to spring again—but the mystery remains unresolved. 'Time passes. That is all' (316). One could put this differently by saying that life is an insoluble mystery in which the only thing certain is the passage of time. This is the same old situation as obtained in *Godot*. What Godot would be like and where he would appear are unknowable. Men come and go, mysterious wait remains. And being a part of that very mystery, there still remains Man—the human spirit, represented by V, the disembodied voice of Bam.

In the premiere production, V was perceptible as a megaphone perched downstage on a higher level to establish its pivotal position as the protagonist. However, since its rim, lit like an eclipsed moon, looked rather frightening, Beckett was not happy with this image. More so because it prompted spectators to see the play only on the political level, ignoring the metaphysical and ontological possibilities. That Beckett was aiming at thematic complexity is more than clear from the closing line but one: 'Make sense who may'. After all, the very idea behind the play is that man is involved in an eternal search that shall never yield an answer. Anyway, since Beckett wanted V to primarily represent the human spirit, in the 1986 Paris production he had it represented by a circle of orange light—something ethereal but by no means ghost-like. Of course, in between these productions, especially in the German television version called 'Was Wo', Beckett had tried quite a few changes. The only thing that he always insisted on retaining was the cyclical pattern through the rhythm of repetition.

Perhaps the emergence and disappearance of characters from places called E, N and W denote the rise and fall of civilizations first in the East, then in the North, and later in the West. Seen thus, the absence of action in the South possibly signifies that in the Southern hemisphere civilization is yet to appear. That Bam, Bom, Bim, Bem are supposed to represent different variations of Man is conveyed by their names: at least some of them figure in *How It Is* and other novels, with slight changes, of course. Aptly enough, they all look alike with long grey hair and similar grey gowns. Indeed, they are, as Alan Schneider calls them, 'successive generations of men'.[7] They are trying to understand the 'what' and 'where' of existence though their continual failure and desperation forces them to torture one another to extract the secret of life. How in the process man has become a bum of the universe is not said in so many words but any intelligent reader should be able to draw that conclusion. The very opening line declares, 'We are the last five', and yet here are only four of them. That prompts one to look for the fifth. Since the names of these B'ms vary in respect of the vowels, inevitably we think of the one vowel that is missing—'u'. And that leads to the deduction that men are all variations of bums torturing one another and being tortured in return—in search of 'it all', everywhere.

In making the play end with 'Make sense who may/I switch off' (316), Beckett possibly meant to speak directly to the audience. Indeed, after 'What Where', he did switch off. At least for the stage he wrote nothing. Perhaps the closing line was a kind of confession that after fifty years of fiction and drama, he was still asking questions because he had failed to get answers to the basic questions with which he had started—the questions about the 'what' and 'where' of Godot.

The 1986 Paris production of 'What Where' was something of a surprise for Beckett enthusiasts. Despite the fact that the theme was still the same old interrogation by tormenting inquisition, the offstage action ceased to be threatening. In fact, the action on the stage was far from morose; it had acquired a light touch and sounded extremely funny at places. The reason was simple enough: the tempo had been speeded up. The possibility of a piece being dead serious in one performance and hilarious in the next one is, indeed, characteristic of Beckett and reminded one of the very first play that Beckett had presented way back in 1931, when he was a 24-year old graduate student at Trinity College, Dublin. Playing Don Diegue, the aged father of the Kid, he had assumed a white beard and put on the period costumes, in a play that he had not only written but also directed.

Le Kid, was meant to be a parody of Corneille's *Le Cid*, with the clear aim of mocking the classical concept of the unity of time. The manuscript has been lost but Beckett's biographer, Deidre Bair, gives a fairly vivid account of a memorable scene.[8] The Don held a small alarm clock and when it suddenly started ringing, the old man, already in the act of delivering his soliloquy, started speaking frantically as if keeping pace with the ring. Thus, the faster went the ring the wilder grew Beckett's delivery. Equally frantic became the up-and-down movements of another man who, engaged to move the hands of a huge clock on the wall, had to climb up and down a ladder. The first night, it was all so hilarious that cascades of unending laughter flowed through the audience. However, the Chairman of the Department, Rudmore Brown, was not amused and reprimanded Beckett for what he considered an irresponsible act. At the performance next night, the same lines were spoken in such a deadpan voice that not a single man laughed. And that was the end of *Le Kid* which, in a way, marked Beckett's start as a playwright. Though it turned out to be a 'false start',[9] one can see here foreshadowed certain features that were to mould, as it were, Beckett's now familiar signature. In a sense, with 'What Where' Beckett's writing has come full circle. In any case, it is worth noting that, in *Le Kid*, already in evidence is Beckett's obsession with clocks (small and large) as well as with ladder. Possibly Beckett was saying in his first play what he continued to say later again and again—that in the process of his evolution, man has to live on two planes of time—eternal and ephemeral—and his progress is like climbing up and down a ladder, frantically as well as purposelessly.

The fate of *Le Kid* could by no means have served as an incentive for more plays. Beckett took five years to recover and launch his next dramatic venture—a play on Dr Samuel Johnson. Despite extensive research, the project never went beyond preliminary decisions about scenarios and writing of just a few pages of the opening scene. This second 'false start' demoralized Beckett so completely that it took him a whole decade to return to drama with *Eleutheria*. Anyway, why did Beckett think of a play about Dr Johnson?[10] The hint lies in the title—*Human Wishes* (1936). The author of *The Vanity of Human Wishes* was to be seen in the ludicrous situation of infatuation at the age of 72 and, thus, epitomize the absurd quintessence of all human wishes—the vanity of 'it all'. That could be possibly extended to the quintessential human wish, viz., Man's ambition of ambitions with regard to evolutionary progress.

Eleutheria was completed all right but it has remained unproduced and unpublished[11]—a veritable discard. However, going by its detailed summary in Ruby Cohn's *Just Play* and comments by John Pilling, Linda Ben Zvi, Fletcher and Spurling in their respective books, I feel that this play also supports my basic thesis—man's determination, like Sisyphus, to continue despite the futility of it all because man's effort at evolution is a value in itself. One hears, as it were, Mankind itself speaking when Victor says, 'I'll tell you how I'll live my life away: rubbing my chains against one another. From morning to night and from night to morning. That faint vain noise will be my life'.[12] He refuses to be like a docile cow; he would at least like to feel free to register his protest. His is, of course, not a social rebellion against bourgeois conventionality; it is, instead, existential revolt to free himself from the prisons of both society and the self. True, he knows not what it means to be free; he just wants to be free. He knows that he will never be free and still he ceaselessly feels himself becoming free. Rejecting both return and suicide, he declares liberty—the freedom to do nothing so as to be nothing. For him, death could not be the right solution because, being dead, one cannot be aware of one's own death.[13] Dr Piouk does advocate the destruction of mankind by every possible method ranging from abortion to euthanasia; but it is not because he hates humanity. Instead, he loves it too much: 'Don't you see we're all circling round something that has no sense? We must find a sense for it, or lower the curtain.'[14] In view of such typically Beckettian motifs in the play, one cannot help feeling that the furniture-stuffed Krap Salone and Victor's bare hotel-room are possibly allegorical representations of the twin realms of macrocosm and microcosm, respectively. Perhaps the idea was to dramatize the fact that, fleeing the company of other uncouth and vulgar species, man has been living all by himself; but his 'desertion' having been resented in the world of nature, there are all kinds of moves to pressurize him into returning 'home'. Since man has not completely broken away from nature, he continues to traverse both the realms and that is why we have contrapuntal action. True, his microcosm has not afforded Man the desired security; rather, he finds himself living in a kind of most vulnerable glass-house where again he has the feeling of being imprisoned—very like Victor in the hotel-room. But, despite all this, man would rather wait here, like Victor, than return to nature and meet inevitable extinction. Even if waiting might not yield any better results, at least it would signify man's freedom to make his own choice to end the way he likes. For all one knows, that freedom might enable him to try again and continue the process of evolution.

There are four more plays which Beckett did not want to be presented—'Theatre I', 'Theatre II', 'Radio I' & 'Radio II'—because they were abandoned before receiving finishing touches. Although he was persuaded to permit their publication, he would not give them proper titles;[15] what is more, he hinted to their incompleteness by dubbing them as 'Roughs'. He also clubbed them as 'odds'—bits which shall remain as odd left-overs after the rest of his work has been categorized. Or could it be that they highlight the odds both in favour and against Everyman's struggle for survival?

In 'Theater I' (1956), a blind beggar, A, is accosted by a one-legged cripple, B, who patronizes the former. For a moment it appears as if their symbiotic partnership would work out to the advantage of both. The cripple could supply 'eyes' to the blind by directing his movements which would, in turn, imply providing legs to the former. But when all appears to go well, B feels so annoyed by A's over-enthusiasm that he strikes A with the pole which he has been using to push his chair. That blow makes blind A lose the sense of direction and he gropes in vain to retrieve his stool and fiddle. Anyway, B's desire for reconciliation, as also A's realization that B's voice might help him recover his lost things, facilitates their coming closer. But even as A tucks the rug under B's feet, the latter's ironic references to the former's past and future irritate A. Infuriated, A wrenches the pole from B's grasp and thus B is rendered as helpless in his movements as is A without his fiddle and stool.

Now, what next? Will they learn from their experience the lesson of peaceful coexistence and mutual cooperation? It is only one of the possibilities—as valid as the other negative one that they stand alienated for good and shall live in fear of each other. The cripple dare not speak because, following his voice, the blindman might direct at him a blow from which he cannot escape. After all, he cannot operate his wheelchair without the pole that is in the blindman's hand. Nor would the blindman do anything voluntarily to restore the pole to the cripple for fear of being beaten once again. In this situation, there is no way the blindman would get back his stool and fiddle or the cripple regain his mechanical mobility. In short, whereas A and B could have complemented each other, they have been rendered not just poorer but perhaps beyond each other's help. Worse, it is now the blindman who is wielding the weapon of power.

To me it appears that in 'Theatre I', too, Beckett is allegorically depicting the same old problem—the ambivalent relationship between visionless Man and Life Force that depends on others to get things done —to 'move', so to say. When man was groping in darkness, his main problem was food, the means of survival. Life Force offered to patronize him but man's excessive zeal and curiosity about things caused annoyance to the pragmatic Life Force. Consequently, what was, in theory, a perfect unit of collaboration has in actual practice led to antagonism. What is more, man has started behaving as if he had Life Force within his power.

In the 'Gloaming' manuscript at the Beckett Archives, the cripple says, '...my only sign of life is to take out my watch, wind it up and put it away again. Otherwise I might just as well be . . . you know (*Pause.*) Well perhaps not quite'.[16] Indeed, the role of Life Force has been reduced to that of the time-keeper of human evolution—

initiating a civilization, waiting for its end, and preparing for the next. In another speech, when the cripple asks, 'Why don't you walk around in a spiral? Have you no system?'[17] we realize why man has been making such a painfully slow progress in his spiral-like evolution. That is the system ordained by Life Force.

In 'Rough for Theatre II' also, the two characters are called A and B, but neither of them is the protagonist. Instead, that honour must go to the silent C, a homeless, unhealthy artist who is the subject of their talk, their investigation, and their verdict. They are sort of Kafkaesque agents of justice who start with a verdict—'let him jump' (78)—and marshall evidence to endorse their pronouncement. They have collected incriminating statements of his mother, his wife, his life-long friends, acquaintances, even himself, and reach the conclusion—'a black future, an unpardonable past' (86).To me it appears that C is not just an individual but Everyman and the testimony pertains to Man's failure as a species in the struggle for existence. Thus seen, A and B are the agents of Life Force who have collected testimonies like the recording angels. To suggest their respective concerns with the good and the evil deeds, they have been named Bertrand and Morvan—the bright one and the darkly morbid. As for the conclusion based on evidence, it amounts to saying that, in view of man's poor track record and bleak prospects, man has no right to survive. Thus, as a species, he must be allowed to 'jump'—that is, go extinct. Significantly enough, C is called Croker—one who is croaking, i.e. dying.

The attributes that characterize C represent humanity at large—sense of humour, sense of proportion, morbid sensitivity to the opinions of others, and an obsession with calamities; his 'disasters', too, are typically human—'work, family, third fatherland, cunt, finances, art and nature, heart and conscience, health, housing condition, God and man' (78). C remembers only calamities—a way of saying that the history of man is a record of catastrophes. That a creature of Man's nature can never really be happy, live passionately, or be sure of survival through his creativity is made clear through the testimony of C's wife. They had passionate exchange during the first 15 minutes of the wedding night, but otherwise there has been not a word of happiness. In the course of their coexistence, they did find themselves on their way to breeding offsprings but those efforts proved abortive. Hence the references to six miscarriages (79). Translated into the lingo of our allegory, it means that Man and Nature are inalienably tied but Man has always hated her: but for the initial courtship on man's landing on the earth, they have never known really happy relationship. Whenever Man has made effort to use Nature in the creating of civilizations, the result has proved abortive. Hence the reference to six miscarriages (79). The impending 'judicial separation' (99) between C and Mrs Croker means therefore the possibility of Man divorcing Nature. That would, of course, spell his doom—extinction.

But, then, the way C stands still throughout, he might be dead already. It is a way of implying that, though not exactly extinct, Man is as good as that. This situation is the result of his not heeding to the repeated warnings from nature. He is, of course, very sensitive; only he cannot retain that sensitivity for long and thus tends to forget the lessons learnt from the past catastrophes. Hence the repetition of his mistakes in respect of the strategies of survival. Things might have been different had man been insensitive like that lovebird in the cage who has the heart to sing even as its partner lies dead. Because of his capacity to feel and then to forget, Man has been behaving like Mr Smith. On the verge of suicide, Smith learnt that his wife had gone under an ambulance; vowing that he couldn't miss that sight, he rushed out and thus survived to lead a steady life. Indeed, on the verge of extinction, something or the other rooted in his sense of humour happens to Man to get him a further lease of life—until he runs away in disgust again only to return once more. No wonder Man has often come close to extinction and yet managed to escape by the skin of his teeth. In this context, Beckett possibly had Vico in mind, or more probably Spengler who believed that man has experienced rise and fall of civilizations some six times.[18]

In my first readings of 'Radio I', it appeared the case of a radio needing repair because two stations relaying music and speech were getting mixed together and the sound from both stations seemed to be growing feebler and feebler as if the set were 'dying'. Or could he be a technician in a broadcasting studio busy mixing the prerecorded music with prerecorded words? Realizing that both music-track and speech-track are getting feebler, he gets panicky and tries to reach the 'doctor', i.e. the studio-engineer who is not available. He turns to the 'producer' of the programme, but he doesn't appear too concerned with the snag. Possibly, being a mere technician, 'He' cannot understand the aesthetic aspect and regards as 'ending' of the sound-system what is in fact a deliberate sound effect—lowered pitch of both words and music to depict the last gasp of death. All this appeared a viable interpretation but it would not explain the She-factor—who was she, what were his 'debts' to her, and what had her visit to do with the snag?

The cue for my present interpretation came from the name of 'He'—Macgillycuddy. The name is repeated and that too with obvious emphasis on its syllables. As Gilly is Scottish for a page and cuddy for a fool, Mr Macgillycuddy should signify servility and idiocy made somewhat respectable. Man is the one who embodies that trait. This is also the conclusion we arrive at via another etymological detour. Gill of the fish is for breathing which is also associated with music, the language of the soul. On the other hand, cudding is ruminating, an activity of the mouth which produces words, the language of the body. As man is always trying to create harmony between the languages of body and soul, he is Macgillycuddy. Here is a creature who is mortal and yet, having managed to survive, he claims a touch of divinity and eternity. His experimental exercises being an existential necessity, he cannot get away from them, but that intrigues Nature. Thanks to his roots in Nature, Man has been indebted to her and therefore 'He' suffers the occasional, uninvited visits of 'She'. But her visits create snags in his microcosm, especially with regard to his evolution. As culture and civilization tend to become one and it would appear as if body and soul had started doing the functions of each other, 'He' gets panicky. Fearing that this might mean that everything is 'ending', he turns for help to Life Force. But being too busy with 'confinements' (births) and 'breeches' (deaths) of the other species, Life Force is rather indifferent to the situation of man. There is, of course, the promise of 'tomorrow noon', and maybe then all would be well. But who knows it might as well be too late. All that 'He' can do is to wait!

'Rough for Radio II' also ends on a similar note of waiting for tomorrow—a note in which, once again, a mere wishful hope seeks to counter an almost certain despair.[19] With the help of the mute Dick who swishes bull's pizzle whenever necessary, an old, urbane, arrogant but romantic Animator is coercing a hooded, gagged and plugged Fox to speak out the requisite information. Whatever the latter says and does is being taken down verbatim and in all details by a young, cool, pretty but pert stenographer. However, this is a game that no one is enjoying because all these torturers are themselves feeling equally tortured. Of course, the nature of torture in their case is more emotional or spiritual than physical, but they are all as helpless as Fox and therefore look forward to that 'tomorrow' when they would be free.

But, then, who are these folks enacting this Kafkaesque scenario? The general notion, led by Martin Esslin, is to treat it as a dramatization of the impetus for creativity in the artistic process—the creative relationship of the writer to his art.[20] For me, the artist involved is Man, his craft being his own evolution. In that business, Man has been a veritable fox—cunningly managing to survive in the struggle for existence. It would be revealing to read closely what Fox speaks out in the play in several speeches. In the context of evolutionary struggle, significant, indeed, are some of the phrases spoken by Fox—'that for sure, live I did', 'all stones all sides', 'all the way up, all the way down', 'age upon age', 'up again, down again', 'living dead in the stones', 'and there took to the tunnels', 'oceans too', 'all ends and farewell', 'farewell and fall', 'farewell seasons, till I fare again', 'down in spring, up in Fall', 'fatigue, what fatigue', 'Me get up, me go on', 'what a hope', 'Have yourself opened, Maud would say', 'I'll give him suck if he's still alive', 'scrabble scrabble', 'Peter out in the stones'. Here are, indeed, clear pointers to stone/cave age, rise and fall of civilizations, succession of generations and man's effort to go on despite fatigue inhering the process of repetition and mutation—all in the hope of reaching Godot stage (what a hope!). Maud is Life Force that is ever prepared to look after the next generation provided it can ensure the continuing of the process of life. This business of climbing up, falling and climbing again—scrabbling—has proved too much for humanity who would rather peter out in stones. That is to say, man would rather commit suicide as a species, but cannot.

To me it appears that, concerned with the 'movements' of man, the animator is anthropologist-historian, who falsifies the record because of a streak of romanticism. On the other hand, like a typical sociologist-journalist, the pretty stenographer would just compile the data rather literally without any attempt at interpreting it. Of course, they discover nothing new: they reiterate the proceedings of the preceding day: '. . . these dicta, like all those communicated to date and by reason of the same deficiencies, are totally inacceptable . . . outlook quite hopeless' (116). This is as good as saying that the chances of man are no better today, or no worse, than they were ever before. Most probably, this futile exercise on the level of existence and its recording would go on and on until Man either goes extinct or becomes Godot. Only then perhaps would the work of both historians and social scientists be over. No wonder, the play ends with Animator telling the Stenographer, 'Don't cry, miss, . . . Tomorrow, who knows, we may be free' (124). Who knows, indeed?

9 Intimations: Poetry and Early Fiction

In this study, I have concentrated so far on tracing the Godot-theme in Beckett's plays, but that does not mean that his poetry and fiction don't have enough to support my thesis. Since detailed discussion of all his poems, novels and stories would need another book-length study, I propose to have just a cursory look for broad hints. In this chapter, I shall deal with Beckett's early works which afford, as it were, 'intimations' of what was to be had later in his dramatic creations.

Significantly enough, the theme of Beckett's most celebrated poem, 'Whoroscope', is Time which is the very core of his canon. Time being a double-headed monster of salvation and damnation, its march involves a circular process of undoing what it has done. Hence a virtual stasis despite incessant mobility. It is like fecundating an oversexed but non-creative whore—mating without breeding, effort without fruit. That makes horoscope (watching the progress of hour/time) a kind of whoroscope. It is possible to see in the never-ending series of civilizations that rise to fall to rise to fall again a sequencing of births, deaths and rebirths which corresponds to the progression of egg-to-chicken-and-back.

'Whoroscope' (1930) is based on Descartes' habit of eating omelette made of such eggs as had been hatched for eight to ten days. This obsession amounted to wilful abortion. Egg is associated with fecundity and putrefaction; its hatching, with maturation and rebirth. In eating an omelette, one saves an egg from putrefaction; but eating an egg that has been hatched for several days means eating chicken before it is born. Indeed, Descartes' habit made him at once a saviour and a murderer. In his capriciously returning an egg to Gillot to mature it further, Descartes was emulating, as it were, the example of Time. Like egg, man as a species could have become a victim of natural decay long ago, but Life Force has saved him from that fate of extinction. But the way a human civilization is eaten up by Time just before its reaching its climactic glory is very like the eating of an egg that is about to yield a chicken. In short, it should be possible to read 'Whoroscope' as an allegory depicting Man being hatched by Life Force to be eaten up by Time when he is about to reach the Godot-stage of superman.

At the heart of Ptolemy-Copernicus dispute was the position of man in the universe. Was he its centre receiving homage from the sun that revolved round his earth, or was it the earth that owed its very existence to the sun? To put it differently, is man moving or himself being moved? Copernican theories gave him the position of a sack of potatoes on the horseback (moving and yet not moving) or that of a river (constantly changing and yet the same). That is the position of man that Descartes would endorse: human body may renew itself like the circular sequencing of chicken and egg, but that is all. Whatever might become the ultimate fate of mankind, an individual blooms and withers—like Anna Maria. A 'chip of a perfect block that's neither old nor new', each man is at best 'a lonely petal of great high bright rose'. It is this realization regarding the futility of individual life that prompted Descartes to end the cycle of birth and death by not letting the egg to mature into a chicken. Thus viewed, evolutionary force, symbolizing at once creation and destruction, is like Christina, the ripper—virile and yet murderous. Indeed, towards the close of the poem, what we hear could be man's own cry—to be spared and given another chance.

As Lawrence E Harvey has pointed out, if there is any single literary and philosophical insight that can be called central to the poems in *Echo's Bones*, it is the perception of flux and the change time brings in the lives of men and women.[1] The title refers, of course, to the myth of Echo and Narcissus's metamorphosis. But Beckett's stress is not on ego-oriented illusions but on life's cruelties. The metamorphic 'precipitates' are born of the frustration of a desire to possess the other when such a possession is absolutely impossible. For Beckett, such is the fate of Man—his absolute necessity to share others' experiences when such a sharing is absolutely impossible. And just as Echo was turned into hard stones and the voice continued, man's voice has continued, albeit it is as hollow as an echo.

In *Echo's Bones*, we have a number of 'enuegs' (nuisances), 'serenas' (evening songs), 'sanies' (songs of wound-pus—the emblem of degeneration of flesh), vexations, etc., as if these were the last cries of human species. But, then, there are 'dawn' poems, too. In 'serenas', dreams are as bad as walking reality and those giving birth feel as if dying. 'Alba' too implies a background that includes ascent as well as descent; in 'Sanies', play becomes reality and fun turns into suffering; 'Cascando' is about the sense of lost opportunities and future uncertainties. Putting all this in the context of my interpretation, I could say that Life Force and Man are engaged in a game in which the latter behaves as a hero while, in fact, he is a mere fool. Man does realize this reality but only when it is too late. Indeed, we hear Man's own cry in

> oh Becky spare me I have done thee no wrong spare me
> Damn thee
> spare me good Becky
> call off thine adders Becky I will compensate thee in full.
> (ll 38-40)

Right from his earliest writing, Beckett's concern has been mankind and each protagonist stands for Man. Belacqua in the uncompleted novel, *Dream of Fair to Middling Women* (1932), was to be such a version of Everyman. An indolent but exasperating character, he is keen to escape body by living in mind and daydreaming but invariably yields to the demands of the body. The novel was never completed possibly because Beckett outgrew Joyce. However, some of its material got adapted into two episodes of *More Pricks Than Kicks* (1933)—'The Smeraldina's Billet Doux' and 'A Wet Night'. Belacqua being common to all the episodes, *More Pricks Than Kicks*[2] has been referred to as a novel. But, in the absence of any integral links beyond cross-references, the ten chapters can also be treated as independent stories. We believe that, in creating this format, Beckett was trying to follow the structure of the story of Man—big events but so marginally connected as to look almost isolated episodes. A creature too lazy to think but full of borrowed ideas, a mortal being who cannot bear to think of his own death, a still hub of both centripetal and centrifugal forces, a lunatic who cannot but talk, Belacqua is a perfect epitome of Man. Indeed, one could say about Man what the different critics have been saying about Belacqua—an indolent, daydreaming, voyeuristic, myopic, queer, and ineffectual dilettante. No wonder he is on the one hand a sterile, impotent, masturbatory narcissist whose life is divided between anesthetized existence and effusion of semen and on the other a balding, introspecting clown bumping around. He is adrift in a world where nothing synchronizes or harmonizes, where facts do not lead to understanding, where causes produce no discernible effects, where accidents prevail and not plans, where things go round and round and round and round, where pointlessness is the point itself.

Seen closely, the themes of the episodes are broadly the quintessential attributes of human existence or institutions—life with friends, love affairs, marriages, diversions, misfortunes, attempts at suicides, etc. Indeed, Belacqua's grotesque growth from youth to maturity through death comprises a veritable summary of the picaresque adventures of Man—an experience of Nothingness. Possibly that is why Belacqua's name means beautiful water—something fascinating and ever-moving but never acquiring solid strength. Aptly, too, his first name is either Shuah which means to be discouraged or Shuach which means to bend or to sink—that is, to be humiliated. No wonder it has been said about Belacqua that, more than a character, he is a theme.

In 'Dante and the Lobster', the best known story in *Pricks*, we find that Belacqua is in the position of God—unable to reconcile pity and piety. Intrigued by a line in Dante, Belacqua asks his teacher whether it should read as 'Here pity lives when it is dead' or 'Here piety lives when it is dead'—that is whether wishing/executing 'its' death would be an act of pity or of piety. In the story, there are so many levels of pity, want of pity or misguided pity—God's for Cain, Dante's for the damned souls, Belacqua's for murderer McCabe and now for the lobster which is to go alive into the scalding water. Mercifully, lobster's was to be a quick death in just 30 seconds; but the narrator adds, 'It is not'. That is to say, death is not always quick. Possibly he is thinking of the death of a man. All men are born a-dying but it is a lingering dissolution, a drag-on affair. What is worse, unlike the lobster, there is in man a consciousness about the impending doom. Likewise, extinction of mankind itself is inevitable, but, open-eyed, Man must await his end consciously. In a situation like this, would Man's decision to commit suicide as a species be an act of pity or of piety?

Belacqua's indolence acquires the form of want of will to work in *Murphy*, the first published novel of Beckett (1938). Though *Murphy* is exceptionally precise with regard to the dates, months and years, the information does not help either in the progression of events or in the understanding of the narrative. Nor do the geographic details, maps and charts. The implication presumably is that, in the context of eternal time and infinite universe, man-made units of time and space are absurdly irrelevant. Indeed, in the world of man, precision is irrelevant, facts do not explain anything, and consequently answer to the dilemma of living does not lie in data. Being a parody of such a world, Murphy's world is almost bizarre. No wonder, instead of being related to one another, individual characters in the novel are basically self-centred. In a sense, man's situation epitomizes the universe in which the planets move in their orbits independently. The parallelism between man and celestial bodies is brought home right in the opening sentence of the novel: 'The Sun shone, having no alternative, on the nothing new' (*M*, 5). Indeed, man, too, has no alternative but to evolve the way he has done, and there shall never be anything new. Murphy's being in a rocking chair might signify his alternately going up and down on the rocker of civilizations.

Like Man, Murphy seeks to redeem his dog-like existence by the pleasures of the mind. Hence his obsession with permutations. Taken in different orders, Murphy calculates, five assorted biscuits may be consumed in 120 ways. How characteristic of man who spends all his life exercising choice in respect of food and livelihood! Similarly, Murphy is intrigued by the phenomena of decimal rendition of irrational numbers like 1/7, √2, π.

The end of Murphy has a long, tell-tale tail. The pulling of a wrong chain releases gas which, lit by a burning candle, incinerates Murphy bound to his chair. It is an ignominious end but, characteristically, Murphy would like to glorify it and so he wills the flushing of his ashes in the lavatory of Abbey Theatre during a performance. But the task is assigned to Cooper whose name literally means dung (= copros). In his drunken state, when he uses the bag of ashes as a missile, it is kicked by others as if it were a football. The bag punctured, ashes lie scattered on the floor of a pub to be swept next morning along with spit, vomit, cigarette butts, and other rubbish. Dust thou art, to dust returnst, says the Bible. Named Murphy, which means potato, the protagonist ends up with potato-skins.

Putting together all the foregoing means rephrasing of what I have maintained in this book as the core of Beckett's vision—the nil-result of man's evolution. In the words of Murphy, 'The syndrome known as life is too diffuse to admit of palliation. For every symptom that is eased, another is made worse. The horse leech's daughter is a closed system. Her quantum of wantum cannot vary' (*M*, 137). Indeed, in a situation like this, man can neither become a superman nor stop making effort. That makes life so like the chess-game between Murphy and Endon. In that, the eighth move brings their play back to the starting point as if they had never begun; even on the forty-third move,

Endon's pieces are back again to the starting situation. He has been playing not with the aim of defeating the opponent but for returning to the starting position. He is indifferent not only to capturing but also to the possibilities of being captured so long as it enables him to continue playing the game. What he enjoys in the game are the rhythms, patterns and shapes of the interim moves. Exactly in the same way, Man has been making move after move with the sole aim of continuing. Man's life is therefore an end-on business—open and uncertain. In such a game there can be no achievement, only expectations. No wonder, too, Murphy's horoscope prepared by an Indian swami promised not accomplishments but only possibilities.

Whether or not Beckett's long silence between *Murphy* and *Watt* (1942) can be attributed to World War II, it is possible to argue that the experience did facilitate his perceiving in the phenomena of the wars the source of man's real trouble in his evolution—the insanity of human sanity. The way Hitler and Mussolini could justify their tyranny, even genocides, appears to have convinced Beckett that man is not a rational animal but a rationalizing creature. To make the readers realize the madness of human reasoning, the novel maddens the reader with excessive reasoning. Things are mysterious and inexplicable not for the want of efforts to explain but because logic has been belaboured to perversity. Man's imperfect intellect engaged in a fight against irrational forces makes his life a story told by an idiot. No wonder *Watt* has been described as a story of a psychotic related by a lunatic, copied by a madman, and edited by a nut.

So far as the story line is concerned, it is quite intriguing, but no less baffling is the manner of narrating it. Watt is a queer, milk-drinking, much-travelled, academician-gentleman who uses tram and train to reach the house of Mr Knott who is a powerful absence like Godot. Here Watt serves on the ground floor and later on the first until he is relieved, and he vanishes as quietly as he had come. Into this narrative are roped several digressive narratives—e.g. the haranguesome monologue of Arsene whom he relieves, account of Lynch clan, Arthur's story of Mr Louit's report, and the epigrammatic addenda at the end. The way the chronology of events is shuffled, the act of telling the story punctured, the language broken and the syntax perverted, the novel becomes as mysterious as the unseen Mr Knott himself.

Sounding what the names do, Watt suggests a question and Knott a negation. Thus, Watt in the service of Knott is a way of saying that man is an ever-questioning creature whose brooding about what-is-life has only led him to perceive Naught, i.e. nothingness at the core of existence. And if Knott signifies knotting, it would mean that the more effort man has put into solving the mystery of the world, through logic, the more complex has become the knot.

Of course, it is possible to interpret the novel as an allegory of man's evolution since primordial times to the modern age. The idea is to show that man's rationalistic strategies of survival have been almost counterproductive because the rise of a civilization followed by its fall has invariably made things worse. The ousting of lovers by prurient Hackett represents the struggle for existence among species. The couple that joins are the vulgar, naked ones who are aptly called Nixons (= Nix-ons). As they interact, there arrives Watt whose most characteristic attributes make him out as Man—milk-drinking, mild, truthful, educated. Indeed, when man arrived on the scene, the earth was full of naked brute animals. Another distinguishing characteristic was man's disproportionate feet which enabled him to walk on two legs—a fact that is represented in the novel by Murphy's staggering funambulistically. The indignities heaped on Watt before and after his service at Knott's house underline the intrinsic vulnerability of man and his proneness to ridicule. Greeted with stones by McCann and the porter's kicks, he is bid 'bye with a knock by the station master and a bucket of slimy water over his head. This is as good as saying that Man, the hero of this ill-told and ill-learnt story, is inevitably a case of ill-come and ill-go. This is the position in Part I when he arrives and Part IV when he departs. In between, it is his turn to feel offended by the chaos and nonsense represented by the inmates of the mysterious house. He represents a quest for order, rationality and meaningfulness as against the absurd goings-on in the pre-civilization state represented by the porter. Then comes the journey from East to West—the way civilization has spread. Here Watt meets Spiro who mixes theology and bawdy, exactly a la pagan mythology. The Galls who come for piano-tuning could be the Gauls representing French culture.

Obviously, Knott's house is human microcosm where several civilizations arrived, served for a while, and then left to be replaced by others who met with similar fate. No wonder Arsene tells Watt, 'Same things happen to us all' (*W*, 44). Thus, Arsene, Erskene, Watt, Arthur, Micks, etc., represent civilizations. The tenor of the coming and going of these servants to Knott's house corresponds to the way modernity of a new age ousts tradition to be ousted, in turn, by the modernity of the next age. The two storeys of Knott's house possibly refer to the humanistic and scientific phases of a civilization. In the case of Watt, during his service on the ground floor, his concern is with food, ringing of the bell, and the mysterious goings-on upstair—problems that could signify man's concern with economics, religion and philosophy. Life on the first floor does not bring Watt closer to Knott; instead, he goes neurotic—the way a civilization loses its values before declining. Anyway, Watt leaves Knott's house and catches a train for the end-of-the-line which could mean either his death or return to primitivism. Since this might imply completion of a Viconian cycle, we are told, 'The coming is in the shadow of the going and the going is in the shadow of the coming' (*W*, 56). No wonder Watt often keeps wondering when and how 'they' came, how and how long they stayed, when and how they went. Nothing is certain here—naught, indeed.

There is no touch of finality about anything, no conclusive answers, because human reasoning is marked by intriguing relativity. Thus, Watt can think of four solutions to the problem of the disposal of the food-remains, but immediately he counters with fourteen objections to these solutions. Likewise, he thinks of as many as twelve possibilities regarding why Knott never complains about food, and whether or not Mr Knott knows of the arrangements obtaining in his house. His guess work regarding who rang the bell takes full ten pages. And one-fourth of the novel has been devoted to explanations that explain nothing. Since this way of thinking, though interesting, does not yield any results, it becomes a kind of game pursued for its own sake. Witness Watt's guesses regarding Knott's movements in the room above, and the placement of furniture there. Every guess is replaced by another in a chain that never ends. Here is a proof of man's absolute inability to know anything with certainty in a situation where the need to know is equally urgent. In an irrational situation like this, man's hope to reach his ultimate goal via rationality is foredoomed; it will land him in madness or else make him go 'dum, num, blin'.

The physically afflicted man's compulsive but unavailing vagrancy in search of a permanent shelter, his effort to get related to others proving as futile as his quest into the self, and this mortal's succeeding in transforming death into a continuum of life—these indeed are the underlying themes of the trilogy of novellas (1946) as well. In each of the stories it is possible to discern the same pattern of expulsion, seeking and falling, a temporary shelter, an interaction with animals, an inability to tell a story of affectional relationship, and return to the original position. True to the tenor of human life, none of the stories depends upon a plot or a point. What is more, the world here is not only without purpose but also marked by diminishing means.

'The Expelled' is possibly a mythical record of man's violent expulsion from the Paradise. Flying through the 'air', he comes to rest in the gutter (earth). After him is thrown his hat—the distinguishing hallmark of Man symbolizing his intellect. The other most conspicuous thing about him is his walk. Indeed, this protagonist's baffled wanderings correspond to the awkward journey of the two-legged man through evolution, sustained by intellect. His tramping around the town and spending the night in a cabman's stable is a metaphorical way of depicting the earliest stages of man's existence as a part of nature. No wonder, like man fleeing Nature, the protagonist here escapes from the window.

'The Calmative' begins with 'I don't know when I died' (*NK*, 25). This could be Everyman recovering his senses after an escape by the skin of his teeth. As his past looks like a dream, he refers to it as a story. The story is about numerous wanderings through a wood and the town, about how he used to collapse, recover and continue his hopeless journey. As even death has not yielded real peace, he seeks calm in the act of story-telling. Thus does he lend to his present the pattern of his past. As for the future, he looks up to the stars. Nothing is clear, however, because the stars are hidden by clouds. That every age feels that it is living better than its predecessor is a life-sustaining illusion of history—man's story. The fact is that man has not achieved much except that, through his factitious existence, he has given himself a fictitious glory.

'I' in 'The End' is sent away from a hospital—not discharged but expelled, as it were. It means that a victim of existential malaise, Man has been behaving so neurotically that he has got on the nerves of those who could have possibly restored his health. The desire to escape his state of despair it is that prompts him to become a carpenter (= an existential artisan). He creates for himself a boat—a symbol of man's small world—which is at once his home, his bed, and even his coffin. Living thus in a boat, the protagonist sees visions of his gliding out to the sea. He is convinced that if it comes to the worst, he would dig a hole in the bottom of the boat and let the water rush in and drown him. Such, indeed, is Man's vision of glorious ending. The reality, however, is that, not being heroic enough to commit suicide, Man shall never have the will to end. More probably he will keep dwindling 'without the courage to end or the strength to go on' (*NK*, 67). He will stay alive not because of any definite purpose but because he wants to remain just alive.

Indeed, like the protagonists of these novellas, ever-homeless man has been busy inventing stories of survival and thus wandering from shelter to shelter. There has been no real change in the human situation, only the quality of the story has undergone some change.

Another work written in 1946 but published in 1970, *Mercier and Camier* was Beckett's first novel with two heroes, a 'pseudocouple' as their creator would call them. Vagrants like Murphy and Watt, they often travel together. As the journeys lead nowhere, the full French title (when translated into English) reads 'The Voyage of Mercier and Camier Detouring Through the Grove of Bondy'. Read closely, the title has two significant pointers to the theme. Firstly, the destination is undefined; secondly, the detour is through the grove of Bondy which, in colloquial French, implies a den of thieves. Putting these pointers together along the references to the thieves in *Godot*, the title possibly means that life is a detour towards an arbitrary salvation or damnation and that the journey of life leads nowhere.[3] In their journeys, one perceives, as it were, man's progress to dissolution as he moves one fruitless age after another. To put it differently, *Mercier and Camier* is yet another indictment of human evolution. Instead of enabling mankind to pass the time better through social interaction, human companionship has created more problems. Indeed, the 'others' have made the journey of life a voyage through hell. Of course, it is a hilarious inferno because the tramp called Man is a red-nosed clown, too.

Like human microcosm, the world of Mercier and Camier is also mysterious; they are driven by a need that is occasionally quite clear but more often impenetrably obscure. The beginning of the novel is fraught with confusion and the entire voyage is enwrapped in a fog of doubt that lifts partially now and then but never completely. Camier's being a detective implies man's having a mind that is at once curious and shrewd. But, alas, its logic is not adequate enough. That is why Camier always wonders about problems that he cannot solve. It is not surprising that as Mercier and Camier walk together, they keep raising the same questions—like philosophers who have been debating the same issues since time immemorial. The questions before Mercier and Camier are: what are they looking for, and whether or not what-they-are-looking-for really exists? This is a veritable epitome of metaphysical concerns and man's effort to know the unknowable. The only thing that really matters for Mercier and Camier and about which they are certain is the need to depart. That is obviously a clear reference to man's inevitable mortality or Man's extinction as a species. In the overall context of Beckett's quintessential theme of man's evolution, it is easy to see why the first day of the couple's journey ends in their original position, why the streets are slippery, why the train is slow, why the co-passenger and the innkeeper are such compulsive story-tellers, why each of them thinks mistakenly that the other has left him, and why they keep meeting again and again.

Although Beckett grouped together *Molloy*, *Malone Dies* and *The Unnamable* as a trilogy, one might as well question the validity of such a clubbing. In the three-decker Victorian fiction, there had to be something common to serve as a unifying link—continuing dynasty, a circumcized social milieu, a spectrum of perspectives on the same events, a unity of theme, or else a multi-tentacled plot. In Beckett's trilogy there is nothing common in terms of time, place, characters, events, or techniques. Surely, Beckett would not have been the modernist that he was if he had hankered after the conventions of the traditional poetics. His links are much subtler and one must look hard and long before one discovers them.[4] It should pay to remember that Beckett is concerned not so much with progress as with disintegration. Only then can one see the real link in the progression of the three novels—a progressive atrophy in respect of places, people, events, things, the world itself. If Molloy is writing in his mother's room, Malone's room is in an indeterminate building, even as the locale of *The Unnamable* is nowhere. Likewise, while the characters in *Molloy* have fixed names and functions, in *Malone Dies* the name changes suddenly from Sapo to Macmann, and the protagonist in *The Unnamable* remains unnamed. Likewise, whereas *Molloy* is full of references to time (seasons and days of the week), *Malone Dies* is vaguer in this respect, despite references to calendar; and in the last novel, time has no more reality than place. There is also a corresponding dwindling in the density of texture in respect of the action. It moves from quest to questions, from discrepancy between events and narration to total doubt. Indeed, the gradual progression from crowd to aloneness, from mobility to stasis, from picturesque landscape to ubiquitous grey, from conversation to aphony, from civilization to shards of words—all these cannot be a matter of coincidence. Once one gets to grasp this pattern of disintegration, one realizes why all these characters have neither achievements nor ambitions. One realizes, too, why they are all physically decrepit—Moran with increasing pain in leg, Molloy with increasing palsy, Malone in a state of total paralysis, and Unnamable totally bodiless.

But, then, one might as well ask why this all-round disintegration? For me this is as it should be in the works of a writer for whom evolution of man has gone hand in hand with his deterioration. Not only does Ruby Cohn talk of a dying sense of civilization here[5] but Eric P Levy also hears in the trilogy the voice of the human species narrating its own persistence.[6] Indeed, the protagonists here are like radio-commentators stationed at different locales relaying the account of what they see—each one taking over from his predecessor and so on. Thus seen, each novel shows things from the standpoint of the species rather than that of the individuals—nameable or otherwise. No wonder their experiences concern not their personal problems but the unmitigated suffering of human existence. Here is, so to say, the common denominator to which the entire mankind can be reduced. Perhaps that is why they keep asserting not their individuality but their humanness. 'I am human', declares Molloy (*MMDU*, 78); 'It's human, a lobster couldn't do it', insists the Unnamable (*MMDU*, 375). As for the connection of Macmann to the species, it is implicit in the name itself—the son of man. Indeed, these Beckettian men have nothing of their own except a resemblance to human species. What these pure narrators share are the characteristics that distinguish man as a species—rationality, will to live, sense of morality, and habit. All this makes Levy identify Beckettian Man with ***humanitas*** which belongs to each man so far as he is a member of the human species.[7]

Now, the fate of the human species is best epitomized in the myth of Sisyphus—going over the same route, bound to the task that has no conclusion, and never getting to completion despite numberless repetitions. That makes every journey as good as the first, but there is somewhere a hopeless hope that it might as well be the very last. Thus stranded, mankind is doomed to revolve as long as there are generations to continue it. Each generation might find itself more tired but, as in the case of Sisyphus, never will the task be given up. That, in a way, makes the progress of human species read like a novel in which the narrator's attempt to find a beginning is as exasperating as his efforts to establish a middle, or his toils to reach the end. Perhaps that is precisely the respective business in *Molloy*, *Malone Dies* and *The Unnamable*. As the pure narrators here represent the voice of the species, they are both the tellers and the told. Expected to express the inexpressible, man too faces the same dilemma as these narrator-writers. They are asking the same, old questions which Linda Ben-Zvi has summed up so succinctly: how can I recognize myself who never made my acquaintance; how can I bring the 'me' and 'I' of the self together under one name and one voice; how can I find words to express the selves I do not know; and, how can I speak my way to the desired end—silence?[8]

That of the two sections of *Molloy* (1947), the second should chronologically precede the first has been the hunch of many a critic. But that, I believe, is unnecessary because, according to me, the action of the twin sections is simultaneous. Moran is sent in search of Molloy precisely when the latter has left for his mother's place and is therefore regarded as missing. In other words, although Moran and Molloy don't actually meet, they are in the same region, at the same time. That is to say, they represent the same stage of man's evolution—an age marked by such existential dichotomy as inheres Cartesian duality. Hence the profusion of bicycles in both the sections and their total absence in the subsequent parts of the trilogy.

True, there is some justification in critics' discovering in *Molloy* echoes of Homer, Virgil, Dante and the Bible. But, as a closer look should reveal, the idea is not to rework the myths but to parody them. It is worth noting that the parody here encompasses at once the epic myth, the pastoral spirit, the picaresque journeys, the detective fiction, the parables, and the scriptures. Possibly the idea is to underline the absurdity of all the archetypes of creativity—not excluding the existential art of man. Indeed, man has been always moving through the world of the Nothing and the more he has tried to adapt it, the more sour, infected, and repellent it has grown. In a parody, the important thing is not what happens but the inverting of an image. Here, too, what Molloy and Moran do is not half as important as what their deeds put to ridicule—the 2,500 years of Western culture.

Only in the context of parody, mother's room can become a tomb as well as a womb and a simple action in a stable imply the Herculean labour for king Augeas. Likewise, Molloy's computing the ways one may assuage one's hunger by sucking 16 stones in different order is only a parody of man's elaborate efforts to invent multiple ways to attain a simple end. That is Beckett's way of indicting the Western logic. When the stones are thrown away as the ultimate solution, it amounts to declaring: so much for human planning and organization! Of course, the oriental hemisphere is not exactly out of the compass of Beckettian parody. Witness, the arguments about the ways one may wear a shirt—the obvious symbol of mortal frame as a garb for the human soul. It is this shirt that, according to reincarnation theory of the Hindus, man changes between death and rebirth.

Once we get on to this wavelength, we don't need a second thought to realize that hobbling and crawling represent the tenor of man's movements on the evolutionary plane. In this state of mind one can understand instantly what Beckett could really mean when Moran moves in circles to proceed in a straight line. In such a framework, does it really matter whether it is the story of Molloy or that of Moran which should be told first? Indeed, here is a situation as intriguing as the fate of the two thieves in the parable—one damned, the other redeemed. Perhaps it is to remind us of those thieves and their situation that, right in the beginning of *Molloy*, we have an account of A and C who resemble thieves. Anyway, if a story can begin at the end, why can't its end assume a beginning? That is the import of the close of *Molloy*. Moran returns to find his hives dry, his chickens dead, and his house abandoned; but everything in the air is proclaiming the season of spring—rebirth. The age of Molloy and Moran may be coming to a close but a new age is about to begin—the next era when other narrators would take over the next phase of the story of Man. No wonder, Moran's son is back in the room—possibly to ask the same old questions : what am I; where, when and how does my story begin—and end?

The protagonist of *Malone Dies* (1948) is yet another M in a series to which belong Murphy, Mercier, Molloy, Moran *et al.*—presumably to represent yet another stage in the history of Man (with capital M). If Molloy and Moran represented the earliest stage when human existence was both oriented in nature and related to spirit, Malone represents the stage when man tried to create a world of his own—a world based on human rather than natural or spiritual values. While other species were content with what nature offered, man insisted on fulfilling his needs through cultivation. That made him, in a sense, saposcat—one who saps 'skatos', i.e. dung.[9] As for Macmann who usurps the position of Sapo in the middle of the story, it literally means the son of man—one further stage in the history of Man.

The room in which Malone lies is somewhat skull-like, possibly to underline its link with human intellect. Malone uses a stick to manoeuvre his dining table and his chamberpot which are associated with the most essential activities of eating and excreting—'dish and pot, dish and pot, these are the poles' (*MMDU*, 185). Convinced that he is going to die, Malone wants to tell himself stories and make an inventory of his possessions. But what he tells makes little sense. Nothing gets elaborated in respect of his past life, present illusions, places visited, or people met. He does not know even who he is, and where. Obviously these questions have metaphysical import—pertaining to the nature of reality, Man's ignorance about his identity, and his position in the universe. In fact, it is possible to treat the novel not as the story of an individual on the point of death but as an allegory depicting either Man preparing to go extinct or some civilization on the verge of disappearance. In that kind of situation, will 'he' really have anything worthwhile to recall? More likely than not, he would end up with the realization that, despite millennia of evolutionary labour and his tall claims of achievements (in the fields of religion, art, philosophy, science and technology), he has no inventory of 'possessions' to offer.

'Malone . . . is what I am called now', the narrator declares (*MMDU*, 223). The use of 'now' is significant in the context of the preceding incarnations/ages.[10] The first story about Sapo pertains to an early stage of civilization. The evolution of man's will is underlined when it is suggested that Sapo was a puppet to begin with but later came to acquire a position of autonomy. Malone could as well be talking about Man when he says about Sapo, '. . . this patient, reasonable child, struggling all alone for years to shed a little light upon himself . . .' (*MMDU*, 193).

Next comes the stage of Macmann. Being literally the 'son of man', he no longer has anything either angelic or natural about him. And what a mess of the world he makes: instead of weeds, he digs out plants and flowers! When scavenging, he leaves the streets in a worse condition and deposits the rubbish in the middle of the road. Through this Swiftian vision, Macmann is perceived as an incorrigible bungler whose attempts to create meaning out of cosmic chaos make things even more confounding. In fact, he has turned the world into a kind of asylum. The irony, however, is that the age of this 'son of man' mirrors the era of the 'Son of God'. Perhaps it implies that life in this asylum of Christian society is loveless, miserable as well as psychotic.

Critics have hailed the end of the novel as a perfect close because one stroke ends all—Macmann's story, Malone's story, Beckett's story, the tellers and the told. But that cannot be. Man cannot die until time itself ceases. It is a comma, not a period. Indeed, out of the coma, Man does emerge again in *The Unnamable* to ask: 'Where now? Who now? When now?' (*MMDU*, 293). Malone himself had forecast: 'My story ended I'll be living yet' (*MMDU*, 285).

Indeed, there he is again in *The Unnamable* (1949), reborn, as it were, to continue man's impulse to 'keep going, going on, call that going, call that on' (*MMDU*, 293). Now, does this reincarnation signify any better prospects? True, he realizes, 'All these Murphys, Molloys and Malones do not fool me. They have made me waste my time . . .' (*MMDU*, 305). But it does not mean that he won't waste any more time in repeating his mistakes. What can one expect from Basil,[11] a creature with an ill-base? 'It's a lot to expect of one creature. It's a lot to ask, that he should first behave as if he were not, then as if he were' (*MMDU*, 337). And these are the words not of Basil but of Mahood who comes after him. As the name indicates, Mahood represents manhood without 'n'—that is, the stage when ill-based creature is further impoverished by the loss of ego. Next step in this process of disintegration is inevitably the stage of irreducible Worm—sans integrity, sans ego, sans name.

Molloy, Moran, Malone belonged to the past marked by 'a ponderous chronicle of moribunds in their courses' (*MMDU*, 310); Basil, Mahood and Worm, on the other hand, pertain to future when, in order not to peter out, it would be necessary 'to invent another fairy-tale' (*MMDU*, 309). Indeed, man will continue to invent illusions to delude himself with the belief that he is here to perform a big task even though he has not the slightest idea of what exactly that assignment is. 'I was given a pensum, at birth perhaps, as a punishment for having been born perhaps, or for no particular reason, because they dislike me, and I've forgotten what it is. But was I ever told?' (*MMDU*, 312). Indeed, that word never came, and so man has to discover the mission of his life somehow. That makes man a kind of puppeteer who has all his puppets around him but has no story to tell. Or, more precisely, he is like a writer who has started telling his story without first deciding what that story is going to be about. In a situation like this, the writer would probably tell the same story again and again, possibly with slight changes. At times he might appear to give up, but would begin again, and yet again—of course, without knowing any better how to proceed even this time. Such a story would never reach an end; in fact, the story may never even get started. Vacillating between a desperate effort to shape the prologue on the one hand and to achieve the silence of the end on the other, the narrator might invent more characters, try varied fictional forms, and move inward and outward in the past and present, but never make any real progress. Such, indeed, is the tenor of the action in *The Unnamable.* And by no means different has been Man's situation. He has been moving in and out of time and space, making and breaking illusions of glory, and assuming different strategies of survival—all without any onward progress, and still continuing without a break. What matters is not what the story-teller tells but the fact that he keeps speaking; likewise, what matters is not how man lives but the fact that he goes on. No wonder, the Unnamable says, 'What was I going to say? Never mind, I'll say something else. It's all the same'. That makes Man a pure narrator in whose case narrating itself is his very life.

Representing different stages of man's evolution in the yet unborn future, Basil, Mahood and Worm are only three of those innumerable puppets whose stories the unnamable puppeteer tries to tell one by one. Mahood, stuck in a jar and producing excreta for manuring the garden, is Man stuck on the earth to fertilize the garden of the universe. His circling round and round in a small, windowless rotunda and moving in slow, converging spirals implies man's repetitive and reiterative existence on this globe. What a pity that, instead of employing his meagre resources to the fullest advantage, man is wasting them in experimenting with his grandiose plans! This, indeed, is the implication of filling one container by emptying another through an elaborate system of pipes and taps. The irony of it is that the container is no bigger than a thimble!

From this state of Mahood, next logical step should lead to worm-like existence—writhing and wriggling, with wild eyes always open and tongue chattering on more and more frenziedly. Unable to speak because he has nothing to say and yet unable to keep silent either!

No wonder the Unnamable goes on and on literally without a period, page after page after page, mixing I and you, subject and object. Even at the end, he avers:

'it will be I, you must go on, I can't go on, you must go on, I'll go on, you must say words as long as there are any . . . where I am, I don't know, I'll never know, in the silence you don't know, you must go, I can't go on, I'll go on' (*MMDU*, 418).

In a situation like this, can man know what he is, how he is related to other objects, and above all how he is destined to meet his end? Indeed, none can tell. Only one thing is sure: man will for ever remain unnamable—without integrity, without identity—and yet he will continue with his egoistic-cum-masochistic, self-mutilating game in the hope of discovering the right rope to build himself: '. . . mutilate, mutilate, and perhaps some day, fifteen generations hence, you'll succeed in beginning to look like yourself, among the passers-by' (*MMDU*, 317). That could, indeed, be regarded as the motto of Man—rather, that of the species which is still unnamable.

To sum up, the Trilogy is just one continuous story—the story of Man. One could say that Molloy represents man before the dawn of civilization—a freak in nature insofar as he is physically weak but spiritually strong. Malone represents the stage of civilization and culture when man felt that he alone could create a world of his own. *The Unnamable* projects the progress of man in future when, instead of becoming a god-like superman, man would be reduced physically and spiritually to the level of a worm. Paradoxically enough, while the immense potential of Man and his endless experimentation to survive have saved him from extinction, these have also led to his gradual disintegration rather than an upward evolution. This progression-cum-disintegration, concomitant with survival-despite-cosmic-opposition, may be something heroic in its own way, but this is a heroism without drama. If the essence of tragedy lies in the identity and integrity of the hero, man's fate is untragic, too, because he has no fixed identity. Maybe, it had some name once upon a time but, with the passage of time, the species has become unnamable. This makes man not a tragic hero but a cosmic clown—a fool looking on a wrong road for a goal that does not exist.

10 Residua: Epiphany as Fizzle

Coming after the trilogy of novels, *Texts for Nothing* (1950) appeared a steep come-down for Beckett. No wonder many of his critics read in the title the author's apologetic hint that the pieces were not to be taken too seriously. That prompted some scholars to treat them as disjecta—possibly unused residua of the trilogy. Some others felt more inclined to treat them as some 'fizzles' that Beckett farted out occasionally and put together because they shared the common core of stinking, airy nothingness. For me, however, the 'nothing' here generically belongs to the 'nothing' in *Godot*—'nothing to be done' followed by a lot of activity that adds up to nothing. Indeed, in the light of Beckett's work, I feel more inclined to see in *Texts for Nothing* a treatise on such Nothingness as inheres human situation—No's knife in Yes's wound, as the concluding Text XIII puts it. Indeed, like the narrator stranded between words and silence, man too has been oscillating between non-being and continuance. Thus seen, the 'texts' are isolated fragments of an epic depicting man's days on the earth. A nightly narration of episodes, the monologues tell how man has been trying again and again to get out of the condition of disintegration. Although he has failed in every attempt, the effort has a core of heroism about it. Here is, as it were, a case of that aesthetics of failure which Beckett had eulogized in 'Three Dialogues': '. . . to be an artist is to fail, as no other dare fail . . .' (*Dj*, 145). The artist here is Man as a species, trying to express himself in an evolution that has yielded no progress but just saved him from the doom of extinction. *Texts for Nothing* presents, so to say, the story of Man narrated by the spirit of Man in a situation when it cannot decide to go on or to give up.

What makes the situation intriguing, the obligation to express is as absolute as the nothingness with which he has to express. It is like making the silence speak without surrendering its silence. A screaming silence appears an impossible task but therein lies the challenge of artistic creativity—making an act of expression the very expression itself. There is, indeed, in *Texts for Nothing*, a pull between language that conceals and silence that reveals. Eric P Levy has very pertinently pointed out that each text introduces a question and ends with a provisional conclusion which does not answer the query but removes the very possibility of the question being asked properly.[1] The answers here thus tend to be not answers but the denial that any answers exist at all. More and more questions are asked in the hope of ultimately gaining knowledge but only to discover the impossibility of ever getting any answer. Every attempt to ascertain truth and falsehood fails because the 'Yes' is found to be as unconvincing as the 'No'. The pity is that No is not content to cut Yes's throat but must cut its own, too.

If we keep in mind the various aspects of Godot theme, it should be easy to see how relevant are the Text-wise questions posited by Levy and the answers—rather, the evasive non-answers—suggested alongwith.[2] In this catechism, I believe, the references to the telling of the story pertain to human evolution, and the questions are being answered by Everyman who is familiar with men of all ages and all climes. Indeed, this Everyman has been always wondering about why, when, where and whence of existence and asking the same questions over and over again without ever getting any final answer.

According to Levy, Text I asks, 'Why did I start the narrative?' and parries the question with 'I am doing the same thing over and over again'. Yes, indeed, although Man has been going on with his story (= evolution), he does not know his aim, his 'story' has made no progress, and his only achievement lies in repeating the same thing again and again. Thus the speaker wonders, 'How can I go on, I shouldn't have begun, no I had to begin' (*NK*, 71). According to Levy, the question raised in Text II is: 'Where can I go with my story', and the answer tends to be: There is no more any hope of going anywhere—neither 'up there', nor 'down here'. In Text III, the question, 'What matter who's speaking?' is evaded with, 'No one has spoken.' That is as good as saying that there has been no real story in the past, and in the future, too, one would always have the same sense of no-event, no-story. Indeed, as in the past, 'Here, nothing will happen here, no one will be here, for many a long day' (*NK*, 86).

Thanks to this tenor of evolution in which departure is as 'impossible' as stay or survival, an evening cannot be told from morning. No wonder in Text IV we have, 'This evening, I say this evening, perhaps it's morning' (*NK*, 88). And the answer to the question, 'Who is narrating, claiming to be me?' is 'As soon as I speak, the voice is no longer mine'. In fact, to want to have a story is a mistake. In any case, the problem is the same old one: 'Where could I go, if I could go, who could I be if I could be . . .' (*NK*, 87). Because of this inalienable sense of failure, man has always felt guilty. Hence the legal imagery in Text V where the narrator is at once the judge and the party, the witness and the advocate, and above all, the court-clerk recording everything and feeling tired of the toil of asking questions. In this interplay of roles, characters may appear to be different, but the result would be always the same. In Text VI, the question is: 'How are the intervals filled between these apparitions?' And the answer is: 'If I could enter an interval and know that I was in one, then perhaps I could at last begin a story that would end.' Since that is not possible, he has to live on hopes and be content even with little achievement. Who knows there may be some stone still unturned. He better make sure before he gives up and reports himself missing. In Text VII, he is likened to a passenger in a third-class compartment who has been waiting for ages for the train to start; he should have reached the destination long ago, but is still at the starting point. Should he give up waiting in despair? No, his ticket is valid for life and if ever the train leaves he will find himself moving. 'Were things always so?' That is the question Text VIII begs with 'I have always been asking that question'. The trouble is that even silence cannot be considered vacant any more: 'But if I were silent the other sounds would start again' (*NK*, 107). If there is no way out, the question arises, 'Why don't I say, "There's a way out there"?' Text IX replies, 'If I could say it, I would pass out of there'. The emergence of man from the inferno of his own making is as far away as ever.

Can effort alone be enough—can mere utterance make sense? Text X answers this question by reminding that the idea behind the attempt is just to go on. In Text XI, the question is 'What am I saying?', the answer being, 'That is all that I can have had to say'. Of course, the choice is again between ending and continuing and the wish once again is, 'I shouldn't have begun'. Characteristically he adds later, 'I have stopped, but I never stirred . . . I am dead, but I never lived' (*NK*, 126). In such a situation, can man ever realize what he is going to be in the long run? The answer in Text XII is, '. . . it's all down the drain, nothing ever as much as begun'. Effort for its own sake, without results—that is how it was in the past and how it will be in future.

The voice does not cease even in Text XIII. In fact, it is here that the dilemma of 'screaming silence of no's knife in yes's wound' (*NK*, 135) concretizes and the ultimate question, 'How do I get out of here?' is answered with 'I am nowhere'. How can there be a voice without a mouth; can one speak of things that don't exist; can one silence the silence itself? Such are the questions that one finds asking oneself when the texts conclude. These comprise, as it were, the coda of the *Texts for Nothing*—and Beckett's credo, too! But more than anything else, they sum up the dilemma of Man, the existential artist.

'From An Abandoned Work' (1956), too, has received from critics little attention because they take its title literally and regard it as a part of the work that was not pursued to the finish. In doing this, it is forgotten that Beckett thought it fit to translate it into French. Surely, no one translates a scrap of abandoned or aborted opus. For me, the reference to the abandonment in the title pertains not to this literary creation but to the creative work of Life Force—man's incomplete evolution. The narrator could be Man, his mother and his father being Nature and God, respectively.

It is possible to take a cue from Ruby Cohn[3] and treat the work as a short picaresque novella recounting three days of journeying—days which get assimilated into Everyday even as the narrator turns out to be Everyman. A compulsive walker and talker, he wishes for the end and yet cannot end; he hates things that move and yet he is always moving; his own realm is chaotic and yet he lectures on cosmology. Aptly enough, this speaker, standing for Man, indicates that although he has no definite destination, he is 'on my way'. Not surprisingly, his (evolutionary) progress is marked either by bursts of speed or by slow steps: 'With me all was slow, and then these flashes, or gushes' (*NK*, 142). Anyway, Man need not necessarily have any regret:

> No, I regret nothing, all I regret is having been born, dying is such a long tiresome business I always found. But let me get on now from where I left off, the white horse and then the rage, no connexion, I suppose. But why go on with all this, I don't know, some day I must end, why not now (*NK*, 142-3).

When the narrator says, 'I was mad of course and still am, but harmless' (*NK*, 144), he is probably referring to man's freakish origin—abnormal but harmless. Indeed, it is ironic that this seemingly harmless being has ravaged his mother (Nature) and killed his father (God).

Aptly, the narrator had had falls aplenty, but every time he would pick himself and go on. But what is the stage that he has ultimately reached? None, for he has abandoned the effort. Such midway 'abandonment' in the very act of progress is as proper a close as any other in Beckett's fiction.

In *How It Is* (1960) we have the 'thing itself'—the tenor of life as it is. Like life, the text here is interesting but difficult to understand, especially because there are no periods and other marks of punctuation. Since life runs eternally without any break, the quality of life is reflected in a voice without pauses; its want of uniformity is suggested through irregular rhythm. Perhaps that is also the reason why, despite a beginning, a middle and an end, there is no plot; nor even the minimal remnants of realism. Indeed, realism would have prompted one to look for meaning in what Beckett believes to be basically unintelligible. In spite of the cataract of words, the narrator continues to claim that he is still without a voice. As I understand it, *How It Is* is a myth about Life Force in its relationship with Man—life before and after the advent of primordial man (Pim) on the earth.

The protagonist's agonizing journey in the dark in Part I ('Before Pim') pertains to life on the earth before man was created—a helpless life. That the reference to 'life up there in the light' pertains to life in Paradise is borne out by the fact that life there was loveless and without free will. In Part II ('With Pim'), we have the stage when the narrator meets Pim—that is, Life Force started its interaction with the new species called Man. In their first meeting, when the narrator places hand on Pim, it recoils—a clear reference to man's being a freakish being. However, soon, the hand settles there with a sense of ownership—a patron's hand, so to say. Frightened, Pim cries which signifies man's ontological insecurity. That is overcome by training in communication through speech and song. Training in speech takes ages and it is followed by that in writing—a matter of ages once again. Since Pim is inconspicuous because of his silence, Kram and Krim—other species—start feeling that Pim is possibly dead. Even the narrator writes END on his back. One could say that the progress of man was so exasperatingly slow that Life Force felt like withdrawing its patronage.

Pim's exit signifies not the extinction of man but the end of prehistoric primitivism. In Part III ('After Pim'), we have a series of Pim-surrogates who symbolize ages in human history. In a way, it extends the Bom-Pim relationship to infinity. One after the other, we have piling of millions of sacks—a suggestion signifying the passing of millennia. When the narrator speculates different ways in which the story could be narrated, it is a way of suggesting the possible ways in which man's evolution could be directed. Implicit in all this are doubts about the wisdom of man's evolution—why these cycles of births and deaths, why God does not leave man in one state permanently, why the procession of tormenting situations, how one age is better than the other, etc. At last everything is swept away leaving behind nothing but mud, darkness and the nameless dying voice.

In short, *How It Is* is an autobiography of Life Force dealing with its uneasy companionship with its protege, Man, whom it gave millions of chances because it had none else to turn to. It is a pity that man has failed to rise to the occasion and is heading towards an impasse when he might die. And with him the Life Force, too! No wonder, the narration closes with, 'I MAY DIE screams I SHALL DIE screams good'. As Pim, Pram, Sam, Bem, etc., who represent successive generations, pass through similar situations of victims and tormentors, the implication is that man's evolution has been beset with problems and counterproblems. After a generation has accumulated some experience, it vanishes; the next generation, instead of making any advance, repeats the previous pattern of relationships and the net result is recurrence rather than progress. The Viconian concept of organic cycles optimistically implies shedding of deadwood and making a new beginning; it is like a circuitous road on the hillside. Beckettian recurrence, on the other hand, implies matrix of surds—meaningless repetition, as in a blind circular alley. Indeed, this is how it is!

But, then, if man were to quit, what would be the resultant position? Even if Life Force continues to patronize some other species, everthing would be so dull and listless. After all, whatever activity there is in the world, it is because of Man. In his absence, there might be more peace but, shorn of colourful variety, earth would be just a white, colourless rotunda. Since Man alone has the discerning eye to perceive beauty and thus monopolizes that kind of imagination, his death would spell the death of imagination itself. Perhaps man alone can imagine the difference his departure would make to the world because imagination is needed even to envision a state in which man (= 'imagination') is no more. Indeed, 'Imagination Dead Imagine' (1965) is an attempt to visualize that state of the earth without man.

As earth would be then like some uninhabited planet, Hugh Kenner has mistaken the description for a space-travel fantasy;[4] but, in fact, the white rotunda is our earth itself. Light and temperature would keep changing to yield days, nights and seasons but, there being no man, there shall be no one to make distinctions. As this kind of existence would be like life in an incubator or in a womb, the male and female of some future species would be just two bodies in two semi-circles lying back to back in a foetal position—perhaps murmuring but not moving. They would open their eyes at intervals, or react to sound with infinitesimal shudders. But, otherwise, there would be no motion, no emotion, no love, no voice, no thought, no trace of what we men regard as life. Must man make an exit and reduce the world to this? The answer is implied rather than stated. No, he must continue to control life through his will, intuition and imagination, howsoever fitful or futile it might be.

'Imagination dead. Imagine!' That is the opening line of 'All Strange Away'. But instead of concentrating on the visual sense, stress here is on the auditory stimuli. Intent on the need to imagine something rather than nothing, the mind here concentrates on sounds. In a hollow glass rotunda, a figure is encased. Surrounded by the mirrored walls and the sounds of his voice, the narrator talks himself to 'silence'. Even otherwise, most of the time, it is sound too faint for mortal ears. In fact, here is a situation in which all senses of perception have weakened to near-absence. As I look at it, the figure represents Man in his microcosm subjected to the tyranny of an endless diminishing cycle.

If *How It Is* presented life with Pim, 'Enough' (1966) presents life with 'him'. The two had worked with and for each other, had the same desires, same needs and same satisfactions. Yet as soon as the word 'leave' was uttered, it was obeyed even without 'his' asking whether it was an injunction for temporary stepping aside or a permanent departure. Now, having lived without 'him' for a long time, the narrator is trying to suppress the regretful memories on the plea that 'his' leaving was inevitable.

But, then, who is this 'he' and how is he related to the narrator? I suggest that the narrator here is Life Force talking about 'him', i.e. Man. It is long after the death of imagination—that is, after man's extinction, following the withdrawal of its patronage by the exasperated Life Force. Man left as soon as he received the order—without argument or pleas for another chance. His departure has really made a difference to Life Force that is now seen recollecting its life with 'him'. Thus seen, 'Enough' is an allegorical version of human history—how mankind and Life Force supported each other, how the former was brought up by the latter and taught to communicate, how, but for their sudden parting, the two could have accomplished something. 'It was then I shall have lived then or never' (*NK*, 157), Life Force is found telling itself. Of course, it is no use regretting now and asking the questions that were never asked then; 'All that goes before forget,' says the opening sentence (*NK*, 153). Anyway, there had to be a parting at one stage or the other. Who knows a later parting might have led them to a far worse situation? It might be interesting to indulge in permutations with regard to those possibilities vis-a-vis partings delayed or immediate, with or without communication; but one thing is certain that there had to be a parting because 'too much at a time is too much' (*NK*, 153). As enough is enough, even now the best thing would be to remain content with the memory of life with 'him'. As for the use of such a memory, it is like the grafting of flowers on a tombstone—or an old woman's feeling a thrill when imagining the touch of her dead lover's old hand on her withered breasts.

If some god, angel or an inhabitant of one of the planets were to view the goings-on on the earth and assess man's role here without applying the human standards, how will the things appear to him? Perhaps the human beings would look to him like some creatures in a laboratory being subjected to Pavlovian experiments. Breathing in a cylinder in which light and temperature keep changing, some of these 'bodies' might appear to move unceasingly, some absolutely still, some circulating when disturbed, and some others moving, halting and moving again. At times there would appear a tendency to go up the ladder but only to jump back to the bottom of the cylinder. Indeed, such is the situation in 'The Lost Ones' (1966).[5] Going by appearances, the goings-on within the cylinder seem absurd—at least without significance. One gets the impression that it is a kind of game in which the main thing is to maintain a certain pattern of movements within the narrow space. However, if one looks at the game, closely and for long, one starts discerning in the movements certain possibilities which gradually provoke one to ask once again all those uncomfortable questions about the who, why, and how of it all. Perhaps it would be helpful to state the bare facts as they appear. Firstly, here is a tribe of naked bodies pursuing a barren existence in forbidding conditions. Secondly, they are incessantly following a certain pattern of respective movements which appear to be compulsive, as if predetermined. Thirdly, the movements are either circular, round and round, or up and down the ladders. Fourthly, there is no fixed goal unless it be the desire of ensuring the continuation of their movements ad infinitum. Lastly, they appear to be seekers seeking nothing in particular and therefore pursuing a search as a habit with unseeing eyes.

When all the above 'facts' are put together, immediately one can perceive in the story an allegorical presentation of human existence in the microcosm of man's own making. Even though he is a victim of necessity, at least in the patterns of his own 'movements', he is exercising his free will. Always busy with one activity or the other, he is just carrying on as if continuation were the end in itself—a situation that has resulted in activity without achievement, repetition without end. Indeed, like the 'climbers' here, men have been going up and down the ladders of civilizations so often that they have forgotten what they are seeking. In other words, the seekers, too, have become the lost ones.

Now, the different parts of 'The Lost Ones' describe various things but, when all is said and done, it boils down to the quality of human life in diverse ages—essentially the same despite slight variations. If light is taken as a reference to intelligence and heat to passion, the allegory points to the advent and exit of civilizations that oscillate with the intelligence and passion of man. As for the ladders, these could signify the rise and fall of civilizations. The want of smooth progress in human evolution is indicated by the fact that there are random gaps in the steps of these ladders. Anyway, the only sound in the near-silence of the cylinder pertains to these ladders being adjusted. It is a way of saying that man's efforts are producing no impact except in the form of the scribbling sounds made by the signatures of different civilizations.

Since the restless movements result from search-motivation of man, the four types of movements in the cylinder correspond to the four groups of searchers—those mobile ones who are always searching; those vanquished ones who search no more and therefore sit along the wall; those who occasionally pause in their search to resume it after a brief halt; and those sedentary ones who start again only when forced to Perhaps these groups can be treated as different stages of man's will to continue the search for Godot, the superman.[6] Indeed, innumerable generations of humanity have been 'seeking' him with varying degrees of enthusiasm, ranging from feverish vigour to total exhaustion. Of course, in certain cases, the mission having been forgotten, the effort has been either given up or else become mechanical. Anyway, the hope is still there so much so that one could say that the ordering principle of the restless movement is some kind of waiting. Will this waiting ever yield the desired result, and will man ever succeed in his mission? Or must the searchers always continue to remain lost in the search and end up as the vanquished? The questions remain unanswered as in ***Waiting for Godot.***

If 'The Lost Ones' presents mankind in a cylinder, 'Ping' (1967) places man in a minimal cell. In fact, Beckett had once declared that 'Bing'—the French title for 'Ping' in English—could be regarded as the miniaturization of 'The Lost ones'. But what exactly is the story told here? Words in 'Ping' are important not for what they tell or mean but what shapes they assume. It is possibly to erase the distinction between form and content that both the content (body) and the container (interior of the box) are equally white so much so that we have the case of 'white upon white invisible'. And precisely like the naked bodies moving in 'The Lost Ones', in 'Ping' the words are juggled around to yield ever-changing patterns. No wonder, just 120 words have been so permuted and combined in different ways as to create a text of a single paragraph of 1030 words. What is more, since the words don't aim at presenting a story—imitation of an 'action' which is usually specified by verbs—there are no verbs at all. Instead, what we have is a collage of phrases. Comprising the same set of words in different permutations, these phrases appear so alike even though they are by no means the same. That has prompted Hugh Kenner to see a kinship between this technique of repeating phrases on the one hand and the scanning of frames in a film on the other.[7] In the latter, individually the differences are infinitesimally small and therefore almost invisible to the naked eye; but cumulatively they project a big, changing perspective. One could extend this suggestion and say that story of human life is like a film-shot in which each successive stage marks an almost imperceptible change. Conversely, one could argue that if each snap corresponds to a generation, it means that, despite the length of its duration, man's evolution has amounted to minimal change. To put it differently, progress of human existence is marked not by big changes, bangs, but by a series of whimpers. That makes an age covering decades or centuries no more than a sonar echo of a bell, a PING.

In *Lessness* (1970), we again have short phrases permuted and combined to create sixty sentences, each of which is repeated twice to produce 24 paragraphs of uneven lengths. In this juggling, the unit is not a word but a phrase—in fact, a whole sentence. Both the number of sentences in a paragraph and their sequences were determined by picking up slips literally out of Beckett's hat. The implication possibly is that such is the random way the elements have been mixed in life to create repetitions with variations. Anyway, most critics have tried to read meaning in the structure itself.In this collage of fragments and segments, allotropic sentences have been recycled to imitate a process in which the whole goes nowhere but just moves round and through itself; what is more, the movement is as slow as it is repetitive and circular.

Reading paragraph after paragraph with similar but not the same contents, one tends to hear in the recycled sentences a kind of chant and perceive in the tenor of the paragraphs a ritual of recurrence. That makes one recall that in the history of man, too, things have happened not once but umpteen times. Even cataclysmic experiences. Every time, man has risen again like the phoenix from its ashes—only, in his case, the restart has always been along a new line. If the opening paragraph exudes a sense of relief that at long last a true refuge has been constructed, one has a feeling at the end that, after the nuclear holocaust, too, man is going to start again—by using the ruins as his refuge. Repeating the past, he would rise again, curse God again, suffer again, until he is punished with yet another cataclysm which would however be yet another starting point, and so on. This makes inexhaustible not only life but 'lessness' too. In fact, here one recalls Zeno's paradoxes—diminishing towards zero but never reaching it. In being too small lies the infinity of a milletgrain; in being all-too-mortal lies the 'immortality' of Man.

When Beckett grouped eight of his shorts under 'Fizzles' (1972), was he dismissing them as stale and stinking work that had failed to rise above the level of meek, inaudible farts? Or was he referring to his own eternal problem as a writer with regard to the expressing of the inexpressible which amounted to creating no more than 'fundamental sounds' in every sense?[8] To me it appears that more than his own art it was in Man's art of evolution that Beckett saw a resemblance to fizzling because man's efforts, too, have been yielding just airy nothing—promising build-ups of big bangs which however end up in whimpersome fiascos.

Now, fizzles are fizzles and their sequence is as immaterial as their nature or the length of their sounds. Each fizzle is independent and scarcely related to the others—something one could say about the eight 'fizzles' here. No wonder Beckett juggled with their orders in different editions and kept changing and reshuffling their titles. In any case, it is interesting to note the nature of the titles as they stand now finally: 'For to End Yet Again'; 'Still'; 'Closed Space'; 'He is Barehead'; 'Horn Came Always'; 'Afar a Bird'; 'I Gave Up Before Birth'; and 'Old Earth'. Obviously, most of them get linked on the one hand to scatological purgation and on the other to man's evolution—the process of ending again to start again. Taken together, these fizzles trace a progress from a restart to another fiasco which bristles nevertheless with a hope of a newer beginning—an endless diminishing cycle. This is as good as saying that even if life is an experience of Nothingness, it is an experience nevertheless. Taken individually, the theme in each piece is either minimum of being or maximum of Nothingness. Unable to accept stasis, man has on the one hand been seeking solace in onward evolution and on the other feeling compelled to 'return to the other terminus and start again'. This amounts to launching another story when the old one is still on. And thus does man's heroic effort inevitably get always reduced to a fizzle—rather, to a series of fizzles.

'A voice comes to one in the dark. Imagine.' That is how *Company* (1977-9) begins. And when this voice asks, 'Are you on your back in the dark . . . Are you in fact alone?' the question strikes, as it were, the keynote of the novel. Is one really alone when lying supine in darkness? How about the company of one's memories—the fizzles of experience? After all, archetypally, company is anything and everything that facilitates escape from oneself. Thus seen, company is never absent. And yet, at the same time, it is never actually achieved even when interacting with others, because one's own self is always in a flux. That makes the need for company as absolute as its impossibility. This paradox inheres the very human condition itself, as epitomized in the medieval image of Everyman who failed to find anyone to accompany him on his last journey. Even otherwise, what is human life if not the process of creation born of man's need to fabricate company? That, however, is countered by the fact of the 'others' being hell. Hence the contrary pulls in the novel.

As the story proceeds with the life of a mute and lonely being in the form of anecdotes about his boyhood, manhood and old age, everything is seen marked by doubt, uncertainty, ambiguity, and dichotomy. Indeed, here is an illustration of how Man's desire to soar is checked by the pull of the earth. That man's ambitious effort is no more than exhaling as well as inhaling of breath is suggested through the name H Aspirate Haitch.[9] The middle name should bring to mind on the one hand blowing of air, in and out, and on the other the act of aspiring to achieve some goal. The H's that precede and succeed it are onomatopoeic sounds of letting the air out—say, when a balloon is pricked. A part of the buttock is also called aitch-bone, and that makes Haitch here a tell-tale name of a man reclining on his arses and letting out air from his fundament. Such, indeed, is the quality of human effort to bring meaning into life through collective efforts, because basically Man is incapable of company and therefore integration. In short, *Company* signifies the expression of the despair of the fragmented soul of man who finds that his aspiration to evolve through integration has yielded results that are as insubstantial as farts and fizzles.

In the next, equally short novel, 'Ill Seen Ill Said' (1981), we have the story of 'this old so dying woman'—a widow in the evening of her life approaching the night of death in a situation when all is lost. She is practically dead even when still breathing, for all her activities are confined to belaboured visits to and from her husband's tomb. At the end, there is 'still life'—an ambiguous expression which tends to cover punningly both life and death. The action of the novel pertains to the fact that whereas her eye stares unseeingly on the physical world, in fact it is on the other world that her mental eye is fixed. That obliterates gradually the distinction between what she sees and what she imagines, where she goes and where she imagines herself going. Indeed, at one stage it becomes impossible to tell whither she is moving and whether she is moving at all. To us it appears that she is old Humanity who claims to be moving ahead while, in fact, she is just where she has always been. Having deluded herself with notions of high significance with regard to her position in the universe, humanity is so cut off from reality that she can no longer tell a fact from the fiction of her own creating. Anyway, before Man started his game of self-deception, the universe was as good as dead—still; after him, too, surely it is going to be still once again—as implied by the end when the globe of the eyes merge with the dying globe of the earth. Indeed, between such extremes of not-being, Man has had his being, but that too has been a version of non-being—'still life'. And all this because, primarily, it has been a case of ill-seen, ill-said.

Ill-seeing and ill-saying became misseeing and missaying in *Worstward Ho* (1983) which is, in fact, a veritable coda for the entire body of Beckett's creativity. Indeed, one hears echoes of many a Beckett protagonist when the voice observes right in the opening sentence: 'On. Say on. Be said on. Somehow on. Till nohow on. Said nohow on.' Or when it adds a little later: 'All of old. Nothing else ever. Ever tried. Ever failed. No matter. Try again. Fail again, Fail better' (*WH*, 7). How his last novel accommodates most of the typically Beckettian motifs would be clear if we put together all the key words or phrases that are juggled again and again to comprise the core of the narrative:

Said missaid. Seen misseen. A body. A place. Try again. Fail again. Dim light source unknown. Stand. Kneel. Head sunk on crippled hands. Void. Boundless. Beyondless. Thenceless. Thitherless. Old man and child. Hand in hand. Unchanged. Each time somehow changed. Bad. Worse still. Battered for worse. Enough. Secretes. Oozes. Blank. Time gone when nowhow on. Back. Praying. Gnawing. Gone for good. Skulll. Gravestones.

True, it is not clear who is speaking and what it is that is said or missaid. But the things that manage to register most on one's mind are parody of the creation followed by an ever-oozing half-life which ends in a situation that is so akin to the opening scenario. No wonder one thinks on the one hand of endless continuance and on the other of birth astride of a grave. It is possible to say that here is an account of the story of an individual as he half-lives at every stage from womb to tomb. All this can, of course, be related also to the history of Man. His existence in the universe as a freakish species had been as insecure as an unborn child suspended in the womb until the stage of birth. Exploiting his erect spine and skull, he has been making efforts to go on and on, albeit in a state of half-living. With things having changed despite the sameness of the essentials, it is difficult to tell whether the process has implied an upward evolution or worstward decline. Thus seen, *Worstward Ho* becomes Beckett's last testament in which he has paid a high tribute to human tenacity—to man's creativity in giving shape to what he had in hand, i.e. 'Nothing'. Aptly enough, the novel ends as it begins—not with a 'no' but with its obverse, viz., 'on'.

At bounds of boundless void. Whence no farther. Best worse no farther. Nohow less. Nohow worse. Nohow naught. Nohow on. Said Nohow on. (*WH*, 47).

Here is, so to say, an affirmation of the boundless void. Man must continue even if it means moving backward towards worse or even the worst. So long as it enables him to move on and on, it is better than nothing. After all, if there is no point in proceeding through life, there is no alternative either. No wonder the voice, despite the longing to be gone, wishes, 'Naught best. Best worse' (*WH*, 31).

11 The End of Rainbow

As maintained throughout this book, Beckett's entire work is an exercise in reiteration, rephrasing and recasting of the same world-view as was projected elaborately in *Godot*. Indeed, most frustrating and endless has been man's waiting for Superman—a hopeless hope which has enabled him to survive somehow. The pity is that he can move neither on nor off the road of evolution. Instead, like Hamm, he 'remains'—remains where he was only to pass through similar, if not the same, experiences. Perhaps, having come 'out . . . into this world . . . before its time', the human race was congenitally too impotent to evolve. In other words, 'Birth was the death of him' and that has made womb and tomb undistinguishable in his case. Subjected to the tyranny of time, the double-headed monster of damnation and salvation, he stands eternally condemned to the forces of both life and death. The evolution of Man is thus a worstward journey in which progressive 'lessness' never reaches the stage of total absence—thanks to Life Force who, willy-nilly, lends a helping hand to keep the rock going. That has made Man's life an exercise in ending the unendable—never quitting and yet never approaching the goal. This game of piercing Yes with No's knife has made human life an endless series of texts for nothing in which man does nothing except ask himself: 'Where would I go if I could go, who would I be, if I could be, what would I say, if I had a voice.' Man will get the answer possibly when he ceases to be man by becoming Superman—that is, Godot. But when will that be and how, nobody knows. At least not Beckett who was amused to find man climbing up and down the ladders of civilization—very like Sisyphus in his unending toil.

Why this hurly-burly of creation-cum-decreation, evolution as well as degeneration? Beckett has never explained. Instead of writing ***about*** the mystique of existence, he has been content with the mystique itself. No wonder, he never takes sides and lets 'perhaps' pass as the core of his philosophy. According to my reading, Beckett sees the source of Man's trouble in his seeking to evolve a world of his own through civilizations. In effect, it amounts to violating the fundamental laws of nature with respect to what Darwin calls natural selection of chance variations. Caught between the pulls of Nature and Civilization, man is a battle-ground where forces of eugenics and euthenics are engaged in a see-saw war which seems fated to run for millions of years. Whether this will end in the emergence of Superman or the extinction of human species is anybody's guess. As things stand, there is scope neither of hoping too much nor of despairing too much because the chance of man's salvation is only as high as that of his damnation. This hopeless hope with regard to man's fate in the context of the rise and fall of so many civilizations is the very crux of Beckett's works. That also explains the profusion of such motifs as quests and questions, journeys and ladders, crawling and cycling, jars and rotundas, ruins and immobility, grey colour and dying light, sounds and stills, solitude and monologuing, story-telling and listening, etc.

Now, if every work had to be a variation of the same theme, why did Beckett keep repeating himself? Surely, it was not a case of aridity of imagination. Somehow one has a feeling that the repetition is akin to creating ever-new variations of the same myth. As soon as one thinks of this possibility, several myths do come to one's mind, and yet none of them would fit the slot. On a closer look, however, it would appear that, consciously or unconsciously, Beckett's aim was creation of a new myth.

In the recorded history, never perhaps did man feel the need for creating myths more acutely than in the twentieth century. Zola's seeking mystique in the literal fact, Yeats's creating a mythology of the lunar phases, D H Lawrence's worshipping the dark fire in the blood are only some of the many attempts at making myths in our century. Understandably enough, none of these enjoyed the universality associated with myths proper. The myths created by Marx, Freud and Frazer did have a more pervasive appeal but not the power and absolute authority of the traditional mythology. After all, mythology being the work of collective unconscious, myths are not created by individuals. Beckett knew this only too well. Thus, instead of undertaking to create a mythological hero that may assume a thousand faces, he preferred to create those thousand faces. The idea was that, taken together, his works might implant in the mind of his reader an outline of that unformulated myth. Instead of assuming an archetype, he attempted a collage of such types as had mutual affinity. As type is not an abridgement but a condensation, piling of types in Beckett leads to a density that almost approximates the wholeness of an archetype. But, then, howsoever numerous, finite parts can never be added up to infinity. No wonder, therefore, Beckett's collage has the quality of a myth but it never acquires the totality and universality of a myth.

Once one concedes mythopoeic dimension to Beckett's imagination, the question arises what it was that he possibly meant to employ as the warp and woof of the myth that he would have liked to create. Since a myth must epitomize the weltanschauung of its age—the collective unconscious, the socio-historical forces, the religious beliefs, the philosophical strands, the scientific theories, the aesthetic approaches, etc.—Beckettian myth also had to be a composite response to the emotional, intellectual, psychological, spiritual and political undercurrents of his times. Tempered by the genius of Marx, Freud, Jung, Bergson, Proust, Laing, Einstein, Wittgenstein, Sartre et al., the twentieth century has been the age of relativity, quantum theory, electronics, vitalism, existentialism, etc. Indeed, accommodating the core of modern physics, gestalt psychology, contemporary sociology and space-age cosmology, any representative myth of this age had to reckon with the divided self, the separation of subject and object, the indeterminacy of time and space, the inevitability of change and movement, the evolution of man and the absurd. In short, Beckett's world view had to be rooted in man's relationship to matter, to his own self, to the others, and to the universe as a whole. It is not surprising, therefore, that in Beckett's works, man's position in the universe corresponds to that of electrons in an atom—always changing and releasing in the process more and more energy in direct proportion to the progressive diminution of matter towards nothingness. Likewise, in Beckettian flux of the 'selves', one may perceive something like the interplay of waves and particles in light. Perhaps that explains why Beckett's works are marked by minimalism and interplay of contraries, why time and space are always changing, why he is obsessed with repetition and recurrence, why there is a constant tendency to go back to the starting point, and why there is perceptual disorientation.

Of course, Beckett never talked about evolving a myth, but each work of his sounds like a myth in the making. What is more, one has a feeling that it is the same myth struggling to be born again and again. Hence the recurrence of motifs. Here are tramps on their eternal journeys moving towards a goal that does not exist. Here are quests for the questers, artists telling stories when they have nothing to narrate, speakers speaking incessantly just to say Nothing. In this world dominated by paradoxes, one encounters heroic impotence, irrational logic, silence that resounds. With voices echoing echoes, images mirroring mirror images, stories about story-telling and myths about myth-making, it is always a most chaotic world. However, when details are forgotten, what remains etched on one's mind is not nihilistic despair but something positive—indomitable spirit of going on, celebration of unconquerable gaiety in the face of the absurd. It is as if the search for zero had led to the discovery of infinity. If evolution climaxes in Nothingness, chaos crystalizes into a dome of many-splendoured glass. To put it differently, the myth which is struggling to express itself in Beckett's works is a myth of impasse—about an antihero who is a hero nevertheless. He is like a colossus astride the shores of Yes and No, only he does not have the stature of Colossus.

As Beckett seems to yoke together Sisyphus and Prometheus, Genesis and Apocalypse, creation and decreation, one feels convinced that the unformulated myth is rooted in man's evolution-cum-regression. No wonder, progress and decadence are so balanced that each and every thing is discovered to be its own antithesis, too. Here, beginning and end, birth and death, growth and decay, survival and extinction emerge as different facets of the self-same phenomenon. In the resultant handy-dandy, fact and fiction, matter and spirit, action and non-action, knowledge and ignorance, impotence and endurance, tend to be interchangeable terms. No wonder, in the paradoxical world of Beckett, it is hard to distinguish between rational and irrational, self and not-I, subjectivity and objectivity, good and evil, silence and speech, salvation and damnation, Nirvana and inferno. Here Yes seems to come out of No, even as No appears to dissolve into Yes. On the one hand it is a case of constantly-dying-but-never-dead and on the other it is a kind of mirage that doesn't exist but is clearly there. It is a hopeless pursuit but full of fun that makes man's paradoxical impasse a source of liberation as well as of frustration. In man's not making any outward progress lies the very chance of his continuing for ever.

Obviously, to express his kind of vision, Beckett needed a different kind of drama. After all, linear perspective of traditional drama was meant to accommodate stability, orderliness, objectivity, cause-effect sequencing. As Beckett's peculiar concerns called for a self-cancelling, circular perspective, there is something spiral-like about his dramaturgy. Since no such dramaturgy was available to him ready-made, he had to evolve it through a series of experiments in which he had to try different possibilities one by one—repetitively, with slight variations. Similar but not the same—that is what one could say about his art, too. Thus, in a way, Beckett as a creative artist was no different from man as an existential artist. Both have been playing the endgame of creation and decreation, going on and on, ever on the verge of ending or quitting but always resuming it forthwith. If there is neither any point in proceeding through life nor any alternative, one could say the same about Beckett's creativity. If life is 'absurd', so is Beckett's work; both are intriguing and mysterious. Indeed, whether we have in mind human life or Beckett's work, we can say with equal justification: sweet are the uses of absurdity.

Finally, does all this that has been said in this book mean anything? Mean? 'What's it meant to mean?' 'That is all I could manage, more than I could.'

'Make sense who may. I switch off.'

Notes

1 GODOT: A NEW INTERPRETATION

1 *The Dismemberment of Orpheus* (Wisconsin: Univ. of Wisconsin, 1982), 238.
2 Quoted in 'In Search of Beckett', *Beckett at 60* (London: Calder & Boyars, 1967), 29.
3 Quoted W Y Tindall, *Samuel Beckett* (New York: Columbia Univ. Press, 1964), 6.
4 Quoted by Peter Bull, 'An Actor's Recollections', *Casebook on Waiting for Godot*, ed. Ruby Cohn (New York: Grove Press, 1967), 39.
5 *Twentieth Century Drama* (London: Hutchinson Univ. Library, 1962), 187.
6 'The Talent of Samuel Beckett', *Casebook* (1967), 59.
7 Review reproduced in *Casebook* (1967), 11-12. What fierce controversies were provoked by the play, how Godotology was haunted by philosophical, anthropological, theological, Freudian, Jungian, Marxist or Bergsonian approaches, and how differently the critics approached the problems of the play with regard to title, situation, genre, characters, meaning, etc., was fairly reflected in Melvin J Friedman's 'Crritic' in a special Beckett number of *Modern Drama* IX, 3 (Dec. 1966), 300-8.
8 Though such a conclave never took place, what follows in the text is based on actual opinions drawn from diverse critical studies.
9 For the origin of this oft-quoted remark, see Alan Schneider's 'Waiting for Godot: A Personal Chronicle' in *Chelsea Review*, No. 2, Sept. 1958—reproduced in *Casebook* (1967), 55.
10 Quoted by Alec Reid, *All I Can Manage, More Than I Could* (Dublin: Dolmen Press, 1968), 34.
11 *Samuel Beckett* (London: Bowes & Bowes, 1965), 94.
12 According to Balwant Gargi, a celebrated Indian playwright and director, what Martin Esslin has recorded about the impact of the play at San Quentin is altogether misleading because it is based on

Herbert Blau's description rather than on Esslin's own observations. Esslin was not present, Gargi was and he found it a hopeless production that just bored. Gargi believes that a play about boredom need not be boring. Polonius and Malvolio, he argues, may be big bores in life but, as characters on the stage, they entertain the audience. Surely, Beckett did not mean his audience to experience boredom; had that been the real aim, why cram this 'tragicomedy' with all those comic antics?

13 *All I can Manage*, 51.

14 See *Beckett: Waiting for Godot*—Casebook Series (London: Macmillan, 1987), 62-7 & 67-70, respectively.

15 *Dismemberment of Orpheus*, 239.

16 *Samuel Beckett: A New Approach* (London: Dent, 1970), 100.

17 'A Public Notice on Waiting for Godot', rep. *Casebook* (1967), 72.

18 M C Bradbrook has made a tickling discovery that in Chinese Didi and Gogo are names meaning big and little brother, respectively.

19 Vladimir, it should be noted, enters the stage with short, stiff strides, legs wide apart. Naturalistically, it is related to prostrate glands which account for his uneasy pissing. But metaphorically speaking, flawed pissing by the mental self should mean imperfect intellection of man and his consequently slow and awkward gait on the journey of evolution.

20 It is not for nothing that Pozzo is an Italian name and his treatment of Lucky brings to mind Hitler's tyranny towards the Jews in general and intellectuals in particular. One may even trace in the play elements of Soviet dictatorship, especially in the way Pozzo is concerned with Lucky's right to the food rather than with his soul.

21 In the original French, Vladimir describes Lucky's dance as 'the death of a lamplighter'. Since lighting receptacle filled with material and wick is called 'God-et', one cannot help seeing some connection between the two. What emerges in the play is the image of a lamplighter sitting on a lamp-post and dying there while waiting in vain for the lighting material to arrive. Translating this image into our interpretation of Godot-theme, it could imply the failure of the human species to realize itself as Superman and make the world bright because of the absence of adequate evolutionary material.

22 See *Modern Drama* IX, 3 (Dec. 1966), 309.

23 In *PMLA* (1960) article, rep. *Casebook* (Grove Press, 1967), 144.

24 'A Public Notice', rep. *Casebook* (1967), 73.

25 In *TLS* (1956) article, rep. *Casebook* (1967), 137.

26 *Samuel Beckett: The Language of Self* (Carbondale: Southern Illinois Univ. Press, 1962), 147-8.

27 See *The Absolute Comic* (New York: Columbia Univ. Press, 1980).

28 *Samuel Beckett* (Boston: Twayne, 1986), 144-5.

29 *Samuel Beckett: A New Approach*, 95.

30 See *Comic Gamut* (New Brunswick: Rutger Univ. Press, 1962), 217.

31 'Samuel Beckett's Waiting for Godot', *Explicator* 35, Fall 1976, 9-10.

32 *The Transformation of Godot* (Lexington: Univ. Press of Kentucky, 1980), 78.

33 That Beckett did have in mind a similar analogy while writing his *Waiting for Godot* is endorsed by the fact that Pozzo is Italian word for 'well'. Frederick Busi who has pointed out this goes on to make a couple of other valuable suggestions. Not infrequently, Pozzo is translated as a pool also. And Puzzo means stench, too. In *The Divine Comedy*, the deep pit in hell is called Pozzo. All this makes Pozzo a kind of cesspool—a symbol of stagnation in which the positive is countered by the negative, and vice-versa.

34 *Angels of Darkness* (London: George Allen & Unwin, 1972), 21.

35 Perhaps that justifies the subtitle of the play—a tragicomedy. It is possible to say that man's effort to persist with his waiting smacks of hubris, but then the protagonist here is by no means a redeemer. Instead of brave deeds and solemn eloquence of a hero, we have the clowning games of a pair of tramps that peter out in dead silence. In a sense, the play is a praody of tragedy, inverting tragic archetypes as if in a distorting mirror. An archetypal hero, according to J Campbell, goes on a journey, encounters adventure, grows wiser by experience, and returns crowned with glory; here Vladimir and Estragon remain on the road and, refusing to move, are condemned to dull routine. And the ones who do move and keep moving are typical comic characters—Pozzo who is boastful like alazon and Lucky who has been cast in the mould of a clown. In short, here are tragically doomed characters caught in funny situations or else clowns caught in the whirlpool of suffering. Here, weighty questions are raised but not pursued, or else they are only turned into nonsense.

36 For example, as mentioned earlier (in the text), Pozzo responds to both Cain and Abel, thus becoming at once the first killer and the first victim of homicide. Likewise, at one stage, Estragon calls himself Adam (*Godot*, 37) and at another compares himself with Christ (*Godot*, 52), which makes him at once the first sinner as well as the redeemer of the sins. Then again, Lucky, who bears the burden of cross, is also the one accused of crucifying Pozzo (*Godot*, 57). In fact, in this handy dandy, it is impossible to tell who is exploiting whom. In another context, Lucky is described as 'Atlas, son of Jupiter', although, in fact, Atlas was a victim of Jupiter's Olympians. The son of Jupiter was Hercules, a human being, while Atlas was god; on the other hand, Atlas was the son of Iapetus, an ancestor of

humanity. Beckett's aim was to stimulate through these confusing associations a balance that should implant in the reader's mind what is perhaps the only logical deduction—that parallel to Viconian transition from the divine to the heroic, there has also been a transition from the heroic to the divine.

37 This state of mind has its root in the structure and style of the play. As James Knowlson has pointed out (Macmillan *Casebook*, 47), 24 per cent of the utterances are questions; stories are never concluded, actions are left deliberately unexplained, and even concrete visual images reveal man essentially befuddled, disoriented, lost and bewildered.

2 PROPHET OF THE MESS

1 Human mind, it must be realized, is neither a manhole where things remain stuck until pulled out, nor is it a cauldron for mixing the ingredients. Nor is it a kind of test tube in which each successive addition would lead to some fresh, transformative chemical reaction. It is customary to trace an influence in isolation, as if the writer had grasped the entire range of the thinker's intellection from the very first day. The way the arguments are built, one would get the impression that nothing whatsoever remained rejected or unassimilated and that either nothing else was ever read and absorbed or all the subsequent readings never made any difference. No less questionable is the assumption that the study of every thinker would necessarily make an impact and that too equally deep in each case. Equally fallacious is the practice of putting all the known influences together as if the writer had read all the books in one sitting and performed, in one long session of meditation, the miracle of evolving associative bridges to integrate all the leading concepts or dissolving all those philosophies to create a world-view. The fact, however, is that the human mind is too individualistic to be similar and predictable. In different cases, entirely different results can accrue. Much should depend on such vital factors as the temper of the writer's age, his own personality, the quality of his mind, his life experiences and attitudes, the previous background, the stage of the growth at the given time, the situation of his accepting a new influence, the order and the mode of reading, etc. The intensity of an impact can vary and so may its duration. One idea might dazzle today but be forgotten within a few days; another might take long to register, then linger on or haunt sporadically, or else impinge spasmodically at most unexpected times. A book read a second time can undo the original impression as easily as it might lead to a greater

understanding, especially if there have been some more formative factors at work. In short, much depends upon the sensibility and specific needs of the person influenced, for these would determine the process of absorption, rejection and assimilation.

2 Quoted by J D O'Hara in 'Introduction' to *Twentieth Century Interpretations of Molloy, Malone Dies, The Unnamable* (Englewood Cliffs, NJ: Prentice Hall, 1970), 9.

3 Beckett to Tom F Driver, quoted O'Hara, ibid., 17.

4 For example, Bruno is quoted in 'Our Exagmination', St Augustine in *Godot*, and Pythagoras and Geulincx in *Murphy*. Likewise, Geulincx is mentioned in 'The End', Kant in 'Three Dialogues', Democritus and Schopenhauer in 'Echo's Bones'. At times Beckett may choose not to mention the names but one may know what his source is. For example, when he refers to two buckets in a well in *Murphy* or to eastward crawling in *How It Is*, a knowledgeable reader cannot miss connections with Heraclitus and Geulincx, respectively. Indeed, whereas 'Our Exagmination' is based on Vico and *Film* on Berkeley's axiom ('to be is to be perceived'), 'Words and Music' parodies Locke and Hume, and *Watt* is a veritable debate with positivists in the vein of Wittgenstein. In 'Whoroscope', the narrator is none other than Descartes himself!

5 Quoted Block & Shedd (eds.), *Masters of Modern Drama* (New York: Random House, 1963), 1103.

6 'Beckett the Magnificent', *Beckett at 60* (London: Calder & Boyars, 1967), 82.

7 *Samuel Beckett* (London: RKP, 1976), 121.

8 Most characteristic of this anti-academic genius was that hoax regarding 'Le Concentrisme' on the Modern Languages Society. It is to this antiacademic core of Beckett's personality that we must turn to realize why he had adapted Corneill's *Le Cid* into a hilarious *Le Kid*, why he was such an inarticulate classroom teacher, and why he gave up teaching altogether even when he had no alternative means of making his living. No wonder Beckett enjoyed spelling academic as 'acacacacademic' (as in Lucky's speech) to hammer home its kinship with that French infantile word for excrement, viz., acaca.

9 A most characteristic trick of Beckett's is implied in Lance St John Butler's suggestion that Beckett is not endorsing the views of Heidegger, Sartre or Hegel but showing what it would mean to live by their respective tenets—a horrible existence in each case. Far from serving as philosophical mouthpieces, Beckett's characters show how ridiculous life would be if the world was really working the way these thinkers believe. Thus, as Butler has demonstrated, Sartre's viscosity becomes ubiquitous mind in *How it is*, Heidegger's 'dasein'

a burial in the earth in *Happy Days*, and royal throne a wheelchair in *Endgame*. In short, Beckett does not adhere to any one school, nor is his a case of eclectic borrowings; instead, philosophical fragments are used for parodic twists or exercises in reduction ad absurdum.

10 See 'Modern Literature . . . a Review for the Teacher', rep. *American Review* (USIS, New Delhi) III, 1 (October 1963), 41-6.

11 *The Modern Temper* (New York: Harcourt, 1956).

12 No wonder, too, the vogue of Darwin, Freud, Nietzsche, Hegel and Marx climaxed in the emergence of the Bergsonian theory of elan vital, Proust's vision of time-in-flux, Hitler's concept of super-race, Frazer's view of cultural anthropology, Camusian version of eternal recurrence in the myth of Sisyphus, and existentialist brand of humanism in Sartre.

13 Published by Macmillan, New York.

14 Ibid., 189.

15 Ibid., 162-3.

16 Evergreen/Grove Press, New York, 1931

17 For example, when it is said that

(a) time is a double-headed monster of damnation and salvation, deformation and transformation (*P*, 1);

(b) man's perceiving self changes from moment to moment and an individual is a succession of individuals (*P*, 8);

(c) memory is a clinical laboratory stocked with poison and remedy, stimulants and sedatives (*P*, 22);

(d) one lies one's life above all to that stranger whose contempt would cause one most pain—one's own self (*P*, 47);

(e) the mortal microcosm cannot forgive the relative immortality of the macrocosm (*P*, 10);

(f) habit is a deadener—the ballast that chains the dog to his vomit (*P*, 8);

(g) when habit fails in its fundamental duty, the boredom of living is replaced by the suffering of being (*P*, 8);

(h) true art is perfectly intelligible and perfectly inexplicable (*P*, 71).

18 See Richard N Coe, *Beckett* in Writers and Critics Series (Edinburgh: Oliver & Boyd, 1968), 18.

19 For Beckett, the absurd inheres not metaphysical emptiness of the universe but in the imperfectibility of human intellect. Attributing irrationality to the universe is a most irrational charge so characteristic of man who, in fact, is himself most irrational. To bring home this point, Beckett frequently ropes in mathematical business. We call a surd an irrational number simply because we don't have the endurance to continue to pursue it to its logical extreme—till

eternity. Irrationality lies in our mind, not in the number. Ditto for the universe. Likewise, we talk of the absolute absence of the Absolute simply because our mind is too determined by relativism to come to grips with the very idea of the Absolute.

20 Quoted by James Knowlson in *Light and Darkness in the Theatre of Samuel Beckett* (London: Turret Books, 1972), 41.

21 Quoted by William Barrett, *Time of Need: Forms of Imagination in the Twentieth Century* (New York: Harper Torchback, 1973), 376.

22 *Shape of Chaos* (Minneopolis: Univ. of Minnesota Press, 1971), 165.

23 Ibid.

24 Quoted O'Hara, loc. cit., 17.

25 Beckett to Tom F Driver, cited *Shape of Chaos*, 165.

26 'Three Dialogues', *Disjecta* (London: John Calder, 1983), 139.

27 See Deidre Bair, *Samuel Beckett* (London: Jonathan Cape, 1978) 209.

3 POETICS OF FAILURE

1 In this context it is interesting to note that time tends to be the theme in practically all his works. Time as hour is the whore in 'Whoroscope'; 'Le Kid' is a farce resulting from the interplay between the wall-clock and the alarm-clock; if the problem in *Waiting for Godot* is how to pass time, in *Endgame* it is how to stop time; concern with time is reflected in the titles of *Happy Days*, 'That Time', even 'All That Fall' (if 'fall' is interpreted as autumn); 'Krapp's Last Tape' is about a man's interpreting the same events at different time-stages of his life; 'Play' also offers three versions of 'that' time; 'Not I' shows openly how 'I' becomes 'Not I' with the passage of time; 'Words and Music' has a speech on the theme of 'Age'; the movements in 'Footfalls' remind one of a pendulum; 'Breath' projects a whole life as a moment in the context of eternity. Indeed, it is possible to say that a Beckettian work is a graph, the twin coordinates of which are Time and Man.

2 Like Clov telling Hamm, 'If they [words] don't mean anything more, teach me others. Or let me be silent' (*Eg*, 32), contemporary writers do have before them that unenviable alternative. But words being their creative tools, they cannot afford to opt for the rhetoric of silence. Ironically, even when George Steiner, Susan Sontag and Ihab Hassan talked about the language, the aesthetics and the literature of silence, they had to use words to show their disgust with words. Indeed, zero-degree writing being impossible, the post-World War writers used words in such a manner as to deny them their traditional role of communicating sense. Chattering and

babbling, for example, has been used as a camouflage of silence. Alternatively, the writers took to experimenting with words to create some kind of new idiom of expression. In the process, the devalued words gained a measure of enrichment through newer patterns of arrangement—something akin to the newer use of dots and splotches in modern painting.

3 See *Modern Tragicomedy and the British Tradition* (Sussex: Harvester Press, 1986), 72.

4 'The Comedy of Samuel Beckett: Something Old, Something New', *Yale French Studies* XXIII, p. 17.

5 See 'Samuel Beckett and the Sheela-Na-Gig', *Kenyon Review* XXIII, 2 (Spring 1961), 299-324.

6 *Dark Comedy* (Cambridge Univ. Press, 1962), 281.

7 And that is as it should be because there cannot be any unilateral response in a work that projects man in the context of both time and eternity. As we view self-at-zero as well as the never-to-be realized dream of a possible absolute, we are struck by an irony. Hence, our wry smile, dry mock or sad laughter. Straddling on the generic borderline, we are intrigued on the one hand by the mystery of life and amused on the other by the mess that man has created in his temerity to mend matters. We raise questions about the limits of man and his world but, finding no solution, express our befuddlement, like a clown, through irrelevant and irreverent blasphemy. Shaken out of both complacency and sentimentality, we laugh at the tragic situation itself. In short, Beckett's plays are parodies of tragedy: instead of offering catharsis or metaphysical solace, they underline the total want of tragic dignity. Indeed, Beckett could not have possibly written tragedy because the trouble with his heroes is that they exist without being born—a situation more comic than tragic.

8 *All I Can Manage, More Than I Could* (Dublin: The Dolmen Press, 1968), 58.

4 ENDING THE UNENDABLE

1 See *Twentieth Century Interpretations of Endgame* (NJ: Prentice Hall, 1969), 51.

2 Quoted Alan Schnieder, 'Letters on Endgame', *Village Voice*, 19 March, 1958.

3 *The Dismemberment of Orpheus* (Wisconsin: Univ. of Wisconsin Press, 1982), 245.

4 Quoted Ruby Cohn, *Back to Beckett* (Princeton, NJ: Princeton Univ. Press, 1973), 152.

5 ALLOTROPES OF ATROPHY

1 That explains why Maddy and Dan have been created as prominently contrasted beings. The former stands for the female drive to live, for the will to procreate, for the struggle to continue, for 'Yea' to life. Dan, on the other hand, representing Nay-saying forces, is determined to depopulate. As they tend to cancel each other, evolution is impeded and everything bogged down.

2 'Krapp's Last Tape and the Proustian Vision', *Modern Drama* IX, 3 (December 1966), 333-338.

3 See *Krapp's Last Tape: Theatre Workbook* (ed.) James Knowlson (London: Brutus Books, 1980).

4 *Samuel Beckett: The Language of the Self* (Carbondale: Southern Illinois Univ. Press, 1962), 157.

5 Of course, the word 'play' has several usages and most of them apply here. For example, it can signify pastime pursued for its own sake. Here, too, playful is the way light shifts from character to character or the buttons of the taperecorder are pressed to switch them on and off. It could as well be a reference to the sports that the wanton gods play with men. The way the narratives have been fragmented and we are expected to piece them together, it is like the game of jigsaw puzzle. It might as well be compared to the game of using the same blocks to create a new structure or possibly something like the creation of ever-new patterns with the same pieces in a kaleidoscope. Maybe, such is the very spirit of all games, all plays—same dices but different matches. Possibly men are to be seen as playthings with which pointless games are being played by Time. If so, the play could be implying a typical oriental concept—life as a 'leela', a play for the amusement of God.

6 There is certainly a lot in the play that underlines ambivalence, dichotomy, diachronicity. Besides the alternation of light and darkness, sound and silence, we have a lot more by way of juxtaposition of the antithetical. Thus incidents stand out even as emotions are played down by telling the story of passionate affairs tonelessly, and by countering slow progress against rapid tempo. No wonder, too, continuous mobility in the text is counterpoised against the fixed image of paralysis in the stage picture before us. In a certain way, the beings in the urns are dehumanized and therefore

absent; but in other ways, they enact an all-too-human situation and are present throughout. This contrapuntal business enables us not only to perceive the incongruity as well as the indispensability of the moral and ontological truths but also to feel the peculiarity of the rhythm of life—totally static despite incessant dynamism.

6 IT GOES WITHOUT SAYING

1 *Samuel Beckett* (Boston: Twayne, 1986), 152.

2 As for the other details, the little tree that descends from the flies is not the Tree of Knowledge with forbidden fruit. That was in the Paradise whereas this is happening on the earth. Possibly it stands for Eros, the will to live. Thanatos is represented by the pair of scissors which man uses to trim his nails (making himself more domesticated and therefore less wild), to cut the rope (with knots facilitating ascent—hence a symbol of civilization), and to slash his neck (marking suicidal despair). Carafe of water stands for the illusions that sustain life. The cubes are the strategies of survival which man learns to exploit through hit-and-trial even though he always takes too long in the process.

3 Going by the fact that, during this period, Beckett had grown fond of 'twins'—'Act Without Words' I and II, 'Radio' I and II, 'Theatre' I and II—one would be justified in wondering if he had possibly planned Film II also. In that counter-experiment, he could have exploited the sound track with minimal movement—a film meant primarily for the ears as against 'Film' that is meant exclusively for the eyes. There is, of course, nothing on record to indicate that the idea of such a companion-piece was ever pursued. However, since in *Eh Joe*, words pour like a cataract while the camera concentrates on a single immobile character, one could venture to suggest that what was originally envisaged as a sort of Film II became a television play later. Possibly 'Film' made Beckett aware of his ineptitude with regard to the cinematic medium—a fact that he openly confessed in the Notes, too. It is worth noting that although Beckett kept writing for radio and small screen, he never tried his hand again on the silver screen. Perhaps 'Film' also deserved to be shelved like the other 'Roughs', but his friend, Alan Schneider, went ahead with its production—with the active cooperation of Beckett, of course. The result only went to confirm Beckett's apprehensions: the premiere-audience booed the film out. The movie is, indeed, marked by such false notes as usually characterize the work of novices. Besides, the audience unfamiliar with the script could not get any meaning beyond a silly chase; on the other hand, those who had read the

script were disappointed to note that Schneider had failed to realize Beckett's detailed project.

4 Surely, as it is, the film abounds in 'eyes'. Credits appear on the close-up of Bustor Keaton's eyelids. The focus throughout is on the eyes—the eyes of the couple, flower-woman, cat, dog, parrot, goldfish, God's image, etc. Even the buttons of the folder and the holes of the headrest were made to resemble eyes. In the photographs, the most conspicuous common feature is the act of visual devouring, seeing, watching, looking up or into—'eyeing', so to say. The final anagnorisis also comprises the discovery of a patch over the left eye. In short, the play seeks to relate filming and perception through the common link of 'eye'.

5 *A Reader's Guide to Samuel Beckett* (London: Thames and Hudson, 1976), 175.

6 So different is 'Quad' from the earlier mimes that perhaps ballet would be a better description. No wonder, too, Beckett declared in the stage-directions that ballet training of the players would be something desirable. Some critics have also called it a kind of modern dance in the tradition of John Cage. Probably, no one traditional label can wholly cover the spirit of 'Quad'. Going back to the quintessential elements of drama, viz., dithyramb and choral dance, Beckett has sought to break, as it were, such artificial barriers between dance and drama as have crept in. Consequently, 'Quad' is not a play with a text but a performance piece in which performance itself is the text. In this connection, it would be helpful to recall that it was around this period that Beckett had written the 'performance poem' called 'Rockaby'.

7 VOICE, FACE AND PACE

1 *Samuel Beckett* (London: Heinmann, 1974), 64.

2 *A Reader's Guide to Samuel Beckett* (London: Thames & Hudson, 1976), 169-70.

3 Clas Zillicus (*Beckett and Broadcasting*, Abo Akademi, 1976, 103) believes that in this radio mock-opera, music is a substitute for action and Croak is a medieval master of Gothic tower whose twin minstrels, Words and Music, are discussing the Seven Deadly Sins, etc. Likewise, the play has been called Beckett's version of 'Saint Cecilia's Day', a tribute to the power of music. Similarly, Croak has been projected as a troubadour or a poet busy creating a work of art out of the struggle to make a work of art. Or is he a 'croaking' Indian classical vocal singer trying to coerce words and melody into producing his *ragas*? Or is he a Prospero with Ariel and Caliban as

his minions? Maybe, he is just a Beckettian version of the senile old man of Jaques's divining? Or shall we be nearer Beckett's intention if we treat him as a psychic necrophile with abnormal, morbid fascination for death and therefore obsessively attracted erotically towards corpses?

4 For example, if most critics believe that at the end Croak leaves in despair disgusted with disharmony between Words and Music, Zillicus (ibid.) feels that Croak is overwhelmed by an offering that is aesthetically too rich for his taste. Likewise, if Words would appear to some to represent the rational element in feeling against the non-rational one of Music, Jean-Jacques Mayoux (Writers & Critics Series) regards the former as a reincarnation of Lucky—a poor thinker, a badly programmed computer. Similarly, to argue that Words and Music represent complementary parts of the same remembering mind is only as valid as to aver that they are mutually exasperating.

5 True, this interpretation of the play is not based on an elaborate discussion of the speeches but, then, just as each character is not a body but an embodiment of some idea, each speech too has significance not in the context of its contents but for the import inhering its general tone, tenor and tempo.

6 There have been innumerable suggestions corresponding to the diverse interpretations of the play—for example, a radio-listener, an operator of taperecorder, a technician mixing the channels of sound and music, a curious intruder opening and closing the doors of a studio, an eccentric warder shutting and opening the doors of a lunatic asylum, an ear, a perceiving part of the self, a creative artist struggling to evolve a story, Beckett himself.

7 For example, like M in *Play*, Joe deserts mistresses without bothering about consequences; like Krapp, he is a lecher visited by a slut even in old age; like Henry in *Embers*, he is a parricide, metaphorically if not literally. In a sense, here is the charge sheet to which 'Not I' could as well be a sort of defence. Or could it be that Joe is another version of O in *Film* while in his own room—listening to what was left to our imagination in the near-silent movie? Anyway, in both *Film* and 'Eh Joe', camera is more than a recorder of events—an active participant in the drama. In the possessive quality of the hectoring voice, one can feel the tyranny of the goad in 'Act Without Words II' or of the light in *Play*.

8 Here is, indeed, a veritable compendium of all Beckett themes—stasis, sterility and absence; emptiness and lessness; anguish, despair and suffering; old age confessions and senile logohorrea of inanities; agony of perceivedness and search for nonexistent salvation; Schopenhauerian immorality of disowning others and Proustian memory rejecting earlier selves; crime of being born and Jungian

disease of living without being born; Cartesian link between body and mind and the ever-new strategies of survival. All this is accommodated in the story of a 'she'—'how it has been . . . how she had lived . . . lived on and on'.

9 There is no dearth of thematic interpretations of Mouth vis-a-vis the Auditor who in any case offers a study in contrast with regard to size, posture, volubility as well as visuality. Quite interesting are the suggestions that seek to explain Mouth independent of the Auditor—vagina of a chronic spinster raped in old age, or the anus producing farts without any break. In conjunction with the Auditor, it has been projected as a sinner before father-confessor or a case of love-denied patient before a psychiatrist, or a performer confronting a critic!

10 It is possible that the interplay of three voices would recall *Play* to one's mind but, then, here voices no longer represent three different persons. Instead, they all belong to the same person. Of course, they are made to look distinct through the different directions from which they appear. Since they are aimed at the silent head—the 'you' in each soliloquy—it is called Listener; but these being his own voices, he is the speaker, too. The sameness of the three voices might remind one of Krapp's three different selves on his spools, but things here are quite different. These are not self-recordings at different points of time, nor is Listener here exercising any mechanical control of opening and closing. In fact, it is a stage beyond all goading—that of free associations. What is more, instead of prerecorded past as it was expressed then, here is expression of the past as it is being experienced now in old age. In fact, the much-cliched Wordsworthian recollection in tranquility has been fused into the Proustian remembrance of things past to make it a case of recollection in senility. Hence fragmented thoughts, fractured fancies and nostalgic images mixed and reshuffled in different permutations, variations and incantatory repetitions.

11 Expression used by Clive Barnes. See Virginia Cooke *Beckett on File* (London: Methuen, 1985), 53.

12 For example, how may one interpret the business in 'Footfalls'? Is it the story of an old dying mother and her daughter who is neurotic, because she was conceived too late, just before the former's menopause? Or is it the story of an unwedded mother whose daughter came to know about sex—about 'it all'—all too soon? Does neurosis stem from self-evasion—insistence on 'Not I' ('I was not there')—or from the shift of identities? Or is it an illustration of the process of artistic creativity regarding transmutation of reality in life to that in imagination and ultimately into fiction? Or is it a ghost telling the story of a ghost? Does revolving here signigy the alternation of the joys of sunny May and the sorrows of winter? Or

could May and Amy be related to 'may' and 'Amen' in a prayer? If so, does May's disappearance at the end therefore signify God's granting a death-wish? Or is it possibly an ironic depiction of what would happen to a she-Christ born out of wedlock—a suggestion that gains vindication from the fact that originally May was called Mary?

Way back in the late seventies, I myself interpreted the play so differently. When I read it for the first time, I perceived a resemblance between May's pacing-and-wheeling and a child's pre-natal movements in the foetus. I tended to feel then that the play had something to do with child-in-the-womb whose movements fill the mother with an urge to hear its foot-falls. On occasions, the mother might even hear its voice even though, in fact, it didn't yet have any tangible existence. Pursuing this hunch I interpreted V as Mother in Everywoman speaking to the child within her womb. Amy, I felt, was the child in Everywoman, 'revolutions' being the recurring process of the mother-in-girl followed by the girl-in-mother. In that line of thought I received support from several speeches. For example, 'I heard you in my deep sleep. (*Pause.*) There is no sleep so deep I would not hear you there' (239). Later, [it] 'bows her poor head against the wall and snatches a little sleep' (241). Or again 'Where is she, it may be asked. (*Pause.*) Why, in the old home, the same where she—(*Pause.*) The same where she began. (*Pause.*) Where it began. (*Pause.*) It all began' (241).

13 Of course, one may hear echoes of the earlier plays, too—for example, from 'Eh Joe' when the dolly moves closer and closer, step by step. In certain ways, this movement is akin to the goings-on in *Film* because camera here also tends to become a character. What is more, in both the cases, the climax lies in seeing the full face of the protagonist. Above all, 'Ghost Trio' is a close cousin of *Waiting for Godot* because the action inheres waiting for someone who does not come but sends instead a messenger boy. In fact, at earlier stages of composition, 'Ghost Trio' was titled 'Tryst'.

14 It has been declared a theatrical elaboration of Beethoven's Fifth Piano Trio, *The Ghost.* On the other hand it has been projected as an autobiography of Beckett, the Nobel laureate, who is doomed to be observed despite all his efforts to hide. Then there is the suggestion that the source of inspiration is T S Eliot's trio of birth, copulation and death in *Sweeny Agonistes.* In this context, door might signify birth, even as rain in the window could be a symbol of copulation, and pallet that of death. Or possibly the trio in the title is supposed to underline the confluence of three arts here—music, painting and literature. Maybe, here is yet another piece about an art media to highlight its quintessence—as in *Film*, *Play*, 'Words and Music', etc. The medium here could be the composite

one of television which combines in one the ghost-like imitative reality of three major performing media, viz., radio, cinema and theatre. Hence the recurring presence of cassette, camera and 'stagey' rectangles on the screen. The three-fold ghostliness of these media not only makes television a 'ghost-trio' but also strains our nervous energy aurally, visually and physically.

15 There is, indeed, God's plenty of trio-combinations. Witness: the structure of the play (Pre-Action, Action, and Re-Action); the narrative frames (television set, visual narrative, and the interior of the mind); the stalking objects (F, camera, and cassette); the characters (F, expected woman, and the boy); the positions of camera (A, B and C); the positions of F (5, 6 and 7); the observers of F on the play (camera, boy, and mirror); the observers of F as a character (audience, 'others', self) the three-time-three rectangles (chamber, floor, wall; door, window, pallet; stool, cassette, mirror).

16 Ghost-sensation is also experienced in several ways—in the ghost music; in the weird interplay of rectangles within rectangles; in the greyness all around; in the luminous light. F's movement without shadow, footfalls or footprints resembles a ghost's gait. There is something mysterious about opening and closing of music. Eery is the atmosphere created by the rain as well as the crescendo and decrescendo of creaking sounds produced by the door and the window. When the mirrors do not reflect F, one feels as if he had no form or substance. The sudden knock and the unexpected appearance of a boy who is all white are as uncanny as the resemblance between F and the boy, as if the latter were a ghost of the former.

17 Indeed, 'shades' link both the plays. In the former, in the introductory speech, V talks about faintly luminous light that leaves no scope of shadows and has all-grey colour—'shades of grey'; in the latter, the set is flooded with a pool of light surrounded by deepening shades. Of course, the shapes are different—rectangular in the former and circular in the latter. Anyway, the obsession with geometrical forms in both the cases is unmistakable.

18 If it is just that, how may one interpret the synchronization of the movements of the imagined, unspeaking lips of the beloved with those of V who actually utters the Yeatsian phrase? Does it mean that, when alive, the beloved used to quote these lines and he can still recollect the movements of those lips when citing? If so, was that done to warn the lover of what would happen to him in old age, as visualized in 'The Tower'? Or does it mean that when V imagines the beloved, she appears to urge him to realize his position as an old man and to 'train his soul' accordingly? Or could it imply that the image of the beloved it is that comes to his mind when he reads Yeats's line about brilliant eyes that 'made a catch in the

breath'? Above all, did Beckett assume that everyone knew Yeats by heart?

19 See *Beyond Minimalism* (New York: OUP, 1987), 165.

20 According to Jonathan Klab in his article, 'Rockaby and the Art of Inadvertent Interpretation' [*Modern Drama*, XXX, 4 (Dec. 1987), 466-79], 'more' is spoken differently each time—first time it is a frightened request, next a plaintive question, followed by an elongated one with a hoarse tremor, and finally abstractly as if uncertain how to speak.

8 ODDS, DISCARDS AND FAGENDS

1 No wonder this piece of monologue was originally titled 'Gone' and it ended then with 'Gone again, gone'. Even in its present form, the word 'gone' is repeated 16 times.

2 Most probably this line of thinking hammered home the fact that, like Ohio, Beckett's own plays start with nothing, end with nothing, and yet say so much that others regard as meaningless—'nothing'. As he brooded over the possibility of writing a play about all these implications of 'Ohio', Beckett appears to have recalled that Moliere, Ionesco and Giraudoux had also written impromptu-plays named after certain cities. In that genre of playwriting, the playwright may talk about his own plays, about his artistic theories, and even parody his critics' opinions. In practical terms, it meant metatheatrical trick of play-within-play. Indeed, it appears quite likely that Beckett meant to address his critics when he opened his 'Ohio Impromptu' with 'Little is left to tell' and ended with 'Nothing is left to tell'. Possibly he meant to declare that after all that the critics had said by way of interpretations, there was hardly anything for Beckett to tell. And yet, had all their talking led to any better understanding? The answer is implicit in the close of the play—Reader and Listener looking at each other, unblinking and expressionless. This is an echo of the close of the narrative, too—'What thoughts who knows. Thoughts, no not thoughts. Profounds of minds. . . . Of mindlessness' (288). Possibly this is Beckett's pronouncement on all seminars: 'What profounds of mind, of mindlessness'. Or could the expressionlessness of L and R be Beckett's oblique comment on the mindlessness inhering the critics' interpretations of the 'profundity' of his plays? Maybe, the theme of narrative itself has something direct for the critics. The ghost visitor comes from the 'dear one' as a total stranger, but as soon as some silent understanding gets established, it is time for parting. Since that is what happens in seminars too, in Ohio, the critics might start understanding Beckett better but, alas, they

would be required to go back home without pursuing the dawning understanding to its logical end.

3 In both the narrative and the stage action, the scene is nightly reading from a worn volume carried in the pocket of a long coat. In both, a Latin Quarter brimmed hat lies on the table. In each, reader and listener gradually grow to be one until the day they realize that they are to meet no more and thus sit as turned to stone. On the other hand, there is nothing to indicate that Listener has suffered any loss of a dear one, that he is living in an unfamiliar room against the wishes of the dear departed, that R is an emissary now under orders not to visit any more.

4 Accommodating the two together, 'Catastrophe' lambasts the political dictators only as strongly as the producers of plays who, in the name of direction, tyrannize over the performers. Thus Director (D) here is a dictator whose inhumanity towards fellow-workers is underlined by his indifference to the fact that P is shivering. Assistant (A) does feel concerned but, going by her obedient acquiscence in everything that D says, she is a younger collaborator in the process of perpetrating artistic tyranny. P (Protagonist in the rehearsed piece and Performer in the frame play) is, of course, a victim, a martyr in both. In short, 'Catastrophe', while raising voice against the political dictators who deny freedom of speech to artists like Vaclav Havel, indicts also directors of political plays who suppress the artistic autonomy of performers by denying them the right to express themselves. When D has got effected all the changes he wants, the invisible audience are heard applauding; but at this point, raising his head, P fixes the audience with his stare and the clapping ceases. P has shamed the spectators through that simple gaze which seems to ask: 'What are you people applauding? Do you really approve of this kind of art? Does my misery make you happy? Am I really a martyr? If so, whose? Is political tyranny any more soul-killing than the artistic tyranny by fellow artists?' It is worth nothing that P is not the only victim of D here; the way D barks at A and she shouts for Luke, the lighting man, one may see the multitentacled tyranny in the field of arts.

5 Maybe, in this single gesture of P, Beckett meant to urge the artists who were aiming to defend other artists to realize the power of the assertion of artistic will. Becoming his own director, P becomes, as it were, a veritable model for other artists. Indeed, when a true artist protests, a single gesture of his might upset the apple-cart of the system. Even a silent gaze can strike terror in the minds of tyrants and thus bring about a revolutionary change. Thus seen, P is a kind of Christ whose crucifixion is applauded by the people around who know not what they do until they are shamed into

realizing how misdirected their appreciation is. Thus Beckett's play speaks not only to the artists but also to the audiences who are expected to realize that it is within their power to withhold their applause and thus force the dictators/directors to change their ends and means.

6 Or, maybe, the play could be interpreted somewhat differently. Most of the action hinges round gradual tinkering by D with respect to the basic structure created by A. This process of 'finishing' touches tends to reverse everything original and reduces the artifact to something grotesque. Possibly this is what Beckett sees in the process of human evolution—the catastrophic consequences of the effort of man to become superman, Godot. Changing bit by bit, civilization after civilization, today man stands changed to a robot. In this result, people might find reason to applaud the advancement of technology but, in fact, it is time it was realized that this situation signifies the defeat of humanism. Let man, therefore, learn to be himself—dignified and defiant like a tragic hero—even if that should spell his catastrophe as a species.

7 See Virginia Cooke, *Beckett on File* (London: Methuen, 1985), 65.

8 *Samuel Beckett* (London: Jonathan Cape, 1978), 127-8.

9 See Ruby Cohn, *Back to Beckett* (Princeton: Princeton Univ. Press, 1973), 122-3. According to Ruby Cohn, 'Human Wishes' and *Eleutheria* had the dubious distinctions of being 'The Play That Wasn't Written' and 'The Play That Wasn't Staged', respectively. For my discussion of these plays, I have depended largely on her *Just Play* (Princeton: Princeton Univ. Press, 1980), 143-62 and 163-72.

10 The enigma has prompted some critics to dig for features common to both the Sams. Linda Ben-Zvi [*Samuel Beckett* (Boston: Twayne, 1986), 51-5] has discovered a number of parallels—Irish origin, stay in London, skin disorders, lonely nature, impenetrable silence, interest in arithmetic, obsession with vacuity of life. Indeed, it would appear as if Beckett were going to write an autobiographical play behind the cover of Dr Johnson. The parallels are, of course, too far-fetched to be convincing—for example, when so much is made of the fact that their respective names have the same number of letters, viz., 13.

11 It has not been included even in *Disjecta* (1983) in which the few pages of 'Human Wishes' have been reproduced. Had Roger Blin opted for *Eleutheria* instead of *Godot*, it is possible that critics would have dismissed it as a commonplace potboiler and convinced the already frustrated Beckett that drama was not his cup of tea. Mercifully the decision went in favour of *Godot*. Nevertheless, despite the poor quality of its writing, the act of writing *Eleutheria* possibly proved a blessing in disguise. It appears to have brought home the

lesson that it is such conventional writing that Beckett must eschew. What is more, in the process, Beckett wrote the traditional drama out of his own system and thus freed himself from the straitjacket of its conventions. Thus, in a way, the freedom of the title applies to the playwright as well. Like Victor Krap deciding neither to commit suicide nor to return to normal life, Beckett also seems to have decided neither to give up playwriting nor to return to conventional drama. It is possible to extend the analogy and say that Victor's problem in life is the same as Beckett's in playwriting—how to explain the inexplicable, express the inexpressible, and do without speech and action.

12 Cited by Ruby Cohn, *Back to Beckett*, 126.

13 This desire of seeing oneself die in Beckett's earliest play is a variant of a dreamer dreaming himself dream in one of Beckett's last plays, 'Nacht and Traume'. That confirms my hunch that all Beckett heroes from Belacqua to Victor through Dreamer are made of the same fibre. Certainly, far from being atypical, *Eleutheria* is full of Beckett motifs—a man on a bed in an empty room; characters with such obscene names as Krap, Piouk, Skunk, Mech, or with such organic malfunctioning as Krap's difficulty with urination and Mme Krap's fallen utreus; search for the self precipitating into one for non-being; repeated plea for destroying humanity; the final option for neither suicide nor normal life; the protagonist looking hard at the theatre audience and lying down with his back turned on them.

14 Cited John Pilling, *Samuel Beckett* (London: Routledge & Kegan Paul, 1976), 71.

15 At least 'Theatre I' did have originally a title that Beckett discarded later—'Gloaming'. In the sense of twilight or dusk, it was possibly meant to signify the mixing of light and darkness—a cross-section of the contraries in which, nothing being certain, one thing is as valid as its opposite. Anyway, the image of gloaming does really sum up the question-mark with which the play closes.

16 Reproduced by James Knowlson & John Pilling, *Frescoes of the Skull*, 231.

17 Ibid.

18 Hence the references to C's jumping from the Sixth floor. Each floor is three-metres-and-a-half high—an allegorical reference to Spengler's putting the duration of a civilization at 350 years! Man's being too concerned with Time and mortality is also allegorically implied in C's contemplating dog-shit for hours on end and being rewarded with a lottery ticket that was to fetch him the price of a perfect watch. That with the passage of time man has alternated on the dark and not-so-dark ages concretizes in the way light in the reading lamp comes and goes.

19 Written around the same time as 'Theatre II', it is a sort of

companion piece in the sense that it gives some idea of the way the evidence against C (on which A and B base their verdict) might have been collected and possibly doctored. That to the same period belong 'Cascando' and 'Words and Music' one gets to know in Animator's being a sort of Opener or Croak, because he too stimulates or stems the speeches of Fox. Although this 'Rough' was published as an 'odd' along with the 'ends', many many years after its composition, yet in spirit it is akin to 'Catastrophe' and 'What Where'. Indeed, Animator and Stenographer here could be early models of Director and Assistant, and what the tormentors here are after is 'what' and 'where' of Fox. Anyway, it is a typically Beckettian piece in having a tone that is at once sinister and funny. No less typical is the daring with which Beckett has roped in a mute character in a radio play in which normally sound alone should matter. And then we have something more that Beckett alone could do: Animator wraps into fiction what is already a fictionalized version of Fox's life—that old game of fiction about fiction.

20 Thus seen, Fox is an artist, Animator his critical faculty, Stenographer his recording consciousness and Dick his determination to stimulate his subconscious suffering. Pursuing this idea along a different line, one might see here efforts to extract the sources of inspiration and influences from an author who foxes his tormentors by intriguing them into further confusion with references to other obsessions. In this framwork, Animator could be an obtrusive literary biographer who interprets everything the way it suits him and who won't mind adding a pinch of salt to make things spicier; Stenographer, on the other hand, could be a younger, modern scientific researcher who is keener on facts than on interpretation.

9 INTIMATIONS: POETRY AND EARLY FICTION

1 See *Beckett: Poet and Critic* (Princeton: Princeton Univ. Press, 1970).

2 This 'novel' had the dubious distinction of being banned in Ireland.

3 Thus viewed, Mercier and Camier appear precursors of Vladimir and Estragon. They have also many other traits common with them—for example, their suffering when together and being afraid of suffering if left alone; their frequently thinking in vain of leaving each other. They too are blessed with a sense of nothingness ('nothing to be done, nothing to be said'). With some other Beckettian protagonists they share the feeling that they are being punished by God and therefore hurl virulent abuses at Him. Witness also their suffering in the present but thinking of the happy days in

the past, and their talking incessantly to fill time while waiting and yet finding words totally inadequate. Here, indeed, is yet another 'salute to entropy' as Hugh Kenner puts it in *A Reader's Guide to Samuel Beckett* (London: Thames & Hudson, 1973), p. 91.

4 According to Ruby Cohn, the protagonists in all the three novels are conscious of their being narrators and each succeeding one assimilates his predecessor(s). (*Back to Beckett*, Princeton, NJ: Princeton Univ. Press, 1973, 113)

5 Ibid., 117.

6 See *Beckett and The Voice of Species* (Dublin: Gill and Macmillan, 1980), 54-71.

7 Ibid., 70.

8 *Samuel Beckett* (Boston: Twayne, 1986), 82.

9 'Sapos' also means soap; that makes man 'sapos-cat'—a soapy cat who is trying to wash the dirt of nature. But Beckett would not be Beckett if he is content with such a simplistic trick as exploiting an adjective as a noun. I, therefore, feel more inclined to pursue our hunch and look for meaning in the noun, cat. Thinking of the rise and fall of numerous civilizations and the innumerable times man has escaped extinction by the skin of his teeth, Beckett possibly thought of man as a kind of cat who proverbially has nine lives. As for the prefix, sapos, it could be implying ironic juxtaposition of two kinds of 'saps'. On the one hand, he is sapping nature dry, and on the other he is acting as the vital sap of the world, because without him the earth would lose all 'life'.

10 Or, maybe, this is in reference to the state in which mankind finds itself at present when it is poised to meet an end. What strikes most in the name Malone is the sound 'alone'—probably to implant in our mind the idea of alienation and aloneness which are supposed to characterize the situation of man in the twentieth century. The idea is reinforced by the fact that the locale is a kind of asylum—a most apt metaphor for the 'modern' age of neurosis. In short, Malone could be modern man pestered with a sense of ending. As he tries to pass time before the end comes, yet another end-game may be seen in progress.

11 Of course, it is possible that Basil might be denoting a reference to basilisk serpent; if so, it all means that man's evolution has been a kind of horizontal dwindling, from serpent to maggot—all inhabitants of graves. And if, instead, Basil is from the Greek Basileus which means king, it is a way of echoing Hamlet's vision regarding the progress of a king to a maggot. Be that what it may, the various possibilities add up to a variation of Beckett's vision of birth astride of a grave, for man's situation appears akin on the one hand to a larva that is conceived but not quite born and on the other to a

maggot which is buried but not quite dead.

10 RESIDUA: EPIPHANY AS FIZZLE

1 *Beckett and the Voice of Species* (Dublin: Gill & Macmillan, 1980), 72.

2 Ibid. All the questions and their answers—as elaborated separately and Text-wise in this section—figure together in a bunch on p. 73 of Levy's book.

3 *Back to Beckett* (Princeton: Princeton Univ. Press, 1973), 241-7.

4 *A Reader's Guide to Samuel Beckett* (London: Thames and Hudson, 1973), 178.

5 True, the incessant activity without end here has been explained differently by diverse critics—the Dantean landscape, the mythical universe of dead bodies, each searching for its lost ones, the ever-changing Proustian 'selves' in a human mind, etc. To me, however, it appears, as usual, an epitome of human situation—yet another Act Without Words, albeit in terms of fiction. No wonder, in 1972, Mabou Mines, New York, could produce out of it a perfect Beckettian mime with the help of 205 mechanical railroad dolls which acquired human proportions.

6 Of particular interest to me (as also to Beckett) are the immobile ones because, having lost the will to seek, they have themselves become the 'lost ones'. However, even though they don't move, their blind eyes do—as if seeking to see what they will never find. What they are looking for is never spelt out; rather, every possible guess is negated. It is possible to say that the lost ones that the other three groups are looking for are those who have given up. But as these mobile ones are wandering unseeingly out of sheer habit, they can't recognise the vanquished ones as the object of their search even when they do meet them. On the other hand, the latter having lost the will to search, they don't realize that they have joined the lost ones whom they were looking for when they could see.

7 *A Reader's Guide*, 179.

8 Or did he mean thus to underline the fact that, instead of imitating action to share an experience, here was the record of memory which is a veritable purgatory through which the experience is purged of its agony? Indeed, an experience as remembered is like a fizzle insofar as it links inner and outer selves, contaminates the present, prevents action, and effects a purgation without affording a lasting relief.

9 The argument is inspired by what Linda Ben-Zvi says in her *Samuel Beckett* (Boston: Twayne, 1986), p. 127.

Bibliography

PRIMARY SOURCES

A. Published Works by Samuel Beckett

All Strange Away. Journal of Beckett Studies. No. 3, pp. 1-9.

Collected Shorter Plays. London: Faber & Faber, 1984.

Company. New York: Grove Press, 1980.

Disjecta. London: John Calder, 1983.

Endgame. London: Faber & Faber, 1964.

For to End yet Again and Other Fizzles. London: Calder & Boyars, 1976.

Happy Days. London: Faber & Faber, 1966.

How It Is. London: John Calder, 1964.

Ill Seen Ill Said. New York: Grove Press, 1981.

Lessness. London: John Calder, 1970.

The Lost Ones. New York: Grove Press, 1972.

Mercier and Camier. London: Calder & Boyars, 1974.

Molloy, Malone Dies, The Unnamable. London: John Calder, 1959.

More Pricks Than Kicks. London: Pan Books, 1974.

Murphy. London: John Calder, 1963.

No's Knife. London: Calder & Boyars, 1967.

Poems in English. London: John Calder, 1961.

Proust. New York: Evergreen, 1931.

Waiting for Godot. London: Faber & Faber, 1965.

Watt. London: John Calder, 1963.

Worstward Ho. London: John Calder, 1983.

B. Beckett in Archives

I Unpublished material at Beckett Archives, University of Reading Library—manuscripts (on diaries, note-books, registers, loose sheets, etc.), typescripts (at different stages of composition), or printed texts with Beckett's own marginal corrections or direction-notes in respect of the following plays: 'Act Without Words II' (1); '. . . but the clouds . . .' (1); 'Catastrophe' (1); 'Come and Go' (2); *Endgame* (3); 'Eh Joe' (8); 'Embers' (1); 'Film' (3); 'Footfalls' (1); 'Ghost Trio' (1); *Happy Days* (7); *Krapp's Last Tape* (4); 'Not I' (1); 'Ohio Impromptu' (1); 'A Piece of Monologue (5); *Play* (7); 'Radio II' (2); 'Rockaby' (3); 'That Time' (3); 'Theatre I' (4); *Waiting for Godot* (1). (Parenthetical figures refer to the number of items/ versions consulted.)

II On Tapes/Audio-cassettes

(i) 'All That Fall'; 'Dead Calm'; 'Eh Joe'; 'Endgame'; 'Footfalls'; 'Ghost Trio'; 'Happy Days'; 'Krapp's Last Tape'; 'Not I'; 'Play'; 'Words and Music' (Courtesy: BBC/Beckett Archives).

(ii) 'Cascando'; 'Embers'; 'Words and Music' (Courtesy: Audio Visual Centre, University of London).

III On Video-Cassettes:
'. . . but the clouds . . .'; 'Catastrophe'; 'Eh Joe'; 'Footfalls'; 'Ghost Trio'; 'Happy Days'; 'Krapp's Last Tape'; 'Not I'; 'Quad'; 'Rockaby'; 'Silence to Silence' (Courtesy: BBC/Beckett Archives/Audio Visual Centre, University of London).

SECONDARY SOURCES

Abbot, H Porter. 'A Poetics of Radical Displacement: Samuel Beckett Coming up to Seventy'. *Texas Studies in Literature and Language* XVII, 1 (Spring 1975), 219-38.

_____. *The Fiction of Samuel Beckett: Form and Effect* (Perspectives in Criticism, No. 22). Berkeley: Univ. of California Press, 1973.

Abel, Lionel. 'Beckett and Metatheatre', *Metatheatre*. New York: Hill and Wang, 1963, pp. 83-5.

Acheson, James and Keteryna Arthur (eds.). *Beckett's Later Fiction and Drama: Texts for Company*. Hampshire: Macmillan, 1987.

_____. 'Chess with the Audience: Samuel Beckett's *Endgame*'. *Critical Qly.* XXII, 2, pp. 33-45.

Admussen, Richard L. *The Samuel Beckett Manuscripts: A Study*. London: George Prior Publishers, 1979.

Ahuja, Chaman. 'Beckett's Theatre of the Seventies'. *Panjab University Research Bulletin (Arts)* VII, 2, pp. 75-82.

Albright, Daniel. *Representation and the Imagination: Beckett, Kafka, Nabokov and Schoenberg*. Chicago: Univ. of Chicago Press, 1981.

Alplaugh, David J. 'Embers and the Sea: Beckettian Intimations of Mortality'. *Modern Drama* XVI, Dec. 1973, 317-28.

_____. 'Negative Definition in Samuel Beckett's *Happy Days*'. *Twentieth Century Literature* XI, Jan. 1966, 202-10.

Alvarez, A. *Beckett*. (Fontana Modern Masters Series). Fontana/Collins, 1973.

Andonian, Cathleen Culotta. *Samuel Beckett: A Reference Guide*. Boston: G K Hall, 1989.

Asmus, Walter D. 'Rehearsal Notes for the German Premiere of Beckett's "That Time" and "Footfalls at the Schiller Theater Werkstatt, Berlin'. *Journal of Beckett Studies* No. 2, pp. 82-95.

Atkins, Anselm. 'Lucky's Speeth in Beckett's *Waiting for Godot*: A Punctuated Sense-Line Arrangement'. *Educational Theatre Journal* XIX, 4 (Dec. 1967), 426-32.

Bair, Deirdre. *Samuel Beckett: A Biography*. London: Jonathan Cape, 1978.

Baldwin, Helene L. *Samuel Beckett's Real Silence*. University Park: Pennsylvania Univ. Press, 1981.

Barge, Laura. *God, The Quest, The Hero: Thematic Structures in Beckett's Fiction*. Chapel Hill: North Carolina Studies in the Romance Languages and Literatures, 1986.

_____. 'Life and Death in Beckett's Four Stories'. *South Atlantic Qly*. Vol. 76, Summer 1977, 332-47.

Barnard, G C. *Samuel Beckett: A New Approach*. London: Dent, 1970.

Barrett, William. *Time of Need: Forms of Imagination in the Twentieth Century*. New York: Harper Torchback, 1973.

_____. 'The Works of Beckett Hold Clue to an Important Riddle'. *Saturday Review* XL, Oct. 4, 1957, 15-16.

Baxter, K M. *Speak What We Feel: A Christian Looks at the Contemporary Theatre*. London: SCM Press, 1964.

Beckett Symposium (held at Reading University in May 1971)—report in *New Theatre Magazine* Vol. XI, No. 3 (May 1971).

Beja, Morris, S E Gontarski and Pierre Astier. *Samuel Beckett: Humanistic Perspectives*. Columbus: Ohio State Univ. Press, 1983.

Ben-Zvi, Linda. *The Devaluation of Language in Avant Garde Drama*. (Microfilm) Univ. of Oklahama Ph.D. Dissertation, 1972.

_____. *Samuel Beckett*. Boston: Twayne, 1986.

_____. 'Samuel Beckett's Media Plays'. *Modern Drama* XXVIII, March 1985, 22-32.

_____. 'The Schismatic Self in a Piece of Monologue'. *Journal of Beckett Studies* No. 7, pp. 7-18.

Bernel, Albert. *Contradictory Characters: An Interpretation of Modern*

Theatre. New York: E P Dutton, 1973.

Blau, Herbert. *The Impossible Theatre: A Manifesto*. New York: Macmillan, 1964.

Block and Shedd (eds.). *Masters of Modern Drama*. New York: Random House, 1963.

Blocker, H Gene. *The Metaphysics of Absurdity*. Washington: Univ. Press of America, 1979.

Bradbrook, M C. 'Beckett, *En Attendant Godot*'. *Aspects of Dramatic Form in the English and the Irish Renaissance*. Collected Papers of Muriel Bradbrook, Vol. III. Sussex: Harvester Press, 1983, pp. 173-86.

Bradby, David. 'The Parisian Theatre II: The New Theatre'. *Modern French Drama*. Cambridge: CUP, 1984, pp. 53-75.

Brater, Enoch. 'The "Absurd" Actor in the Theatre of Samuel Beckett'. *Educational Theatre Journal* XXVII, May 1975, 197-207.

_____. *Beckett at 80/Beckett in Context*. New York: OUP, 1986.

_____. *Beyond Minimalism: Beckett's Late Style in the Theatre*. New York: OUP, 1987.

_____. 'Fragments and Beckett's Form in "That Time" and "Footfalls"'. *Journal of Beckett Studies* No. 2, pp. 70-81.

_____. 'The "I" in Beckett's "Not I"'. *Twentieth Century Literature* XX, July 1974, 189-200.

_____. 'Noah, Not I and Beckett's Incomprehensibly Sublime'. *Comparative Drama* VIII, 254-63.

_____. 'The Thinking Eye in Beckett's *Film*'. *Modern Language Qly* XXXVI, June 1976, 166-76.

_____. 'Towards a Poetics of Television Technology: Beckett's *Nacht and Traume* and *Quad*'. *Modern Drama* XXVIII, 1 (March 1985), 48-54.

_____. *Why Beckett?* London: Thames & Hudson, 1989.

Brienza, Susan D. *Samuel Beckett's New Worlds: Style in Metafiction*. Norman: Univ. of Oklahoma Press, 1987.

Brombert, Victor. *The Hero in Literature*. Greenwich, Conn: Fawcett Premier, 1969.

Bruns, G L. 'The Story-teller and the Problem of Language in Samuel Beckett's Ficion'. *Modern Language Quarterly* XXX, 2, pp. 265-81

Burkman, Katherine H (ed.). *Myth and Ritual in the Plays of Samuel Beckett*. Rutherford: Fairleigh Dickinson Univ. Press.

Burrow, D. 'A Study of the Plays of Friedrich Durrenmatt and Samuel Beckett as Anti-Tragedies'. (Microfilm) Ph.D. Thesis: State Univ. of New York at Stony Brooks, 1978.

Busi, Frederick, 'Joycean Echoes in *Waiting for Godot*'. *Research Studies* XLIII, 2 (June 1975), 71-86.

_____. 'Lucky, Luke and Samuel Beckett'. *Research Studies* XLV, June 1977, 100-4.

_____. *The Transformation of Godot*. Lexington: Univ. Press of Kentucky, 1980.

Butler, Lance St John. *Samuel Beckett and the Meaning of Being.* London: Macmillan, 1984.

_____ and Robin J Davis. *Rethinking Beckett: A Collection of Critical Essays.* London: Macmillan, 1990.

Calder, John (ed.). *Beckett at 60: A Festschrift.* London: Calder & Boyars, 1967.

Calderwood, Jame L. 'Ways of Waiting in *Waiting for Godot*'. *Modern Drama* XXIX, 3 (Sept. 1986), 365-75.

Chabert, Pierre. 'The Body in Beckett's Theatre'. *Journal of Beckett Studies* No. 8, pp. 23-8.

Chase, N C. 'Images of Man: Le Malentendu and En Attendant Godot'. *Contemporary Literature* VII, 3 (Autumn 1966), 295-302.

Chevigny, Bell Gale (ed.). *Twentieth Century Interpretations of Endgame*, Englewood Cliffs, NJ: Prentice-Hall, 1969.

Cleveland, Louise D. 'Trials in the Soundscape: The Radio Plays of Samuel Beckett'. *Modern Drama* XI, 3 (Dec. 1968), 267-82.

Coe, Richard N. *Beckett.* Writers & Critics. Edinburgh: Oliver & Boyd, 1968.

Cohen, Robert S. 'Parallels and the Possibility of Influence Between Simone Weil's *Waiting for God* and Samuel Beckett's *Waiting for Godot*'. *Modern Drama* VI, Feb. 1964, 425-36.

Cohn, Ruby. *Back to Beckett.* Princeton, NJ: Princeton Univ. Press, 1973.

_____. 'Beckett and Shakespeare'. *Modern Drama* XV, 3 (Dec. 1972), 223-30.

_____. 'Beckett's Recent Residua'. *Southern Review* V, 4 (Autumn 1969), 1045-54.

_____. (ed.). *Beckett: Waiting for Godot.* Casebook Series. London: Macmillan, 1987.

_____. (ed.). *Casebook on Waiting for Godot.* New York: Grove Press, 1967.

_____. 'The Comedy of Samuel Beckett: Something Old, Something New'. *Yale French Studies* Vol. 23, pp. 11-17.

_____. *The Comic Gamut.* New Brunswick, NJ: Rutgers Univ. Press, 1962.

_____. *Currents in Contemporary Drama.* Bloomington: Indiana Univ. Press, 1969.

_____. *Just Play: Beckett's Theater.* Princeton, NJ: Princeton Univ. Press, 1980.

_____. 'Play and Player in the Plays of Samuel Beckett'. *Yale French Studies* Vol. 29, pp. 43-56.

_____. (ed.). *Samuel Beckett: A Collection of Criticism.* New York: McGraw Hill, 1975.

'Commentary'. *Comparative Drama* III, 3 (Fall 1969), 219-35.

Connor, Steven, *Samuel Beckett: Repetition, Theory and Text.* Oxford: Basil Blackwell, 1988.

Cooke, Virginia. *Beckett on File.* London: Methuen, 1985.

Copeland, Hannah C. *Art and Artist in the Works of Samuel Beckett.* The Hague: Mouton, 1975.

Cormier, Ramona and Janis L Pallister. *Waiting for Death: The Philosophical*

Significance of Samuel Beckett's En Attendant Godot. Univ. of Albama Press, 1979.

Cornwell, Ethel F. 'Samuel Beckett: The Flight from Self'. *PMLA*, 88, Jan. 1973, 41-51.

Currie, Robert. 'Beckett's Transcendental Nihilism: The World of Habit'. *Genius: An Ideology in Literature*. London: Chatto & Windus, 1976, pp. 171-93.

Dearlove, J E. *Accommodating the Chaos: Samuel Beckett's Non-relational Art*. Durham, NC: Duke Univ. Press, 1982.

_____. 'Allusions to Archetype'. *Journal of Beckett Studies* No. 10, pp. 121-33.

_____. 'The Voice and Its Words: How It is in Beckett's Canon'. *Journal of Beckett Studies* No. 3, pp. 56-75.

De Sollar, John P. 'Sound and Sense in Samuel Beckett's Drama and Fiction'. *Irish Studies* I (ed.) P J Drudy. London: CUP, 1980, pp. 133-52.

Dobree, Bonamy. 'The Melting Pot'. *Sewanee Review* LXVI, Winter 1958, 149-52.

Dobrez, L A C. 'Beckett: The Task of Saying Nothing'. *The Existential and Its Exits: Literature and Philosophy: Perspectives on the Works of Beckett, Ionesco, Genet & Pinter*. London: Athlone Press, 1986, pp. 261-80.

Doherty, Francis. *Samuel Beckett*. London: Hutchinson Univ. Library, 1971.

Doll, Mary A. *Beckett and Myth: An Archetypal Approach*. Syracuse, New York: Syracuse Univ. Press, 1988.

Drama Critique Vol. 6, No. 2 (Spring 1963)—a special number on Absurd Drama.

Duckworth, Colin. *Angels of Darkness: Dramatic Effect in Beckett and Ionesco*. London: George Allen & Unwin, 1972.

_____. 'Beckett's Dramatic Intensity'. *New Theatre Magazine* XI, 3 (May 1971).

_____. (ed.). *En Attendant Godot*. London: Harrap & Co., 1966.

Dukore, Bernard F. 'Krapp's Last Tape as Tragi-comedy'. *Modern Drama* XL, 4 (March 1973), 351-4.

_____. 'A Non-Interpretation of Godot'. *Drama Survey* III, 1 (May 1963), 117-19.

_____. 'The Other Pair in *Waiting for Godot*'. *Drama Survey* VII, 133-7.

_____. Dutton, Richard. *Modern Tragicomedy and the British Tradition*. Sussex: Harvester Press, 1986.

Eliopulos, J. *Samuel Beckett's Dramatic Language*. Series Practica 100. The Hague: Mouton, 1975.

Ellman, Richard. *Samuel Beckett: Nayman of Noland*. Washington: Library of Congress, 1986.

Esslin, Martin. *Brief Chronicles*. London: Temple Smith, 1961.

_____. *Mediations: Essays on Brecht, Beckett and the Media*. Baton Rouge: Louisiana State Univ. Press, 1980.

_____. (ed.). *Samuel Beckett: A Collection of Critical Essays*. Twentieth

Century Views. Englewood Cliffs: Prentice Hall, 1965.

_____. *The Theatre of the Absurd*. Harmondsworth: Penguin Books, 1977.

Estabrooks, G H. *Man: The Mechanical Misfit*. New York: Macmillan, 1941.

Estess, Ted L. 'Dimensions of Play in the Literature of Samuel Beckett'. *Arizona Qly*. XXXIII, 1 (Spring 1977), 5-25.

Federman, Raymond. *Journey to Chaos: Samuel Beckett's Early Fiction*. Berkeley: Univ. of California Press, 1965.

_____ and John Fletcher. *Samuel Beckett and His Critics: An Essay in Bibliography*. Berkeley: Univ. of California Press, 1970.

Finch, Roy. 'The Reality of the Nothing: The Importance of Samuel Beckett'. *Lugano Review* I, 3-4 (Summer 1965).

Fletcher, Beryl S, John Fletcher, Barry Smith and Walter Bachem. *A Student's Guide to the Plays of Samuel Beckett*. London: Faber & Faber, 1978.

Fletcher, John. *The Novels of Samuel Beckett*. London: Chatto & Windus, 1964.

_____. *Samuel Beckett's Art*. London: Chatto & Windus, 1967.

Fletcher, John and John Spurling. *Beckett: A Study of His Plays*. London: Eyre Methuen, 1978.

Foster, Paul. 'Beckettian Impasse: A Zen Study of Ontological Dilemma in the Novels of Samuel Beckett'. Ph.D. Dissertation, Heidelberg Univ., 1980.

Fowlie, Wallace. 'The New French Theatre: Artaud, Beckett, Genet, Ionesco'. *Sewanee Review* LXVII, Fall 1959, 643-57.

Fraser, G.S. *The Modern Writer and His World*. Calcutta: Rupa, 1961, Indian Reprint.

Freedman, Morris. *The Moral Impulse: Modern Drama from Ibsen to the Present*. Crosscurrent Modern Critiques. Carbondale: Southern Illinois Univ. Press, 1967.

Friedman, Melvin J (ed.). *Samuel Beckett Now*. Chicago: Univ. of Chicago Press, 1970.

Frische, Jack E. 'Endgame: A Play as Poem'. *Drama Survey* III, 2 (Oct. 1963), 257-63.

Garner (Jr.), Stanton B. 'Visual Field in Beckett's Late Plays'. *Comparative Drama* XXI, 4 (Winter 1987-8).

Garzilli, Enrico. *Circle Without Center: Paths to the Discovery and Creation of Self in Modern Literature*. Cambridge, Mass.: Harvard Univ. Press, 1972.

Gascoigne, Bamber. *Twentieth Century Drama*. London: Hutchinson Univ. Library, 1967.

Gassner, John. 'Broadway in Review'. *Educational Theatre Journal* X, May 1958, 122-31.

_____. *Directions in Modern Theatre and Drama*. New York: Holt, Rinehardt & Winston, 1965.

_____. 'The Modern, The Modernist and The Absurd'. *Drama Critique* VI, 2 (Spring 1963), 50-5.

Gidal, Peter. *Understanding Beckett.* London: Macmillan, 1986.

Gilbert, Sandra M. 'All the Dead Voices'. *Drama Survey* VI, 3 (Spring 1968), 244-57.

Gilman, Richard. 'Beckett'. *Partisan Review* XLI, 1 (1974), 56-76.

_____. *The Making of Modern Drama: A Study of Buchner, Ibsen, Strindberg, Chekhov, Pirandello, Brecht, Beckett, Handke.* New York: Farrar, Straus & Giroux, 1972.

Glass, Peyton. 'Beckett: Axial Man'. *Educational Theatre Journal* XXIX, Oct. 1977, 362-73.

Glicksberg, Charles I. *The Ironic Vision in Modern Literature.* The Hague: Martinus Nijhoff, 1969.

Gluck, Barbara Reich. 'Me to Play'. *Beckett and Joyce: Friendship and Fiction.* Lewisburg: Bucknell Univ. Press, 1979, pp. 141-63.

Gontarski, S.E. 'The Anatomy of Beckett's *Eh Joe*'. *Modern Drama* XXVI, 4 (Dec. 1983), 425-34.

_____. *Beckett's Happy Days: A Manuscript Study.* Columbus, Ohio: Ohio State Library, 1977.

_____. *The Intent of Undoing in Samuel Beckett's Dramatic Texts.* Bloomington: Indiana Univ. Press, 1985.

Graver, Lawrence. 'Guides to the Ruins'. *Partisan Review* XLI, 4, pp. 622-5.

_____. *Samuel Beckett—Waiting for Godot.* Landmarks of World Literatur Series. Cambridge: CUP, 1989.

_____ and Raymond Federman (eds.). *Samuel Beckett: The Critical Heritage.* London: Routledge & Kegan Paul, 1979.

Grossvogel, David I. *Four Palywrights and a Postscript: Brecht, Ionesco, Beckett, Genet.* Ithaca, New York: Cornell Univ. Press, 1962.

Hale, Jane A. *The Broken Window: Beckett's Dramatic Perspective.* West Lafayette: Purdue Univ. Press, 1987.

Hamilton, Kenneth and Alice. *Condemned to Life: The World of Samuel Beckett.* Grand Rapids, Mich.: William B Eerdmans Pub., 1976.

Hampton, Charles C. 'Samuel Beckett's *Film*'. *Modern Drama* XI, 3, December 1968, 299-305.

Harvey, Lawrence E. *Beckett: Poet and Critic.* Princeton: Princeton Univ. Press, 1970.

Hassan, Ihab. *The Dismemberment of Orpheus.* Wisconsin: Univ. of Wisconsin Press, 1982.

_____. 'Joyce and Beckett: A Scenario in Eight Scenes'. *Journal of Modern Literature* I (1970-71), 7-18.

_____. *The Literature of Silence: Henry Miller and Samuel Beckett.* New York: Alfred A Knopf, 1967.

_____. Modern Literature . . . a Review for the Teacher', rpt. from *NEA* in *American Review* (USIS, New Delhi) III, 1 (Oct. 1963) 41-6.

Hasselbach, Hans-Peter. 'Samuel Beckett's Endgame: A Structural Analysis'.

Modern Drama XIX, 1 (March 1976), 25-34.

Hayman, Ronald. *Samuel Beckett.* Contemporary Playwrights Series. London: Heinmann, 1974.

_____. *Theatre and Anti-Theatre: New Movement Since Beckett.* New York: OUP, 1979.

Henning, Sylvie D. *Beckett's Critical Complicity: Carnival, Contestation and Tradition.* Lexington: Univ. Press of Kentucky, 1988.

Hermathena, Trinity College Dublin Review CXLI (Winter 1986)—a 'Beckett at Eighty' tribute issue.

Hesla, David H. *The Shape of Chaos: An Interpretation of the Art of Samuel Beckett.* Minneapolis: Univ. of Minnesota Press, 1971.

Hoffman, Frederick J. *Samuel Beckett: The Language of Self.* Carbondale: Southern Illinois Univ. Press, 1962.

Homan, Sidney. *Beckett's Theatres: Interpretations for Performance.* Lewisburg: Bucknel Univ. Press, 1984.

Hooker, Ward. 'Irony and Absurdity in the Avant-Garde Theatre'. *Kenyon Review* XXII, 3 (Summer 1960), 436-54.

Iser, Wolfgang. 'The Pattern of Negativity in Beckett's Prose'. *Georgia Review* XXIX, Fall 1975, 706-19.

_____. 'When Is The End Not the End? The Idea of Fiction in Beckett'. *The Implied Reader: Patterns of Communication in Prose Fiction from Bunyan to Beckett.* Baltimore: John Hopkins Univ. Press, 1974, pp. 257-73.

Jacobsen, Josephine and William R Mueller. 'Beckett as Poet.' *Prairie Schooner*, XXXVII, 3 (Fall 1963), 196-216.

_____. *The Testament of Samuel Beckett.* London: Faber & Faber, 1964.

Jadwiga, Uchman. *The Problem of Time in the Plays of Samuel Beckett.* Lodz: Wydawnictwo Uniwersytetu Lodzkiego, 1987.

Jones, Louisa. 'Narrative Salvation in *Waiting for Godot*'. *Modern Drama* XVII, 2 (June 1974), 179-88.

Journal of Beckett Studies Nos. 2-12.

Journal of Modern Literature. Vol. VI, No. 1 (Feb. 1977),—A special number on Samuel Beckett.

Kaelin, Eugene F. *The Unhappiness Consciousness: The Poetic Plight of Samuel Beckett.* Dordrecht: D Reidel Pub., 1981.

Kalb, Jonathan. *Beckett in Performance.* Cambridge: CUP, 1989.

_____. '*Rockaby* and the Art of Inadvertent Interpretation'. *Modern Drama* XXX, 4 (Dec. 1987), 466-79.

Kantra, Robert A. 'Beckett's Little Voices of Conscience'. *Journal of Popular Culture* VI, 4 (Spring 1973), 731-9.

Karl, Frederick A. 'Waiting for Beckett: Quest and Re-quest'. *Sewanee Review* LXIX, 4 (Autumn 1961), 661-76.

Kennedy, Andrew. 'Beckett'. *Six Dramatists in Search of a Language.* Cambridge: CUP, 1975, pp. 130-64.

_____. *Samuel Beckett*. Cambridge: CUP, 1989.

Kenner, Hugh. *The Mechanic Muse*. New York: OUP, 1987.

_____. *A Reader's Guide to Samuel Beckett*. London: Thames & Hudson, 1976.

_____. Samuel Beckett: A critical Study. London: John Calder, 1961.

_____. *The Stoic Comedians: Flaubert, Joyce and Beckett*. Berkeley: Univ. of California Press, 1962.

Kern, Edith. *The Absolute Comic*. New York: Columbia Univ. Press, 1980.

_____. 'Beckett'. *Existential Thought and Fictional Technique: Kierkegaard, Sartre, Beckett*. New Haven: Yale Univ. Press, 1970. pp. 167-243.

_____. 'Beckett's Knight of Infinite Resignation'. *Yale French Studies* Vol. 29, pp. 49-56.

_____. 'Drama Stripped for Inaction: Beckett's Godot'. *Yale French Studies*. Vol. 14, pp. 41-7.

Klawilter, Robert Louis. *Being and Time in Samuel Beckett's Novels*. (Microfilm). Yale University Ph.D. Dissertation, 1965.

Knowlson, James. 'Beckett as Director: The Manuscript Production Notebooks and Critical Interpretation'. *Modern Drama* XXX, 4 (Dec. 1987), 451-65.

_____. (ed.). *Happy Days: Samuel Beckett's Production Notebook*. London: Faber & Faber, 1985.

_____. *Krapp's Last Tape: Theatre Work Book*. London: Brutus Books, 1980.

_____. *Light and Darkness in the Theatre of Samuel Beckett*. London: Turret Books, 1972.

_____. 'Practical Aspects of Theatre, Radio and Television: Extracts from an Interview with Billie Whitelaw'. *Journal of Beckett Studies* No. 3, pp. 85-90.

_____. (ed.). *The Samuel Beckett Collection: A Catalogue*. The Library, Univ. of Reading, 1978.

_____. (ed./cat.). *Samuel Beckett: an Exhibition*. London: Turret Books.

Knowlson, James and John Pilling. *Frescoes of the Skull: The Later Prose and Drama of Samuel Beckett*. New York: Grove Press, 1980.

Kott, Jan. 'A Note on Beckett's Realism'. *Tulane Drama Review* X, 3 (Spring 1966), 156-9.

_____. *Shakespeare Our Contemporary*. London: Methuen, 1967.

Krutch, Joseph Wood. *The Modern Temper*. New York: Harcourt, 1956.

Lake, Carlton, Linda Eichhorn and Sally Leach. *No Symbols Where None Intended*. A Catalogue of Books, Manuscripts and Other Material Relating to Samuel Beckett in the Collections of the Humanities Research Centre. Austin: Univ. of Texas at Austin, 1984.

Lamont, Rossette C. 'Death and Tragi-comedy'. *Massachussetts Review* VI Winter/Spring 1965, 381-42.

Langburn, Robert. 'Beckett: The Self at Zero'. *Georgia Review* XXX, 4 (Winter 1976), 884-905.

Langdale, Kay. 'God, the Narrator and the Quest for an Aesthetic in Samuel

Beckett's Prose Fiction'. D.Phil. Thesis, Oxford University, 1987.

Langhlin, Karen. 'Beckett's Three Dimensions—Narration, Dialogue and the Role of the Reader in *Play*'. *Modern Drama* XXVIII, 3 (Sept. 1985), 329-40.

_____. ' "Looking for Sense. . .": The Spectator's Response to Beckett's *Come and Go*'. *Modern Drama* XXX, 2 (June 1987), 137-46.

Lann, Thomas F Van. '*All That Fall* as Play for Radio'. *Modern Drama* XXVIII, 1 (March 1985), 38-47.

Lawley, Paul. 'Beckett's Dramatic Counterpart: A Reading of *Play*'. *Journal of Beckett Studies* No. 9, pp. 25-42.

_____. 'Counterpoint, Absence and the Medium in Beckett's *Not I*'. *Modern Drama* XXVI, 4 (Dec. 1983), 407-14.

Lee, Warren. 'The Bitter Pill of Samuel Beckett'. *Chicago Review* X, 4 (Winter 1957), 77-87.

Leventhal, A J. 'The Beckett Hero'. *Critique* (Minnesota) VII, 2 (Winter 1964-5), 18-35.

Levy, Eric P. *Beckett and the Voice of Species: A Study of the Prose Fiction*. Dublin: Gill and Macmillan, 1980.

Libera, Antoni. 'Beckett's Catastrophe'. *Modern Drama* XXVIII, 3 (Sept. 1985), 341-7.

Lyons, Charles R. 'Beckett's Major Plays and the Trilogy'. *Comparative Drama* V, 4 (Winter 1971-2), 254-68.

_____. 'Perceiving Rockaby—As a Text, As a Text by Samuel Beckett, As a Text for Performance'. *Comparative Drama* XVI, 4 (Winter 1982-3), 297-311.

_____. *Samuel Beckett*. Modern Dramatists Series. London: Macmillan, 1983.

Lukacs, George. 'The Sociology of Modern Drama'. *Tulane Drama Review* X, 4 (Summer 1965), 146-70.

Marinello, Leone J. 'Samuel Beckett's *Waiting for Godot*'. *Drama Critique* VI, 2 (Spring 1963), 75-81.

Mayoux, Jean-Jacques. *Samuel Beckett*. Writers and Their Work Series. Harlow: Longmans, 1974.

_____. 'The Theatre of Samuel Beckett'. *Perspectives* XI, 3 (Autumn 1959), 142-55.

McCarthy, Patrick A (ed.). *Critical Essays on Samuel Beckett*. Boston: G K Hall, 1986.

McMillan, Dougald and Martha Fehsenfeld. *Beckett in the Theatre: The Author as Practical Playwright and Director*. Vol. I. London: John Calder.

Mcmullan, Andrey. 'The Space of Play in L'Impromptu d'ohio'. *Modern Drama* XXX, 1 (March 1987), 23-4.

Mercier, Vivien. *Beckett/Beckett*. Oxford: OUP, 1977.

_____. 'Samuel Beckett and the Sheela-Na-Gig'. *Kenyon Review* XXIII, 2 (Spring 1961), 299-324.

Metman, Eva. 'Reflections on Samuel Beckett's Plays' (1960). Offprint.

Modern Drama IX, 3 (December 1966)—special Beckett number.

_____ XIX, Sept. 1976—mini-special Beckett number.
_____ XXV, 3 (September 1982)—special Beckett number.

Modern Fiction Studies Vol. 29, No. 1 (Spring 1983)—special Beckett number.

Moore, J.R. 'Some Night Thoughts on Beckett'. *Massachussetts Review* VIII, Summer 1967, 529-39.

Moorjani, Angela B. *Abysmal Games in the Novels of Samuel Beckett.* Chapel Hill: North Carolina Studies in Romance Languages & Literatures, 1982.

Morot-Sir, Edouard. 'Samuel Beckett and Cartesian Emblems'. *Samuel Beckett: The Art of Rhetoric*, 1976. Offprint.

Morrison, Kristin. *Canters and Chronicles: The Use of Narrative in the Plays of Samuel Beckett and Harold Pinter.* Chicago: Univ. of Chicago Press, 1983.

Murch, Ann C. 'Quoting from Godot: Trends in Contemporary French Theatre'. *Journal of Beckett Studies* No. 9, pp. 113-29.

Murphy, Vincent J. 'Being and Perception: Beckett's *Film*'. *Modern Drama* XVIII, 1 (March 1975), 43-8.

Murray, Patrick. *The Tragic Comedian: A Study of Samuel Beckett.* Cork: Mercier Press, 1970.

Nicol, Bernard de Bear. '"The Absurd" Dramatists' (Discussion on Dramatic Forms and Themes Between Stanley Evernden, Roger Hubank, Thora Burnley Jones and Bernard de Bear Nicol). *Varieties of Dramatic Experience.* London: Univ. of London, 1969, pp. 249-64.

O'brien, Eoin. *The Beckett Country: An Exhibition of Samuel Beckett's Birthplace.* Dublin: The Black Cat Press, 1986.

_____. *The Beckett Country: Samuel Beckett's Ireland.* Dublin: The Black Cat Press, 1986.

O'Dair, Sharon K. '"The Countless Passion of an Unfruitful Wind": Irony and Laughter in *Endgame*'. *Criticism* XXVIII (1986), No. 4, pp. 165-78.

O'Hara, J D (ed.). *Twentieth Century Interpretations of Molloy, Malone Dies, The Unnamable.* Englewood Cliffs: Prentice Hall, 1970.

Oliver, William I. 'Between Absurdity and the Playwright'. *Educational Theatre Journal* XV, 3 (Oct. 1963), 224-35.

_____. 'After Absurdity'. *Educational Theatre Journal* III, 3 (Oct. 1965), 196-205.

O'Neill, Joseph P. 'The Absurd in Samuel Beckett'. *Personalist* XLVIII, 1 (Jan. 1967), 56-75.

Ormerod, Beverley. 'Beckett's Waiting for Godot'. *Explicator* 32, Item 70.

Paine, Sylvia. *Beckett, Nabokov, Nin: Motives and Modernism.* Port Washington, New York: Kennikat Press, 1981.

Paul, Leslie. 'The Writer of the Human Condition'. *Kenyon Review* XXIX, 1 (Jan. 1967), 21-8.

Peter, John. *Vladimir's Carrot: Modern Drama and the Modern Imagination.* London: Andre Deutsche, 1987.

Pilling, John. *Samuel Beckett*. London: RKP, 1976.

Postlewait, Thomas. 'Self-Performing Voices: Mind, Memory and Time in Beckett's Drama'. *Twentieth Century Literature* XXIV, 4 (Winter 1976), 473-92.

Pronko, L. *Avant-Garde: The Experimental Theatre in France*. Berkeley: Yale Univ. Press, 1962.

Rabinovitz, Rubin. *The Development of Samuel Beckett's Fiction*. Urbana: Univ. of Illinois Press, 1984.

Radke, Judith J. 'The Theatre of Samuel Beckett'. *Yale French Studies* Vol. 29, pp. 57-64.

Raghavan, Hema V. *Samuel Beckett: Rebels and Exiles in His Plays*. New Delhi: Arnold Publishers, 1988.

Ramakrishna, Lalita. 'Time and the Self in Beckett'. (Typescript) M. Litt Dissertation. CIEFL, Hyderabad, 1980.

Read, David. 'Artistic Theory in the Work of Samuel Beckett'. *Journal of Beckett Studies* No. 8, pp. 7-22.

Reid, Alec. *All I can Manage, More Than I could: An Approach to the Plays of Samuel Beckett*. Dublin: The Dolmen Press, 1968.

Renton, Andrew. '"He All But Said. . ." Evasion and Referral in the Later Prose and Drama of Samuel Beckett'. Unpublished Thesis—Reading Univ., 1989.

Robinson, Michael. *The Long Sonata of the Dead: A Study of Samuel Beckett*. London: Rupert Hart-Davis, 1969.

Rose, Marilyn Gladdis. 'The Irish Memories of Beckett's Voice'. *Journal of Modern Literature* II, 1 (Sept. 1971), 127-32.

Rosen, Carol. 'A Dream of Order'. *Plays of Impasse: Contemporary Drama Set in Conflicting Institutions*. Princeton, NJ: Princeton Univ. Press, 1983, pp. 260-81.

Rosen, Steven J. *Samuel Beckett and the Pessimistic Tradition*. New Brunswick: Rutgers Univ. Press, 1976.

Savory, Jerold J. 'Samuel Beckett's Waiting for Godot'. *Explicator* Vol. 35, 1 (Fall 1976), 9-10.

Schlossberg, Edwin. *Einstein and Beckett: A Record of an Imaginary Discussion with Albert Einstein and Samuel Beckett*. New York: Link Books, 1973.

Schoell, Konard. 'The Chain and the Circle: A Structural Comparison of *Waiting for Godot* and *Endgame*'. *Modern Drama* XI, 1 (May 1968), 48-53.

Schulz, Hans-Joachin. *This Hell of Stories: A Hegelian Approach to the Novels of Samuel Beckett*. Hague: Mouton, 1973.

Scott, Nathan A. *Samual Beckett*. London: Bowes & Bowes, 1965.

_____. *Man in the Modern Theatre*. Richmond: John Knox Press, 1965.

Sen, Supti. *Samuel Beckett: His Mind and Art*. Calcutta: Firma K.L. Mukhopadhayay, 1970.

Starnes, Patrick. 'Samuel Beckett, the Novelist: Three Complementary

Approaches'. Doctoral Dissertion, Cambridge Univ., 1973.

States, Bert O. 'Catastrophe: Laboratory/Theatre'. *Modern Drama* XXX, 1 (March 1987), 14-32.

_____. *The Shape of Paradox: An Essay on Waiting for Godot.* Berkeley: Univ. of California Press, 1978.

Stempel, Saniel. 'History Electrified into Anagogy: A Reading of *Waiting for Godot*'. *Contemporary Literature* XVII, 2 (Spring 1976), 263-78.

Styan, J.L. *The Dark Comedy: The Development of Modern Comic Tragedy.* Cambridge: CUP, 1962.

Suvin, Darko. 'Beckett's Purgatory of the Individual. . .' *Tulane Drama Review* XI, 4 (Summer 1967), 23-36.

Sypher, Wylie. *Loss of the Self in Modern Literature and Art.* New York: Random House, 1962.

Szanto, George H. 'Samuel Beckett: Dramatic Possibilities'. *Massachussetts Review* XV, Autumn 1974, 735-61.

Tanner, James T F and J Don Vaun. *Samuel Beckett: A Checklist of Criticism.* Kent State Univ. Press, 1969.

Tharu, Susie J. 'Samuel Beckett: Revealing a World as Deprived as His Stage'. *The Sense of Performance: Studies in Post-Artaud Theatre.* New Delhi: Arnold Heinemann, 1984.

Tindall, William York. 'Beckett's Bums'. A brochure privately printed, 1960.

_____. *Samuel Beckett.* Columbia Essays on Modern Writers No. 4. New York: Columbia Univ. Press, 1964.

Velissariou, Aspasia. 'Language in "Waiting for Godot"'. *Journal of Beckett Studies* No. 8, pp. 45-57.

Weales, Gerald. 'The Language of Endgame'. *Tulane Drama Review* VI, 4 (June 1962), 107-17.

Webb, Eugene. *The Plays of Samuel Beckett.* London: Peter Owen, 1972.

_____. *Samuel Beckett: A Study of his Novels.* Seattle: Univ. of Washington Press, n.d.

Wellwarth, George. 'Samuel Beckett: Life in the Void'. *The Theatre of Protest and Paradox: Development in Avant-Garde Theatre.* New York: New York Univ. Press, 1964, pp. 41-56.

Wilcher, Robert. 'What's it meant to mean? . . . An Approach to Beckett's Theatre'. *Critical Qly* VIII, 2 (Summer 1970), 9-37.

Wilson, Robert N. 'Samual Beckett. The Social Psychology of Emptiness'. *The Writer as Social Seer.* Chapel Hill: Univ. of North Carolina Press, 1979, pp. 134-44.

Worth, Katherine (ed.). *Beckett The Shape Changer: A Symposium.* London: RKP, 1975.

_____. *The Irish Drama of Europe from Yeats to Beckett.* London: Univ. of London, 1978.

_____. *Waiting for Godot and Happy Days: Text and Performance.* London: Macmillan, 1990.

Worthen, William B. 'Beckett's Actor'. *Modern Drama* XXVI, 4 (Dec. 1983), 415-24.

Zeifman, Hersh. 'Being and Non-Being: Samuel Beckett's *Not I*'. *Modern Drama* XIX, 1 (March 1976), 35-46.

Zillicas, Clas. *Beckett and Broadcasting: A Study of the Works of Samuel Beckett for and in Radio and Television*. Abo: Abo Akademi, 1976.

_____. 'Samuel Beckett's *Embers*: A Matter of Fundamental Sounds'. *Modern Drama* XIII, 2 (Sept. 1970), 216-25.

Index